THE LAWYER'S GUIDE
TO WRITING WELL

Tom Goldstein
Professor, Columbia School of Journalism
Columbia University

Jethro K. Lieberman
Associate Dean for Academic Affairs,
Professor of Law, and Director,
The Writing Program
New York Law School

SECOND EDITION

University of California Press
Berkeley / Los Angeles / London

University of California Press
Berkeley and Los Angeles, California

University of California Press, Ltd.
London, England

© 2002 by
The Regents of the University of California

Library of Congress Cataloging-in-Publication Data
Goldstein, Tom.
    The lawyer's guide to writing well / Tom Goldstein and Jethro K.
Lieberman.—2nd ed.
        p.   cm.
    Includes bibliographical references and index.
    ISBN 0–520–23472–3 (cloth : alk. paper). — ISBN 0–520–23473–1
(paper : alk. paper)
    1. Legal composition.   I. Lieberman, Jethro Koller.   II. Title.
    KF250 .G65 2002
    808'.06634—dc21

                                                    2002009717

Manufactured in the United States of America
10   09   08   07   06   05   04   03   02   01
10   9   8   7   6   5   4   3   2   1

The paper used in this publication is both acid-free and totally chlo-
rine-free (TCF). It meets the minimum requirements of ANSI/
NISO Z39.48–1992 (R 1997) (Permanence of Paper). ∞

To Leslie and Jo

CONTENTS

The first edition of this book was written in 1988, at a time when many critics were bemoaning the state of legal writing but few were doing anything about it. Between October 1987 and June 1988, we asked 650 people familiar with legal writing—practicing lawyers, judges, professors, writing instructors, and journalists who report on legal topics—what bothered them most about the way lawyers write. We do not pretend that our survey was scientific: We sent a four-page questionnaire to people listed on our Rolodexes. As journalists we had covered law and the legal profession since the early 1970s for a variety of news media, and our list included thoughtful lawyers and writers in half the states and every major city; most major law firms, scores of smaller firms, and courts; law schools; and newspapers, magazines, and broadcast stations across the country. The answers from 300 respondents inform a portion of this book. People named in the text but not identified in the notes were respondents and are identified in the acknowledgments. Unattributed statements about what lawyers, judges, professors, writing instructors, and journalists "think," "feel," or "believe" are drawn from the statements of these respondents, as are some of the displayed quotations.

In the dozen years since the first edition appeared, there have been vast changes in the technology of communications—the ways in which lawyers produce and distribute their letters, memoranda, briefs, and other documents. In the late 1980s, desktop computers were beginning to find their way into lawyers' offices, but probably few lawyers used them regularly or proficiently. (Indeed, lawyers at some firms told us they were forbidden to touch a computer; managing partners in those days viewed the "word processor" as a tool for secretaries and typists, not professionals.) By today's standards, early desktop computers were clunky machines, though surely useful and already then revolutionizing the production of legal paper. Although laser printers became available, few offices had hooked them to their computers or were realizing their potential to supplant the print shops to which at least the more formal of their documents continued to be sent. The desktops of the 1980s were only beginning to be networked; e-mail was scarce or nonexistent; lawyers were untrained in computerized legal research; and no one in the legal world had then heard of the Internet.

For all of the rapid improvement in communications technology since 1988, legal writing has improved little, if at all. Law offices around the country, busier than ever, have largely defaulted in training their newcomers. The large law firms hired so many new associates during the 1990s that they found it impossible to provide the one-on-one training in writing and editing that had been customary until sometime in the 1960s. Government legal offices and smaller firms have little time and few resources to devote to the task. Their response to poor writing by their young lawyers is to blame the law schools.

The law schools, of course, would assign the blame elsewhere. During the 1990s most American law schools established (or beefed up) their legal writing programs, usually a yearlong course in writing and research. These programs and courses were spurred by the "MacCrate Report" of the American Bar Association in 1992.[1] Named after its chairman, New York lawyer Robert MacCrate, the Task Force on Law Schools and the Profession called on the law schools to add communication skills to their educational objectives. The cry for greater clarity in communication, however, has not led to serious curricular reform. Most law school classroom instruction remains oral, and full-time professors devote almost no time to critiquing their students' written work. Even in legal writing courses, writing often takes a back seat to legal analysis, research, and the formats for motions, briefs, and other legal documents. For all the talk about legal literacy, writing instructors have the lowest prestige and the smallest claim on the resources of the law schools in which they work. The consequence is that the law schools remain unequipped to deal with a generation of increasingly ill prepared college graduates who clamor for admission.

Our hearts sank when we read in the Columbia law school newspaper in 2001 about a well-meaning but flawed effort to educate Columbia law students about writing. Professor H. Richard Uviller, a published author of nonfiction intended for a broad audience, did what no other Columbia law professor had ever done—offered a course on basic writing. "I call this the tenth-grade English class that you never took," Uviller told the newspaper. "It's a class in basic grammar, syntax, style and usage."[2] Remarkably, 160 students—just under half the first-year class—enrolled for this noncredit course. They were divided into two sections, an impossibly high number of students. Writing needs to be taught in small sections, preferably no more than 15. In this course, no papers were required—surely an odd way to learn a skill for which practice is obligatory.

Nearly fifteen years after we began the first edition of this book, lawyers still write poorly.

PART I

WHY LAWYERS WRITE POORLY

Most lawyers write poorly.

That's not just our lament. Leading lawyers across the country agree. They think modern legal writing is flabby, prolix, obscure, opaque, ungrammatical, dull, boring, redundant, disorganized, gray, dense, unimaginative, impersonal, foggy, infirm, indistinct, stilted, arcane, confused, heavy-handed, jargon- and cliché-ridden, ponderous, weaseling, overblown, pseudointellectual, hyperbolic, misleading, incivil, labored, bloodless, vacuous, evasive, pretentious, convoluted, rambling, incoherent, choked, archaic, orotund, and fuzzy.

Many critics amplified: Lawyers don't know basic grammar and syntax. They can't say anything simply. They have no judgment and don't know what to include or what to leave out. They do not know how to tell a story—where to begin, when to end, or how to organize it. They get so carried away with their advocacy that they distort and even deceive.

> *The difficult task, after one learns how to think like a lawyer, is relearning how to write like a human being.*
> FLOYD ABRAMS

So what? Does poor writing matter? It's commonplace to say that it does.

What are its consequences? That's a harder question to answer.

Justice Alvin F. Klein of New York State Supreme Court in Manhattan once embarrassed opposing lawyers in a divorce case by saying in open court that he could not understand the papers filed by either of them.[1] He ordered the lawyers to rewrite their motions and objections.

The judge's impatience stands for more than the passing mortification of two practitioners or the wasting of several hours in drafting undecipherable papers. Judges rarely comment on the style or intelligibility of documents they read, though not for want of opportunity. Perhaps judges are reluctant to do so because they know their own prose could be ridiculed next. In admonishing the lawyers, Justice Klein rambled a bit himself: "Upon a careful reading of all the voluminous papers submitted herein, the court is frank to state that it cannot ascertain the basis for the relief sought by the plaintiff on the motion and by the defendant on the cross-motion." But Justice Klein diagnosed a soreness that afflicts the practice of law throughout the country. Perhaps it is not a fatal disease but a wasting one: a canker if not a cancer.

The consequences of poor legal writing are simple to state though difficult to prove:

- It wastes the valuable time of judges, clients, and other lawyers, who must constantly reread documents to figure out what is meant.
- It costs law firms a lot of money; they must absorb the time of senior lawyers who are forced to rewrite the work of junior ones.
- It costs society; we all pay for the lost time and the extra work.
- It loses cases. Briefs and memoranda and letters that do not adequately convey a writer's point give adversaries who are better writers the opportunity to portray their own positions more persuasively and sympathetically.
- It can lead to disrespect for or indifference to law. The public can't understand what lawyers are saying because the law itself is almost always obscure, and the lawyers' attempts to explain it are rarely clearer.
- It erodes self-respect. Hurried, careless writing weakens the imagination, saps intelligence, and ultimately diminishes self-esteem and professionalism.
- It impoverishes our culture. Writing well in a calling that prides itself on professionalism in pursuit of justice ought to be an end in itself.

Despite these consequences, many lawyers fail to connect good writing to good lawyering, probably because it is rarely possible to quantify the costs. We doubt that lawyers would offer to reveal, or that accountants would leap at the opportunity to prove, the dollar value a particular document cost the firm or the client or society because it was poorly written. And who can measure the injustice that obscurity fosters? So lawyers dismiss the consequences of their inability to express themselves well.

Writing to me is just writing—not legal or otherwise.
LOUIS S. AUCHINCLOSS

"Writing is a waste of time," said a young associate at a midsized New York firm, which had hired us to tutor incoming lawyers. "We sell time, not paper." He could not be more mistaken. Good lawyers may rightly measure the value of the paper they sell by the time it takes to put words onto it, but if the document is unreadable, clients are not impressed—or should not be—that a lawyer has spent endless hours on their behalf. Good lawyers must devote their time to producing effective prose, but that is time well spent.

The more important a lawyer, judge, or case, the more important clear writing becomes.

One can be a good lawyer or judge and a bad writer,
but not a great one without being a good writer.
STUART BERG FLEXNER

Good lawyers are genuinely interested in words, in their nuances, in the subtle distinctions between them, in the growth of the language. Good lawyers browse through usage books now and again, not from pedantry but from fascination with language and the power of writing. Good lawyers revere English—and edit their work one more time to ensure that they have expressed their thoughts with the clarity and felicity that they owe to their clients, to the public, and to themselves.

Those for whom writing is unimportant are doomed to be second-rate lawyers. The connection between good writing and good professional work is not peculiar to lawyers. But because lawyers' work, more than that of other professionals, consists of writing, a lawyer's disinclination to write well is the more disheartening—and potentially the more disastrous. Bad lawyers scorn the craftsman unremunerated for his pains. These lawyers, at best, produce workmanlike prose—they know some rules of usage—and settle for the pedestrian. Bad lawyers, neglecting their craft, risk their livelihood—or certainly their clients'.

Lawyers who ignore the art of writing, who leave their prose rough, murky, and unedited, are not simply foolish; they are guilty of malpractice. Unhappily, this form of malpractice is widespread.

George D. Gopen, a lawyer and director of the writing programs at Duke University, uses an elaborate metaphor—the "toll booth syndrome"—to describe how lawyers write. Late on an arctic night as you drive home from an exhausting day's work, you toss your last quarter at the toll basket—and miss. You can back up and pay the toll collector in another lane, or you can go through the red light just ahead of you. Your choice depends on what you think the toll is for. If it is to help finance road repairs, then you should back up and pay. But if you suppose the purpose is simply to divest drivers of loose change, you will go through the light. The money is not in the road authority's hands, but it is not in yours either.

So, says Gopen, lawyers write, without thinking about the purpose of doing so:

> You cast all of your knowledge on the subject out of your mind onto the paper, not caring if the audience will actually receive your 40¢ worth of wisdom, but caring only that you unburden yourself of it. It's all out there—on the paper, in the gravel—and that is what matters.
>
> Of course, that is *not* what matters. . . . [Lawyers] get all the relevant information down on the paper; they refer to all the possible issues and suggest a number of different approaches and counterapproaches; and

all the while they have no perception of how a reader not already knee-deep in the case will be able to wade through it all.[2]

The widespread feeling that good writing does not count is puzzling in a profession that demands its practitioners be well educated. Every state requires prospective practitioners to spend three years at law school, where students learn the substance of law. But the schools largely neglect the skills of practice. Although most law schools offer "clinical" courses, showing how to build a client's case and how to guard against an adversary's, they are costly and can enroll relatively few students. In theory, the law schools offer somewhat more in writing instruction: At most law schools all first-year students take a required "writing" course. But these courses, often taught by low-status writing instructors without tenure or hope of getting it, carry few credits and deliver little in the way of a sustained critique of writing. The accrediting rules of the American Bar Association require that law students complete two "rigorous writing experience[s]," a term the accrediting arm has never defined.

When pressed, law schools offer excuses: Our professors don't want to teach writing. Teaching writing effectively is costly. Or time is limited, and students come for law, not for a refresher course in what they should have mastered years before. Teaching writing is the responsibility of colleges (or high schools or elementary schools). Students will develop their writing skills on the job.

These excuses are inadequate. The Navy scarcely tolerates a sailor's inability to swim because he should have learned it elsewhere, nor does it assume that a sailor will discover how to float when his ship is sunk. Worse, these excuses keep students from learning that most lawyers do not know how to write effectively and that good writing really does matter. The message to students is clear: Your writing is good enough for whatever tasks come your way once you leave school's sanctuary.

In practice, the problem worsens. Most firms offer only a few hours' training to their recruits, even though the best recruits are mediocre writers. Some large firms invest fair sums of money and large amounts of time on substantive training—a workshop on advocacy, a seminar in the fine points of securities trading, the art of taking depositions— a measure of what they think is valuable. Many bosses have been poorly trained themselves and cannot improve upon the inept writing of their juniors, so the prose deteriorates further. The occasional partner out- raged at some bit of mangled syntax might circulate a memo on "the five rules of good writing," as if these idiosyncratic rules (themselves quite likely to be wrong) solve the problem. Solo practitioners and lawyers at small firms receive little guidance; what they see is the often marginal, convoluted prose of their adversaries and judges.

The lawyer's writing problem is compounded by the different forms that poor writing can assume. When lawyers discuss bad—and good— writing, they mean diverse things. Solving minor difficulties, they may believe they have overcome all. At a prosperous West Coast law firm we visited, a fourth-year associate bragged about how well she and some of her colleagues wrote. Of her boss, she said, "He knows how to write; he knows the difference between *that* and *which*."

The "that-which" distinction is an occasional issue in English usage, but this knowledge is scarcely the height of the writer's skill. The writer must contend with scores of other usage problems, and usage itself is only one of many elements a skilled writer must master. Yet all too many lawyers believe that good writing means only mastering a few simple rules.

To prove that they are good writers, or at least that they care about well-ordered sentences, many lawyers, including the West Coast asso- ciate, point to a tattered copy of Strunk and White sitting on the bookshelf. *The Elements of Style,* that venerable volume on good usage, was published in 1918 and rediscovered in 1957 when one of William Strunk's students, E. B. White, reminisced about the book in the *New Yorker.* For many lawyers, it epitomizes the craft of writing. The U.S. Court of Appeals for the Eleventh Circuit in Atlanta gives a copy to every lawyer admitted to practice. Thomas W. Evans, a senior partner in a large New York firm, told us: "Over the years the only aid that I have found particularly useful in writing is to reread occasionally *The Elements of Style.* Immediately after these readings, my sentences seem to become shorter and clearer. In time, I drift back into bad habits until I am led to pick up that little book again."

The Elements of Style is a good "little book," as Strunk himself called it in 1919 when it was first circulated on the Cornell campus. As a brief summary of some useful rules, it does belong on a writer's shelf. But *The Elements of Style* is also unsystematic, chaotic, limited, and sometimes unhelpful. Here, for example, is how Strunk and White explain *that* and *which*: "*That* is the defining, or restrictive pronoun, *which* the nondefining, or nonrestrictive." Accurate, surely, but how does it help?

Lawyers' misplaced reliance on Strunk and White is emblematic of a limited perspective on writing. Good writing is more than adherence to elementary rules of usage. The good legal writer must consider these subjects, among others:

- Vocabulary—the choice of appropriate words
- Organization—the effective arrangement of thought
- Topic flow—the appropriate articulation of concepts
- Transitions—the connections between ideas
- Structure—the proper elements of a document
- Audience—the knowledge held by the expected readership
- Tone—the manner or spirit of addressing readers
- Style—the types of sentences and the cadence of prose
- Clarity—the fit between idea and expression
- Accuracy—the fit between expression and reality
- Timing—when to write and when, and how often, to edit

In this book we write for lawyers who wish to improve their writing—for practitioners who seek to refine their skills and for students who hope to develop them. We look at writing from many perspectives to offer concrete solutions to difficulties of which readers may be unaware. We do not suppose that those who absorb the contents of this book will match Brandeis, Cardozo, or Holmes as stylists. But we do believe that diligent readers will become better writers and that they will be equipped with the means of improving further on their own.

Three more observations about the book's aims:

1. Because writing is an art and a skill, a process and a business, an end in itself and a means to other ends, we do not confine our discussion to rules of usage. We propose that readers consider context and process as well. In Chapter 2, we discuss the causes of poor writing and the historical critique of legal writing; in Chapters 3 through 7, the way writers write—individually and in the office; in Chapters 8 through 11, the rules and techniques for polishing prose; and in Chapter 12, how to make your writing memorable.

2. Because every lawyer composes for many purposes and different audiences, our advice should not be taken to apply equally to every kind of document and under every set of circumstances. We know that lawyers are busy and that they do not have the novelist's luxury of time. The lawyer who must prepare overnight a response to a motion for a preliminary injunction obviously cannot put the draft aside for days before returning to reconsider it. Rules of grammar and usage apply to every brief, memorandum, and pleading, but the process by which those papers are composed will depend on the time and resources available.

3. With minor exceptions, we do not consider the art of drafting legislation, contracts, or other legal instruments in "plain English," understandable to the lay public. Our premise is that lawyers' thoughts and manner of expression are so disordered that even *other lawyers* cannot understand them. As lawyers learn to write well, inevitably the public will learn to understand them also. But that is not the starting point. Lawyers must first learn to talk to each other.

Mindful that we have chided scores of lawyers by using their writing to illustrate problems and solutions, we have sought assiduously to eliminate our own mistakes. But writing about writing errors is always dangerous because the critics invariably commit their own. Sally Powell, the book review editor of *Business Week* for many years, never let her writers attack typographical errors in the books they were reviewing, because as soon as they did, she said, similar mistakes would creep into the magazine.

On occasion, we confess, we have led with our chins. In our survey, for example, we asked the question: "Do you have other thoughts on legal writing that you would like to share with us?" David L. Shapiro, a professor at Harvard Law School, chided: "Only that the 'sharing of thoughts' should be left to the headmasters of progressive secondary schools."

We hasten to acknowledge that mistakes are sometimes just mistakes and that not every wooden phrase or fuzzy thought means that the writer is thoughtless or poorly trained. We recognize that mistakes inevitably remain in this book too. We hope that by adhering to the principles we propound, we and you can learn to become more acute at spotting and eliminating the mistakes that slip through.

Around the country, a select group of court watchers indulges an arcane hobby: collecting lawyers' dreck. A West Coast journalist sent us this specimen:

> That on November 10, 1981, at 1:00 p.m. while plaintiff was a business invitee and customer, present at that certain real property, a Ralph's Market, located at 1725 Sunset Blvd., Los Angeles, California, and that at said time and place, the defendants, and each of them, carelessly and negligently owned and operated and maintained and controlled the said real property and particularly a shopping cart thereof, and the said cart was at said time and place in a dangerous condition, because there was no "seat flap" in the "upper" basket and a can fell through, breaking plaintiff's foot and it was unsafe for use by persons, including plaintiff, and directly because of such condition, and the negligently and carelessly maintained condition thereof the plaintiff was caused to and did sustain injuries and was proximately injured thereby as hereinafter set forth.

Fred Graham, a former Supreme Court reporter for the *New York Times* and CBS-TV and now chief anchor for Court TV, collected examples of particularly ghastly "questions presented," the required statement of the issues in each petition for certiorari, "until," he says, "I got discouraged." Here are two of his favorites:

> Whether, consistently with the due process clause and the equal protection clause of the fourteenth amendment, a state court may deprive a party, without compensation of his or its constitutional rights to property by validation of an invalid court determination through the aegis of res judicata, wherein such principle of res judicata was actually a premise for invalidation and nullity rather than the aforementioned validation.

> Does it violate the fourteenth amendment of the United States Constitution for the highest court of the state, here the supreme court of

Pennsylvania, when a petition for leave to appeal to it from a decision of an intermediate appellate court, here the superior court of Pennsylvania, to refuse allocatur even though the petition for such sets out clearly and unambiguously a claim of denial of due process of law guaranteed by the fourteenth amendment, and a claim that such refusal violated the Pennsylvania constitutional prohibition against impairment of contract, and a claim that a refusal of such a review is a violation of the corporation's right to a jury trial guaranteed at some stage of an arbitration proceeding by local case law where the jurisdiction of an arbitrator has been challenged?

Teachers, too, have their collections. On a constitutional law examination, one hopeful student referred to a "probable certainty." Another cleared his throat: "First of all, the first problem to address is . . ." A classmate opined that "the right to publish and distribute political ideas is a tenant of the Constitution." Another declared: "Treating AIDS sufferers and carriers as a suspect class would most likely not fly." Still another informed her bewildered professor that "the state has a valid and compelling interest in keeping its locals clean and thus affixing stickers to telephone poles and lampposts may be valid." The professor's eyes widened upon reading: "Concededly, the AIDS epidemic is a compelling governmental objective," and stayed wide upon encountering: "The state has a conceivable interest in preventing bigamy or family values." Other students noted that the statute could not "past muster" and that an assumption may help "to access the situation." One advocated "repealment"; another spoke of a policy's "wiseness."

I want every law student to be able to read and write. Half my first-year students, more than a third of my second-year students, can do neither.
KARL N. LLEWELLYN

Much of the current dismay over lawyers' writing reflects a belief that their writing went to hell only recently, that lawyers were once known for their elegant style. This view misses a good deal of history.

It reminds us of the story Edward I. Koch, the former New York City mayor, has often told about the elderly woman who stopped him on the boardwalk at Coney Island. She poignantly related how life had deteriorated. Crime was up, the air was dirty, the water befouled. "Make it like it was," she implored. "I'll try," Koch responded. "But it never was the way you think it was."

A Short Retelling of the Attack on Legal Prose

Historically, lawyers' prose has never been free from attack. In fifteenth-century England, Chief Justice John Fortescue declared that the judges were giving effect to forms written in unintelligible language even though none could remember the reason for the language. In the sixteenth century, the lord chancellor stuffed a plaintiff's head through a hole cut in a stack of pleadings and marched him around Westminster Hall with the pages drooping over his shoulders. This public humiliation was a double insult: The pleadings were drawn by the plaintiff's lawyer, who had padded them with an extra hundred pages and then had the effrontery to charge his client more. A century later the practice continued: Chief Justice Hale denounced padding as serving "no other use but to swell the attorney's bill," and Sir Francis Bacon urged editing of cases—"prolixity, tautologies and impertinences to be cut off."[1]

In the eighteenth century, Jonathan Swift rebuked lawyers for their odd speech: "a peculiar Cant and Jargon of their own, that no other Mortal can understand." Jeremy Bentham was blunter, characterizing lawyers' language as "excrementitious matter" and "literary garbage," even though his insistence on nouns in place of verbs contributed to the opaque quality of modern legal prose. Henry Fielding put in the mouth of one of his characters that "nothing is more hurtful to a perfect knowledge of the law than reading it."[2]

In America, the critique of legal style is older than the republic. Thomas Jefferson, a pellucid writer of legal as well as ordinary English, mocked as "lawyerish" the orotund style of the day. Late in his career, long since retired as president, Jefferson wrote to a friend about a bill he had drafted in simple language:

> You, however, can easily correct this bill to the taste of my brother lawyers, by making every other word a "said" or "aforesaid," and saying everything over two or three times, so that nobody but we of the craft can untwist the diction, and find out what it means; and that, too, not so plainly but that we may conscientiously divide one half on each side.[3]

Similar criticisms echoed through the nineteenth century, an age when reformers began to purge from the common-law system the worst of the archaic forms of pleading. The rules of pleading, as stylized as movement in a Kabuki play, had contributed to the prolixity and pedantry of legal writing. But centuries of bad habits had dulled lawyers' ears and addled their brains. Simpler procedures would not yield simplified writing.

In the twentieth century, criticism of lawyers' language intensified. In the early 1920s, for example, Urban A. Lavery, chief legislative draftsman for the Illinois Constitutional Convention, scolded his fellow practitioners:

> How many lawyers ever consult once a book on grammar or on good use of English, where they consult a lawbook a hundred times? . . . The lawyer too often is a careless writer; and he, before all men, might write well if he but strove to do it. But he does not strive; he "dangles" his participles, he "splits" his infinitives, he scatters his auxiliary verbs, he leaves his relative pronouns and adjectives to die of starvation far removed from their antecedents; his various parts of speech are often not on speaking terms with their best friends.

In the 1930s three prominent law professors deplored the general illiteracy of the bar. In 1935, Karl N. Llewellyn, a professor at Columbia Law School, said: "I want every law student to be able to read and write. Half of my first-year students, more than a third of my second-year students, can do neither." In 1936, in "Goodbye to Law Reviews," a famous article in the *Virginia Law Review,* Professor Fred Rodell of

Yale Law School wrote: "There are two things wrong with almost all legal writing. One is its style. The other is its content. That, I think, about covers the ground." In 1939 William L. Prosser, then teaching at the University of Minnesota Law School, said of his students: "Very, very many of them are hopelessly, deplorably unskilled and inept in the use of words to say what they mean, or, indeed, to say anything at all."[4] Prosser illustrated his lament by reprinting this passage, among others, from a final examination:

> The buyer has an action for breech of warenty if he has gave notice to the seller in a reasonable time Uniform Sales Act sec. 48 after he knows of the defect there is a trade name here but here he does not give such he has an action no action for breech of warenty also after he reasonably ought to of known the warenty would be implied warenty of merchentable quality here thirty days is too long. You could not bring fitness for the purpose here because there is a trade name Holden's Beer is a trade name buyer took initiative in asking for it so reliance on seller's skill and judgement not here but merchentable not excluded according to Cardozo if this is sale and not service I think it is sale and merchentable quality in spite of trade name but no notice and so no action for breach of implied warenty of merchanteble quality in spite of trade name.

In 1950 Arthur T. Vanderbilt, then Chief Justice of the New Jersey Supreme Court and formerly dean of New York University Law School, acknowledged "the well-nigh universal criticism respecting the inability of law students to think straight and to write and speak in clear, forceful, attractive English."[5] Nine years later, another frequent critic of legal writing, Dean William Warren of Columbia Law School, said at a symposium of the American Association of Law Libraries:

> I know that some of my colleagues in other institutions have taken the position that their students are able to write. However, I can only tell you what the Bar thinks about this since I have talked rather extensively with many practitioners. Most members of law firms tell me that the young men who are coming to them today cannot write well. I think the situation has reached almost epidemic proportions.[6]

Carl McGowan, a Chicago practitioner later to become a distinguished federal appeals judge, complained in 1961 of the inability of lawyers to express themselves in English: "Most of the time our lights are hidden under literally bushels of words, inexpertly put together."[7]

As academic and professional law journals have continued to denounce the "epidemic" of bad writing, the academy and the bar have responded by shelling out cash. Remedial writing entrepreneurs have launched businesses to tutor practicing lawyers. Law schools have almost universally added basic writing courses to their required curricula. A new professional discipline, the teaching of legal writing, has evolved, accompanied by its own journals and murky jargon ("reader-protocols" and "revision feedback"). Language columns have proliferated in bar journals, and books for students and practitioners have flooded the market.

Almost everyone who discusses law school students—or even, it may be added, young law school graduates—has an unkind word to say about their lack of adequate powers of oral and written expression in their native tongue.
ARTHUR VANDERBILT

Even the government has found it politic to act. In 1978 President Carter signed an executive order that federal regulations be written in "plain English and understandable to those who must comply with them." Many states followed. Some large corporations began to rewrite consumer documents in plain English, both as a reaction to legislative pressures and as a public relations gimmick. But these initiatives have not proved long lasting. Principles of composition do not receive priority when new staff members are trained, and over time institutions forget the purpose of plain English and lose the skills to provide it. Every few years some government agency or another rediscovers the problem and promulgates yet another plain English requirement, as if the subject were new.

In 1998, for example, the Office of Investor Education and Assistance of the U.S. Securities and Exchange Commission published *A Plain English Handbook*. In his preface to the 77-page guide, the billionaire investor Warren E. Buffett confessed that after more than forty years of studying public company documents, "too often I've been unable to decipher just what is being said or, worse yet, had to conclude that nothing was being said." SEC Chairman Arthur Levitt recommended that legalese and jargon "give way to everyday words that communicate complex information clearly."[8] The primary author of the manual, William Lutz (an English professor at Rutgers who has edited the *Quarterly Review of Doublespeak*) offers succinct advice: Use the active voice. Keep sentences short. Avoid legal and financial jargon, weak verbs, and superfluous words. Instead of "capital appreciation," write "growth."

Fourteen Causes of Bad Legal Writing

Critics of legal writing discern not one but many causes of the "epidemic" of bad writing. To bring some order to an often confused discussion, we have distilled from the literature fourteen explanations of why lawyers write badly:

- *Sociological.* Every profession needs its own symbols and codes.
- *Professional.* Lawyers are trained to be exhaustive researchers.
- *Competitive.* A competitive society demands prolixity.
- *Legal.* The law requires "legalese."
- *Economic.* Lawyers make more money by writing poorly.
- *Historical.* Creatures of precedent, lawyers do what was done before, solely because it *was* done before.
- *Ritualistic.* People must believe in the majesty of the law, embodied in its ritualistic language.
- *Technological.* Modern machines are responsible for slovenly writing.

- *Institutional.* The pressure of business is responsible for unclear writing.
- *Deterministic.* The way lawyers write is the best way to accomplish the law's goals.
- *Pedagogical.* Lawyers never learned to write well.
- *Cultural.* Lawyers don't read enough or know enough of their heritage to write better.
- *Psychological.* Lawyers are afraid to reveal themselves.
- *Intellectual.* Lawyers don't think clearly enough.

Sociological

To function as a profession, every group of practitioners needs its own symbols, rituals, and practices to set it apart from the rest of the world. Stuart Auerbach, who covered legal affairs at the *Washington Post,* has speculated that lawyers' language serves "as a secret handshake in a fraternity, letting others know you are one of the tribe." Or as Professor Lawrence M. Friedman of Stanford Law School said, a "specialized vocabulary reinforces the group feelings of members. . . . Legal style and the vocabulary of lawyers . . . are indispensable for the cohesiveness and the prestige of the profession."[9]

This cultish quality of the language takes possession of all lawyers early in their training. What lawyer was not struck to learn in the first year of law school that "an action sounds in tort"? We were stepping away from our friends and college classmates, leaving them behind. They were becoming—"nonlawyers." Since they were not lawyers, they were something much less: They were the laity. Alone among professionals, lawyers exclude the rest of the world in their very name for others. Who has ever heard of a "nonteacher," a "nonjournalist," or a "nondoctor"?

"Strange style," as Professor Robert W. Benson has called it, binds lawyers, in their own eyes, into a fraternity.[10] In short, lawyers conform to a way of writing so that colleagues will not think the worse of them.

The sociological explanation suggests that lawyers will never rid themselves entirely of their technical language. That lawyers, like all professionals, desire fraternity does not, however, explain writing that is incomprehensible even to lawyers themselves.

It would be desirable that each student who graduates from this school know how to read and write. I do not consider this objective to be a modest one; on the contrary, it is extravagantly ambitious.
GRANT GILMORE

Professional

The professional explanation purports to justify verbosity, obscurity, and vagueness. Lawyers are trained, as the cliché goes, to leave no stone unturned: The diligent lawyer will search through every case that even remotely bears on the problem and will digest each one in a brief or memorandum. It is considered less than professional—it might even be malpractice—to omit any possible strand of argument, or any case that strengthens that strand, no matter how tangential. Hence verbosity.

Likewise, lawyers allege professionalism to justify much of the cryptic quality of their prose. Knowing they have a losing case or a difficult message, they express themselves opaquely to keep the courts or others from acting contrary to their clients' interests. The difficulty with this explanation is that it presumes that much that is cryptic has been made so deliberately. There is little evidence for this proposition. Nor is there evidence that intentional obfuscation is a sound strategy. Furthermore, purposeful obscurity is difficult to accomplish; it takes a writer who knows how to write clearly to achieve a convincingly murky style and still stay out of trouble.

Moreover, this explanation fails to distinguish between a style that is unnecessarily opaque and the expression of critically important concepts that are by their nature vague. Consider the following two legal concepts:

The legal requirement that a person act "reasonably." The word expresses a legal standard impossible to define precisely. That is not a fault of the writer but a virtue of the law. Norbert Wiener, the eminent mathematician, argued that the law should always say exactly what it means; it should never use ambiguous concepts.[11] But some legal concepts—due process, equal protection of the laws, executive power—are inherently vague; to fix their boundaries for all time would rob us of the flexibility necessary to a free society.

The Supreme Court's 1955 ukase in *Brown v. Board of Education* that school desegregation proceed "with all deliberate speed."[12] Legitimately or not, the Court chose that vague phrase to avoid the serious dangers it foresaw had its language been more concrete.

Compare these examples with this recall notice to automobile owners, a favorite example of Joseph Williams, author of *Style,* one of the best books on clear writing: "Sudden hood fly-up beyond the secondary catch while driving . . . could result in vehicle crash."[13] The concept is not at all complicated; rather, the drafter chose cloudy language to mask the danger. Even if the client demanded this obscurity to inhibit purchasers from demanding free repairs, the notice is irresponsible—and nothing in the law requires that kind of dismal prose.

Defenders of the verbose style of statutory language—those overblown sentences dozens of lines long, with series of subjects ("person, organization, company, association, group, or other entity")—insist that verbiage closes loopholes. If statutes were not verbose, they argue, courts would exploit the loopholes they are so adept at discerning. Sometimes that argument is true, and sometimes lengthy statutes are necessary. But this sense of professionalism does not justify the *style* in which the statutes are written; nor does it justify prolixity in documents that are not legal instruments.

Competitive

In our competitive society, the client wants every edge. Some lawyers and their clients insist that no argument, no matter how trivial, be overlooked or underplayed. If contracts are to be airtight, their clauses tend to be prolix, multiple, and often redundant. Language in an adversary culture evolves into a precision tool for accomplishing a range of ends. But the symptoms are broader than the cause. A litigious society will depend on lawyers who follow every byway of a case, but it does not dictate the writing of every point at maddening length or in obscure style.

Legal

Sometimes lawyers justify legalese by pointing to the law itself. Many words have settled meanings; substituting plain language—that is, words other than those to which the courts are accustomed—can lead to litigation. For some terms, the argument has merit. The common example is the medieval requirement that a fee simple could not be transferred unless the land was sold "to X and his heirs." A sale "to X and his children" would not be effective. But the courts are less formalistic today, and fewer words have rigid meanings. Moreover, few words, even the most arguably precise terms of art, have escaped being broken on the interpreter's rack: The meanings of *herein* and *whereas,* for example, have stirred up plenty of lawsuits.[14]

In any event, the legalistic approach yields a policy at cross-purposes with itself. If legalese is so refined that it prevents litigation, the wording will probably be unintelligible to the clients who sign the instruments. Because it is unintelligible, the clients may go to court claiming that they did not understand what they were signing. At best, the term of art may win the case, but it will not prevent a case from being filed. A clearly worded contract, on the other hand, may keep the parties out of court altogether.

Economic

There are two economic explanations. First, lawyers use language as a tool to maintain their economic perquisites, and second, legalese is a tool to save time and money. Steven Stark, who has taught writing to lawyers and law students, argues that "lawyers write badly because doing so promotes their economic interest. . . . If lawyers stopped writing like lawyers, they might have trouble charging as much for their work." As long ago as 1939, Fred Rodell insisted that the legal trade "is nothing but a high-class racket" because the public is "scared, befuddled, impressed, and ignorant."[15] That is why lawyers write in legalese and produce mounds of paper—at least when paid by the hour. If clients knew what the Latin phrases meant, they would never pay for the lawyer's services.

Such arguments are speculative. Whatever may once have been the truth about Latin incantations, law has become so complex that clients who receive advice in the form of memoranda or letters, or who buy legal instruments such as wills, are more likely to be grateful if they can understand what they have paid for. Although lawyers were once paid by the word, in America this practice died out long before the turn of the twentieth century. Billing is based on time, not on word counts. But it takes more time to produce a shorter, clearer, more readable document, because revising and editing are time-consuming. If generating higher legal bills were the goal, lawyers would produce shorter documents, not longer ones.

A second economic point is made by Lawrence Friedman, who suggests that legal terms of art were invented as helpful shortcuts.[16] Legalese is thus an efficient way to write, one that saves lawyers time and saves clients money. The validity of the argument depends on how much legalese is used and if the audience for whom it is intended can understand it. Using technical terms in front of the court surely does save time—lawyers would appear foolish, and feel foolish, testing out synonyms for *stare decisis* or *collateral estoppel.* But an opinion letter filled with such terms is not necessarily efficient. "Why force your reader to parse and chart your prose?" asked Mark Matthewson, an Illinois practitioner, in an article addressed to prospective lawyers: "The writer should be doing that work, not the reader. Think of it in economic terms—there will almost always be fewer writers of a document than readers, and the interests of efficiency will surely dictate that the writers, not the readers, translate the prose into simple form."[17]

Historical

Lawyers are conservative, innately cautious, and often do what was done before solely because it was done before. As Jacques Barzun suggested to us, lawyers use strings of synonyms out of habit. We all know that the hold of habit is strong, but it rarely justifies what we are doing. Justice Holmes once wrote in a different context, "It is revolting to have no better reason for a rule of law than that so it was laid down in the time of Henry IV. It is still more revolting if the grounds upon which it was laid down have vanished long since, and the rule simply persists from blind imitation of the past."[18]

Ritualistic

Because law is a system of social control, it depends in a democracy on faith—not guns—to achieve its purposes. People must believe in the *majesty of the law.* The language of the law is, according to this argument, a form of magic, a ritual incantation. (Centuries ago, the ritual function was all there was. The litigant or lawyer would recite a formulaic defense, and if he stumbled or misspoke, his misstatement was taken as a sign from God that his cause was wrong.) In some contexts even today, such as the taking of an oath ("the truth, the whole truth, and nothing but the truth"), ritual phraseology "is designed to convey, not information, but emotion—fear, awe and respect," says Lawrence Friedman.[19] But in a secular age, such talismanic purposes of language will necessarily be few.

Some defenders of legalese argue, however, that customers may draw comfort from the archaic. An employee of Siegal & Gale, a New York firm that specializes in simplifying the language of legal instruments, told us that some clients distrust documents that do not have the reassuring "whereases" and "heretofores." And Peter Lubin, a Cambridge writer and lawyer, wrote in the *New Republic* that he was quite impressed when the lawyer representing him in answering an unfair small claims action produced the following lines: "Now comes the Defendant and for his answer denies, Each and every allegation of the Plaintiff's complaint. And further answering says, that if he ever owed the Plaintiff anything, he owes the Plaintiff nothing." Lubin extolled this language as "beauty on the level of the Bible and Shakespeare,. . . . part of what creates the mystery and majesty of the law."[20]

What is disturbing is that law schools . . . find themselves in the situation that even the good writers do not know the difference between "its" and "it's."

DAVID G. TRAGER

This is more whimsy than sense. There are few such phrases and, we suspect, even fewer admirers of them. Again, magic explains only phrases, not the panoply of writing faults in which lawyers regularly engage.

Technological

In the early 1960s, David Mellinkoff blamed the typewriter for contributing to verbosity: fingers waltzing along a keyboard could turn out copy far faster than a hand cramped from dipping a pen in an inkwell. He also noted that electronic data retrieval, like its predecessors "in the arts of availability," is "ruled by a corollary of Parkinson's Law: the data to retrieve increases as it becomes more retrievable."[21] Since then, the photocopier, the computer, the optical scanner, the facsimile machine, and the Internet have contributed to the ease with which lawyers can quickly create long documents. Because they can get words down on paper so easily and without scanning every line, lawyers may be less likely to take the time to consider style and content.

Institutional

Modern law practice is a business, with institutional imperatives of its own. Few law firms working at a leisurely pace survive. From the most senior partner to the most junior associate, private law firms (and most public law offices too) are pressured to crank out paper. The pressure of business means that human energies are focused more on technical matters—meeting deadlines, checking footnotes, getting documents printed—than on thinking. Fewer hours are available for thinking through a problem, writing down one's thoughts, and editing a series of drafts. It is far easier, and seemingly safer, to borrow from previous documents than to rethink and rewrite. Add the lawyer's fear of originality, and the consequence is that lawyers reproduce not just words from a document but its tone and style as well. To be sure, boilerplate may be appropriate, but it does not belong everywhere.

Students seem more than ever to think that some kind of human right is violated when we hold them to high writing standards.
RICHARD K. NEUMANN JR.

The institutional pressure can be even more unremitting on the small-firm and solo practitioners. Always pressed for time, often competing with large firms that can drown them in paper, the small-firm practitioners understandably, if unfortunately, are inclined to regurgitate old copy.

Other institutional habits also diminish the quality of writing. One is the tendency, observable at nearly every level of every institution (it is by no means confined to law firms), to ask someone lower on the organization chart to write for someone higher. Outside the legal profession, this practice often goes by the name ghostwriting. A generation ago, Carl McGowan commented on "the extraordinary degree to which the successful lawyer may get out of the habit of writing anything himself. . . . Some of our best men at the bar may be doing very little initial composition; and we all know how the first draft tends to set the style and tone of any piece of writing."[22]

Still another development that multiplies words is the expansion of staff. Many of the lawyers and judges we have spoken to have pointed to the baneful effect of more law clerks on the length and quantity of judicial opinions. Former Justice Richard Neely of the West Virginia Supreme Court said that hiring more clerks increases the level of "pseudoscholarship": "While judges used to be good old boys who penciled out their opinions in longhand, now they simply figure out the bottom line and tell some magna cum loudmouth smartass clerk to cobble up the reasons in an opinion. The clerk has little idea how everything comes together. But he knows how to use a library. Thus, the ever rising level of crap in reported cases." Similarly, Patricia M. Wald, long-time Chief Judge of the U.S. Court of Appeals for the District of Columbia Circuit, told us that judges are understandably reluctant to disappoint the clerk who has researched and written a lengthy memorandum about a pending case. So they incorporate the pages in the opinion.

Deterministic

Some critics say that lawyers' abstruse writing reflects their abstract way of thinking about the world. Steven Stark concluded that "poor writing is as much a consequence of the way lawyers look at the world as is their ability to read a contract and find consideration."[23] This bent toward abstraction, Stark argued, prevents lawyers from writing clear stories that others can follow.

In the heels of the higgling lawyers, Bob,
Too many slippery ifs and buts and howevers
Too much hereinbefore provided whereas,
Too many doors to go in and out of.
CARL SANDBURG

Law professor Richard Hyland rebutted Stark's notion in a lengthy defense of legal writing.[24] Storytelling, Hyland observed, is one of many levels of discourse, and it is not the level most deserving of a lawyer's time. Instead, lawyers must focus on the higher conceptual plane. Rather than blame lawyers for writing what the public cannot understand, Hyland suggested that the public recognize that the conceptual complexity of legal writing is necessarily beyond general understanding.

But even at the conceptual level, lawyers fail. Lawrence Grauman Jr., a San Francisco–area writer and editor with a special interest in law, expressed it best:

> Most lawyers appear to regard language and prose as merely an inconvenient vehicle (what they would term "style") for the accommodation of ideas or argument (what they think of as "content"), rather than as the very fiber of, and inseparable from, thought (or at least distinctive perception) itself. Few lawyers would wear a second-hand suit, but most are comfortable wearing well-worn or mass-produced language. And frequently the same lawyers who select their clothes to make a visual impression use language merely to make a verbal impression or to inflate their self-importance.

Every time a lawyer writes something, he is not writing for posterity, he is writing so that endless others of his craft can make a living out of trying to figure out what he said.
WILL ROGERS

Hyland's concern with whether the public understands legal writing diverts attention from the more vexing problem: even *other lawyers* cannot fathom what their colleagues are writing.

Pedagogical

The simplest explanation of why lawyers write badly is that they were never taught how to write well—not in high school, not in college, and not in law school.

Participants in a symposium in the *Yale Alumni Magazine* in 1976 expressed a familiar complaint of the 1970s and 1980s: "Anyone who reads student writing today knows that students can't write."[25] The students of 1976 who could not write are today's partners who, in turn, are responsible for supervising the writing of new associates. At that

symposium, A. Bartlett Giamatti, who later became president of Yale
and then commissioner of baseball, explained how cultural longings
denied students their ability to express themselves:

> Today's college students—the former grammar and high school students
> of the late 1960's and early '70's—have lost touch with the language. . . .
>   . . . They have come out of the sentimental '60's . . . out of a primary
> and secondary world where "personal development" was said to be worth
> more than achievement, where "creativity" was the highest goal and was
> often completely divorced from one of its essential components: disci-
> pline. . . .
>   What has happened? I believe that of all the institutions attacked in
> the past dozen years—governmental, legal and educational—the one
> that suffered most was the institution of language itself. . . . This insti-
> tution—language—was perceived as being repressive. It was thought to
> be the agent of all other repressive codes—legal, political, and cultural.
> Language was the barrier that blocked—blocked access to pure feeling,
> blocked true communal experience of the kind that flowered at Wood-
> stock, blocked the restoration of Eden.[26]

Many schools are now focusing on language skills courses, but their
rigor is open to question.

Still, too much can be made of what happened in the late 1960s.
Even a nodding acquaintance with the complaints of educators over
the years shows that the quality of too much student writing, in general,
and law student writing, in particular, has always been problematical.
In 1953, speaking of past generations, Jacques Barzun, the eminent critic
and scholar, asked, "How do people write who are not professionals or
accomplished amateurs?" His answer: "Badly, at all times."[27]

The time traveler can easily confirm Barzun's observation. In the
seventeenth century, leading British intellectuals clamored for admission to the new Royal Society, dedicated to scientific discovery and
invention. In their history of the period, Jacob Bronowski and Bruce
Mazlish have said: "More important than any formal symbolism, however, scientific work, to be understood, needs a clear expression in
words. This the Royal Society stressed from the outset. . . . The Fellows
of the Royal Society were exhorted to report their findings 'without

amplification, digressions, and swellings of style.'" When the poet John Dryden was admitted to the Royal Society, he was promptly put to work simplifying the scientists' prose.[28]

Each generation of critics has despaired anew over the ostensible decline of English and has blamed the deterioration on the failures of an earlier generation to teach it well. To spare law faculty from having to give instruction in grammar and composition, the University of Chicago Law School created the first legal writing course in the late 1930s;[29] many other law schools adopted the practice in the 1940s. But even after decades of complaints and reforms, most legal writing courses devote little attention to reading good writing or to criticizing bad writing. During three years of law school, the required readings—appellate opinions—are selected for their substantive meaning, not for their quality of expression. As it happens, many judicial opinions are dreadfully composed, in no small part because the profession has no mechanism for criticizing the prose style of opinions. Writing is learned by imitation, and yet generation after generation of law students are given poor models to emulate. Consider, for example, the following paragraph from *Pennoyer v. Neff*, 95 U.S. 714 (1877), a basic case in civil procedure read by all first-year law students, often in the first week of school:

> The force and effect of judgments rendered against non-residents without personal service of process upon them, or their voluntary appearance, have been the subject of frequent consideration in the courts of the United States and of the several States, as attempts have been made to enforce such judgments in States other than those in which they were rendered, under the provision of the Constitution requiring that "Full faith and credit shall be given in each State to the public acts, records and judicial proceedings of every other State," and the Act of Congress providing for the mode of authenticating such Acts, records and proceedings, and declaring that, when thus authenticated, "They shall have such faith and credit given to them in every court within the United States as they have by law or usage in the courts of the States from which they are or shall be taken." In the earlier case, it was supposed that the Act gave to all judgments the same effect in other States which they had by law in the State where rendered. But this view was afterwards qual-

ified so as to make the Act applicable only when the court rendering the judgment had jurisdiction of the parties and of the subject-matter, and not to preclude an inquiry into the jurisdiction of the court in which the judgment was rendered, or the right of the State itself to exercise authority over the person or the subject-matter. . . .

Robert Leflar, a former justice of the Arkansas Supreme Court, has observed that the opaqueness of judicial writing is rarely challenged or criticized. The judge "may receive no real criticism of his writing for months or years. Unlike ordinary editors or publishers, the state reporters and the West Publishing Company never refuse to print his opinions, nor do they even edit them. His writing is published whether good or not. Almost no one except law review editors and losing litigants criticize his work, and even these critics usually dwell only on the correctness of his legal analyses rather than on the quality of his presentation."[30]

One style held out as a model is the law review essay. It should not be. In his characteristically blunt fashion, Fred Rodell blamed legal style on what lawyers learn as law review editors, when they are "brainwashed" into thinking they must write in a "straitjacket" style, the lawyers' "brand of professional pig Latin."[31]

Like judicial opinions, law review articles are seldom criticized for their density and opaqueness. As law reviews proliferate—more than 650 are now published—the law review style spreads. Journal editors move on to clerkships, and in those jobs they re-create what they have learned: unending essays, numerous footnotes, suffocating prose—all taught by people who are themselves far from being students of good writing. Many lawyers say they learned how to write and edit on a law review. But the question is *what* they learned. If you are taught by people who prefer long-windedness, you will likely adopt that long-windedness. In criticizing law review writing, we do not mean to be anti-intellectual, but we do mean to observe that good writing is rarely taught, bad writing usually absorbed. Although many lawyers deplore the style of law reviews, few suggest how to improve the style, and few pledge to refrain from writing for the reviews.

Cultural

Two centuries ago, the tiny social elite that could write also tended to read. The intellectuals of the day, including the learned professionals—lawyers, clergy, and doctors—read the classics and the leading contemporary works. By the mid–twentieth century, that common culture had vanished. In 1950 Arthur Vanderbilt lamented that "no instructor in any class in any law school can make a reference to Plato or Aristotle, to the Bible or Shakespeare, to the *Federalist* or even the Constitution itself with any real assurance that he will be understood."[32] Today, most learned professionals are drowning in technical literature and have little time for reading outside their field.

Lawyers who do not read broadly fail to develop the nimbleness of mind that distinguishes good from bad writers. Carl McGowan recalled the comments of a Supreme Court justice who complained that the quality of briefs and oral arguments before his court was "distressingly low." The justice, whom McGowan did not name, lamented "the narrowing cultural range of the profession," which he attributed to "the restricted reading habits of lawyers, both in terms of the small amount of time devoted to general reading and the ephemeral character of what is read."[33]

They have no lawyers among them, for they consider
them as a sort of people whose profession it is to
disguise matters.
THOMAS MORE, *Utopia*

What lawyers do encounter in their narrow reading is bureaucratic double-talk (among McGowan's examples: the Pentagon's description of appropriations not already spent as "unprogrammed in no-year accounts"). As George Orwell pointed out in "Politics and the English Language" (1946): "[Our language] becomes ugly and inaccurate because our thoughts are foolish, but the slovenliness of our language makes it easier for us to have foolish thoughts."[34] Beset by euphemisms ("terminations with extreme prejudice" for "kill"), obfuscations ("inoperative statements" for "lies," and "revenue enhancements" for "tax increases"), and other forms of Newspeak (presidential quibbles about "what the meaning of *is* is"), lawyers find it difficult to think or write clearly.

Psychological

As representatives, lawyers hesitate to intrude their personalities into the affairs of their clients. Trained to identify more with process than value or outcome, exhorted to refrain from vouching personally for their clients' bona fides,[35] lawyers are distanced from the merits of their causes. But writing is a personal act, which reveals the writer in the act of writing. To avoid or minimize the revelation, lawyers transfer the masks that they wear in public to the prose that they put on the page.[36] The passive voice, the fuzzy phrases, and the circumlocutions that permit the lawyer to sidestep the simple "I" may all be understood as lawyers' attempts to keep themselves from being on display.

Intellectual

The final explanation is the most devastating: Lawyers lack the aptitude, or at least the training in logic, to think clearly, and their muddy writing reflects their muddled thinking. Hyland, for example, concluded that many lawyers suffer from a disorder far more serious than lax style: they succumb to "the irrelevancies that reveal the absence of disciplined thought."[37] Unable to assess the validity of an argument, they toss in every point they can think of, hoping one will capture the justices' fancy.

I know you Lawyers can, with Ease,
Twist Words and Meanings as you please;
That Language, by your Skill made pliant,
Will bend to favour ev'ry Client;
BENJAMIN FRANKLIN

True, the more complicated a legal problem, the more likely a lawyer will flounder, but Hyland's diagnosis is flawed (as is his bizarre notion that most lawyers are incapable of thinking clearly because they have not been trained in Latin, Greek, or comparative law). Many legal problems are simple enough for any practicing lawyer to grasp. Failure to organize a document logically cannot be attributed solely to an empty head. Poorly organized thought and cloudy concepts are also products of laziness and inadequate grounding in what constitutes clear expression.

Poor writing is often just that. Lawrence Friedman, after discussing the purposes that legal language rightly fulfills, notes that "law books are full of incredible quantities of plain bad style—clumsy, pompous legalese and tedious, obscure prose—which is neither good law, good magic, nor good history."[38]

That it is imperative for lawyers to learn how to express themselves more clearly—against all the social and personal forces we have just explored—is, we think, almost a tautology. Some have doubted it, however. In 1986 Richard Hyland asserted that good writing makes little difference because "prose itself seems to be losing its hold as the prime medium for the communication of thought"; in 2000 Professor Richard K. Sherwin concluded that "print-based culture" has been replaced by an "image-saturated culture," in which people look "*at* the signs and symbols that flow by, rather than *through* printed words for whatever meanings they may offer."[39] We reject the implications of this "McLuhanacy."[40] Despite all the new technology, with its powerful capacity to organize and display graphic enhancements on the page, despite torrential story-telling told in television and movies, language still matters. If a picture is worth a thousand words, a few words can summarize, organize, and explain a thousand pictures. The lawyer's job is, as it always has been, to communicate legal thought in understandable prose.

"What is writing for?" we ask a roomful of lawyers.

"Communication," someone pipes up.

"Anything else?" we continue.

Blank stares. Determined to get an answer, we change our question.

"Quick now, how much is two plus two?"

Singled out by name, the lawyer hesitates, weighing the simplicity of the question against the odious possibility of a complex trick. Finally, the answer: "Four."

"Good."

Singling out another lawyer, we ask: "How much is ten times five?" "Fifty," hurled back in the next breath.

"Very well, then," pointing this time to a lawyer who has sat silent all afternoon, "how much is 1,324 times 967?"

The wiseguy, overcome with his brilliance, announces that the product is 57,246,589. Polite laughter, from us too.

We point again to the perplexed lawyer, who stares ahead gloomily, not understanding what has turned a writing tutorial at a law firm into a mathematics exercise from which he had fled years before.

"I cannot do that math in my head," the wriggling lawyer grunts. "I'm no idiot savant."

"What, then, should you do? We want an answer."

"Multiply," he replies, still resisting the obvious.

"Multiply where?"

"Here," he says, stabbing at a notebook.

"Oh," we say, "you mean on paper!"

We've engaged in this colloquy dozens of times to show that before

In the first edition, we called this chapter "The Ten Steps of the Writing Process." Jacques Barzun wrote us to complain of the unnecessary use of "process."

communication is possible, the writer must know what he wants to say. Just as most of us cannot solve a complicated math problem in our heads, so most of us need paper to solve the problems that are put to us as lawyers. Before communication, in other words, comes *problem solving.*

How much anguish we would all have been spared had we known when we were young what we were supposed to do when we had to write. Told to compose an essay on Shakespeare, Charlemagne, or the Declaration of Independence, we gnawed at our pencils, wondering how to get words to resemble the essay example in our textbooks. The methodical writer constructed an outline, dutifully scribbling "I. Shakespeare, the Man." The impatient jotted down thoughts in spurts and whooped when the last ruled line was filled in. The furtive pulled down the encyclopedia, copying the most relevant article, aware on occasion of the need to paraphrase, though unclear why. Wasn't the object of the exercise to make sure we stayed in at night? Any words on the page would prove the next morning that we had.

When the papers came back to us, the teacher annotated in bold marginal red about the need to avoid so many irrelevancies, or to organize our thoughts better, or to refrain from copying quite so liberally, but few teachers could explain what we were supposed to do and why we couldn't seem to do it. Even fewer acknowledged the pain of writing and showed us how to ease it.

Lawyers need to know what writing is about and how to vanquish the pain, without aspirin. You need to know that you are not the only one who suffers from chaos, uncertainty, and false starts. All writers do, and there is a sound reason for your difficulties in writing clearly and smoothly and logically on demand. That reason lies in the very nature of writing.

Polished writing requires many steps. First, in the composing stage, you think through a problem and get your thoughts on paper. Second, in the editing stage, you shape what you have written to communicate it to an audience. When you sit down to compose, you have nothing to communicate, nothing, at least, about a subject of even moderate complexity, for you have not yet figured out what to say or even what you know. Just because you stare blankly at a piece of paper does not mean that your mind is defective; it is not a warning to take up another line of work. It means that your work *as a lawyer* is about to begin. Writing is thinking on paper.

Though problem solving is the essence of a lawyer's job, that skill is barely taught in law school. Classroom discussions focus on small points. Indeed, one cannot expect more from classroom time: To take on a larger problem, students would have to write it out, and no time in the classroom is set aside for that. With few exceptions, law schools call on students to solve problems only on final exams, and by then class has been adjourned for the semester. Students thus learn little about writing from their exams. For the most part, the schools teach doctrine, not skills.

Different skills are required at the two stages of writing. The goal of the first stage, composing, is to solve problems; the goal of the second stage, editing, is to express the solution clearly, to communicate. Most instruction in writing emphasizes the second stage, by teaching rudimentary editing skills. Writing instruction, at least in law schools, rarely emphasizes problem solving or composing.

Skill in composing entails proficiency in thinking: First, you must have the talent to put concepts into words—to wield logic, use analogy, and employ metaphor. Second, you must exercise judgment—to evaluate, select, and weigh.

> *There is an accuracy that defeats itself by the overemphasis of details . . . The sentence may be so overloaded with all its possible qualifications that it will tumble down of its own weight.*
> JUSTICE BENJAMIN CARDOZO

In solving math problems, you need plenty of scrap paper once you move beyond simple arithmetic, because the solution is uncertain and mistakes are unavoidable. So, too, in solving a logical or conceptual problem, you will rarely get it right the first time. You stumble, you back up, you weave this way and that because you are hunting for the solution as you go. That is why the most successful writers are those with well-stocked minds open to experimentation.

Few people solve problems the same way. Carl Stern, former law reporter for NBC-TV, compared the approaches taken by two Supreme Court justices, William Douglas and Harry Blackmun, in their dissenting opinions in *Sierra Club v. Morton,* 405 U.S. 717 (1972). (The Court ruled that the Sierra Club had no standing to challenge the U.S. Forest Service, which had approved a plan to build a vacation complex in California.) Stern observed:

> Douglas wrote passionately of "these priceless bits of Americana" which might be forever lost. He eulogized the "valleys, alpine meadows, ridges, groves of trees, rivers, lakes, estuaries, beaches, swampland or even air that feels the destructive pressures of modern technology and modern life," of water ouzels, otter, deer, elk and bear, and of the Tuolumne Meadows and the John Muir Trail. He wondered who would speak for "the core of America's beauty" before it is destroyed.
>
> Justice Blackmun, on the other hand, a one-time Harvard math major, computed the number of cars that were likely to pass a given point in the road each hour (300). "This amounts to five vehicles per minute," he said, "or an average of one every twelve seconds." Really, one every six seconds, he noted, because cars must return to leave the park. And that does not include service vehicles and employees' cars, he added, in his concern about preserving the beauty, solitude and quiet of the wilderness.
>
> Two judges with one point of view, but vastly different writing styles.

> *Diversionary tactics on the part of lawyers come from*
> *their fear that their expertise won't seem very special if*
> *they write it down in plain English.*
> ANDY ROONEY

The ability to write is neither an innate talent nor a learned skill, concludes Susan R. Horton, an authority on writing. "It is," she writes, "more a matter of attitude than of skill, and the attitude most essential is that of welcoming the mess and the mystery" that give life to writing:

> If you are uncomfortable getting your hands dirty and your desk messy, you will cheat yourself out of the chance to discover something new and wonderful to say. Mess is material: material for thinking; for shaping into essays. . . .
>
> We know that "writing" does not begin when we first put pen to paper. Instead, writing is actually only the final stage of a long process. Ideas are born . . . partly in the act of writing—writing itself generates them—but they are also born out of that rich, primordial slime where we alternatively go after them with our big guns (like definition, compare/contrast, distinction-making) and lie in wait for them to raise their heads out of the smoky swamp like some Nessy. The truth is that all of the lists of procedures in the world will not help you write better if you do not acknowledge that the idea, the hypothesis, the new synthesis, the organization for an essay is likely to appear not so much as a result of applying a rigorous set of procedures, but just when you were not looking for it at all; as you stumbled half asleep to the front door at 4 A.M., to let the dog in, or out.[1]

Once you understand that composing is a messy hunt for a solution to a problem, you should feel less frustrated over the stubborn refusal of the first draft to write itself. You will find it slow going because you are wrestling with unyielding concepts, not because you are foundering on the words. That is why you cannot sensibly begin with a formal outline, as some teacher somewhere along the way insisted you must (even though an informal outline is usually helpful). A formal outline represents an ordered and logical structure, an organization that you will not be able to impose until you have solved the problem.

Since composing is thinking on paper, a first draft is, at best, the scrap-paper solution to your problem, showing the signs of trial and error. You can never count on a first draft to communicate your solution to your intended audience.

From these considerations emerge two key principles to mastering writing:

- Compose early.
- Edit late.

There is no trick here, but adhering to these two simple principles will have a magical effect on your writing. Solve your problem as early as you can, and delay rewriting and editing as long as you can. You need this intermission to forget about composing and problem solving, to gain some distance from your draft, and to prepare yourself to edit. As you'll see, the secret to editing is to come to your draft not as its writer but as its reader.

To write well, the writer must take ten steps in two stages. In stage one (steps 1 through 6), the writer searches for ways to solve the problem. In stage two (steps 7 through 10), the writer dresses up the solution to communicate it clearly to the reader.

1. Develop a theory; write it down.
2. Research; take notes.
3. Jot down a rough outline.
4. Reassess your theory; explain it to yourself on paper.
5. Set down a formal outline.
6. Compose.
7. Reorganize.
8. Rewrite.
9. Edit and edit again.
10. Proofread.

For the most complex assignments, we recommend that you proceed step by step. For less complex assignments, you may need to jumble the steps or even take two steps at once. Often, for both simple and complex assignments, you may need to repeat some steps several times.

Here, we briefly describe the ten steps; we discuss them at length in later chapters.

Step 1. Develop a theory.

You must begin with some idea of direction, purpose, or goal, though you need not know exactly how you're going to get there. When Jessica was in the eighth grade, her history assignment was to write a thousand-word essay on "the impact of European colonialism on African economic development." She didn't know quite what that meant, and she didn't ask. Consequently, her research amounted to no more than a random collection of quotations that she jerry-built into an answer. She gave the draft to her father, the writing teacher. He didn't take kindly to it. She didn't take kindly to him. Moral: Know where you're going.

Ordinarily, step 1 in legal writing is the easiest step because the nature of the case or your discussions with the client or a supervising attorney determine the objective: "We want summary judgment"; "he breached the contract"; "let's see if we can get specific performance"; "do we have a good case of copyright infringement?" You will surely fail if you do not know at the outset what your aim is. If you are unsure of the aim, ask. Lawyers who fail to ask questions, fearing to look stupid, are doomed to prove that they are stupid when they turn in their drafts. Of course, you want to be intelligent about the questions you ask. The young lawyer who wonders "What exactly is summary judgment?" will raise a supervisor's eyebrow. But to ask "Why do you think we should seek summary judgment in this case?" will force the supervisor to articulate a theory, a starting point for the work to come.

Step 2. Research.

With a goal in mind, you can begin to research. You are not looking just for quotations to adorn your brief. Writers absorbed in hunting for quotations sacrifice time for thought; the more sparingly you quote, the better your writing. Research should stimulate thought; you read cases not to write a history of the law but to force your mind to respond to something relevant, to begin thinking about the problem at hand, to let ideas flow.

As you research, keep your mind open to all possibilities. In a letter to a friend who had complained of an inability to write, the poet Friedrich von Schiller offered advice that remains sound:

> The reason for your complaint lies, it seems to me, in the constraint which your intellect imposes upon your imagination. . . . Regarded in isolation, an idea may be quite insignificant, and venturesome in the extreme, but it may acquire importance from an idea which follows it; perhaps in a certain collocation with other ideas, which may seem equally absurd, it may be capable of furnishing a very serviceable link. . . . In the case of a creative mind . . . the intellect has withdrawn its watchers from the gates, and the ideas rush in pell-mell, and only then does it review and inspect the multitude. You worthy critics . . . are ashamed or afraid of the momentary and passing madness which is found in all creators, the longer or shorter duration of which distinguishes the thinking artist from the dreamer. Hence your complaints of unfruitfulness, for you reject too soon and discriminate too severely.[2]

How the mind solves a problem remains mysterious, so no one can give you a formula for telling how many pieces of the puzzle you need and how to lay them out. But we do know that it is crucial to begin the writing process early. You need not actually sit down to compose, but you must have the project in mind. You need time for conscious reflection and for subconscious rumination. That is why thinking about a memorandum due on Monday morning must not be left for Sunday night; you need to have time for reflection, for mental processing, for second thoughts, or for intermediate solutions that lead to still better solutions. Even if you do not have the time to start *composing* until Sunday night, try to read the assignment and begin thinking about it the day you receive it.

Step 3. Jot down a rough outline.

Before you progress too far in your research, you should begin to jot down notes for a rough outline. This rough list will help you direct and organize further research. You will not yet be able to see the entire structure of your solution, so you cannot compose a formal outline. But you should begin to list the topics you plan to discuss. Later, when you know what all your topics will be, you can rearrange them into a logical sequence.

Step 4. Reassess your theory.

Your initial theory of the case suggested certain avenues of research. Your research may have suggested new avenues. You should constantly be asking whether your initial assumptions were correct or whether your research requires you to modify them.

Step 5. Set down a formal outline.

When you are satisfied that your research has given you the main direction for your document—and that you have not overlooked any byways—you should write a formal outline. By now you will know, for instance, that there are two elements to proving copyright infringement, that courts have accepted six circumstances in your case as proof of those elements, that there are several procedural hurdles, that you have ways to surmount each, and that none of the available defenses is well-founded. You may have solved your problem already, or you may solve it as you are working out your formal outline. Don't become too attached to this outline, however; there's a good chance that it will not be the final one.

Step 6. Compose.

You have completed five steps, and only now should you begin to compose. Now you will see whether your solution to the problem will work. If you are not yet sure you have a solution, now you will discover what you need to create one.

The time it takes to reach this step depends on the complexity of the assignment and the amount of research you must undertake, but you must always leave plenty of time for steps 6 through 10. As you compose, you will learn what you know and, even more important, what you have yet to discover. The sooner you start writing, the sooner you can see the holes in your argument. You can read statutes and cases forever, but you will not know whether your reading is sufficient or germane until you try to make sense of it by writing your first draft.

When you now sit down to compose—or stand up, if you are like Justice Holmes, who said "nothing conduces to brevity like a caving in of the knees"[3]—you may feel blocked. We distinguish two kinds of writer's blocks. The first is the psychological difficulty many people have in *beginning* any protracted and solitary intellectual enterprise. The second kind of block is conceptual: it is a signal of inadequate preparation. You stop because you do not have the information you need, or because you cannot discern logical connections within the materials you have assembled. Once you identify the source of a conceptual block, you can stage unblocking maneuvers. You may need to do more research or more thinking about your argument (How does *this* fact connect to *that* rule?).

Again, the earlier you start to compose, the earlier you will encounter these blocks, and the more time you will have to do more research, interview more witnesses, talk to the client, or rethink some aspect of the problem. If you have waited until Sunday night, you will be denied these options, and your document will be empty—or late.

You can also learn to write around small gaps in your knowledge. If you are missing a minor fact, one whose presence will not affect the concepts you are developing or their consequences, leave the fact checking for later. Once you begin to compose, you should not interrupt your train of thought to locate a date, a name, a middle initial, a line of cases, or the "right" word. Give yourself as much uninterrupted time to compose as possible.

Here's a simple trick that journalists use. When they are momentarily stumped, they jot in "TK," meaning "to come." So a sentence in a first draft might read: "On May TK, a witness, TK Jones, saw the defendant step out of the drug store wearing, in Jones's words, 'TK.'" The three missing points (the date, Jones's first name, and Jones's precise words) will not affect your argument, nor will their absence prevent you from proving your point. The important thing is to write. Don't hold back the big ideas; don't bog down in minutiae. Shut your door, turn off your phone, keep the radio low, tell your kids to play in the street, don't get up to sharpen a pencil or look up a word in the dictionary— just write.

When you are composing, try not to even look at your notes. You have read through cases, previous memos, and the record of the case, and you have a general impression of the facts and the law. Let that impression suffice as you strive to make sense of the whole. Usually the important points will rise to the surface, and you'll avoid becoming bogged down in details. You can always go back later and add what's missing.

Step 7. Reorganize.

Let's assume you have solved your problem. You know why summary judgment should be granted, why your client's copyright has been infringed and how to prove it, why your client was not an inside trader. When your draft is done, you have completed your problem solving. Now it remains to communicate that solution to your readers.

The first draft is *your* solution to the problem; the final draft must be the *reader's*. What may be clear to you may appear ambiguous to a reader who does not know how you think, how you arrived at what you wrote, and what you intended. Your words are the reader's only window into your thinking. When you edit your work, you must put yourself in the reader's place—you must come to your work without any preconceptions about its meaning.

> *Your business as thinkers is to make plainer the way*
> *from some things to the whole of things.*
> OLIVER WENDELL HOLMES JR.

That is why you must *edit late,* why you must allow as many hours or days as possible to elapse after you have reorganized your document so that you still have time to prepare a final product on deadline. For as time passes, as your words grow colder, your memory of what you intended will dim. The halo of meaning will dissipate. After enough time has passed, you will read the document more as an outsider would, seeing the ambiguities and having to guess at the meaning. Edit a paper five minutes after you have drafted it, and you will not see how it flunks its ultimate mission, to communicate your solution to its readers. Edit five days (or even five hours) later, and you will begin to see which sentences and paragraphs are murky.

Your schedule will never permit the lengthy intermission John Kenneth Galbraith enjoyed during his work on *The New Industrial State.* He was about to send the manuscript to his publisher when President Kennedy called, asking him to serve as ambassador to India. Galbraith put the manuscript in a drawer and returned to it two years later, appalled to discover deficiencies he had never imagined. The best thing for a writer, he concluded, was to accept a long overseas appointment.[4]

Failing that, allow as much time as possible for the document to sit, out of sight and out of mind. That is another reason that you should begin your writing early. The earlier you write, the more time you will have to clear your mind before you begin editing.

Editing well—transforming your writing from draft to polished prose—requires several steps; it cannot be done in a single sweep of the red pencil across all the pages. Your first concern is whether your document proceeds in a logical order. Read through the entire draft and look at the sequence of the major parts and the sequence of topics within each of the major parts. To help you keep track of the sequence, jot down in the margin of each paragraph its main points and compare these marginal headings throughout the document. You should quickly see what belongs together and what is out of order.

Don't fret if much of your draft is jumbled. In fact, be suspicious if everything seems well ordered. Problem solving is messy, and as you compose you will rarely think of every issue and every fact in time to place them just where they belong.

Move your sentences and paragraphs around. Draw arrows; use scissors and tape or the cut-and-paste features of your word processor. To spare yourself extra work, avoid the temptation at this point to correct grammar, sentence structure, punctuation, word choice, and the like.

Concern yourself with organizing the whole. Fixing a sentence or paragraph before you move it will almost surely require you to modify it further once you have put it in a new place.

Confusion of expression usually results from confusion of conception. The act of writing can help clarify one's thoughts. However, one should spare the reader having to repeat one's own extrication from confusion. The object is to be clear, not to show how hard it was to be so.
GEOFFREY C. HAZARD JR.

Step 8. Rewrite.

Read through the document again. This time, look at the major elements: introduction, conclusion, topic sentences, headings, transitions. Does your introduction give your readers a road map for the entire document? Is your conclusion obvious and inescapable? Does each paragraph contain only one major point, does the topic sentence state that point, and do the sentences that follow make the point? Do your headings and transitions tie your paragraphs together? Will the reader understand why paragraph 24 follows paragraph 23?

Although *you* know that you have solved the problem assigned to you, the reader remains to be convinced. You have satisfied yourself; now satisfy the reader.

Step 9. Edit and edit again.

In successive readings, look for specific types of writing problems: word order, word choice, grammar, passive voice, and other impediments to clear communication. Editing is not simple work, and you will not be able to identify and fix all the errors and difficulties in one pass. You should edit until you are satisfied, or until you run out of time. You should press on friends and colleagues as many of your documents as their time and patience will permit. No matter how long you let your own writing lie inert, you will still retain some faint wisp of meaning that your audience can never have. An outsider who tells you that something is unclear is therefore a valuable ally. There's little point in arguing with someone who says, "I don't understand this." *You* may fully understand it, but *your* understanding is not the goal. If one person misunderstands, others may as well. Rewrite some more.

Step 10. Proofread.

When you have finished, either because you have exhausted your patience or your deadline is fast upon you, you must read the document at least once more, to ensure that the final product—the actual paper to be delivered to your reader—is as formally perfect as you can make it. In the days before word processors, proofreading was generally understood to be vital: typists and typesetters could make mistakes, so words might have been misspelled, punctuation might have been missing, a whole line might have been dropped.

Today all too many writers are gulled into complacency by the seeming infallibility of the computer: what you see on the screen is presumably what you get on the printed page. Alas, the correspondence between screen and printer is not always complete, and the writer who refrains from proofreading forgoes one last opportunity to perfect what the reader will see. You would not press a suit for work and then forget to put it on before leaving for the office. Neither should you fail to check that your edits have been faithfully transcribed on the final printed page.

The hardest lesson of all remains. You must learn how to allocate your time between research, composing, and editing. We have talked to enough lawyers to conclude that most misconceive the relative importance of these phases of producing a document. When presented with novel issues, most lawyers spend between half and three-quarters of their time on research. That is a mistake. Research in a vacuum, without the hard thought that comes from composing, is often a wasted effort.

The information you have gathered is useless if you do not effectively communicate it to judges, adversaries' lawyers, or clients. If you are responsible for producing a first draft from scratch, you should devote no more than 30 percent of your time to research and up to 40 percent to composing. During your composing time, you may have to break away to conduct more research. That's not only permissible, it's imperative, as long as you are continuing to compose while researching. The remaining 30 percent of your time should be spent editing. Editing is that important, and it's likely that you will fail in your most important task of effectively representing your client if you do not reserve the time to polish your prose.

Writing is hard work. But that's what you do. It's why you're paid.

4 OF DAWDLERS AND SCRAWLERS, PACERS, AND PLUNGERS

GETTING STARTED AND OVERCOMING BLOCKS

Jay Topkis, who has represented Spiro Agnew, large corporations, and death row inmates, is a tenacious courtroom advocate and an elegant craftsman admired for his spare prose, apt analogies, and colorful images. This is how Topkis, who has practiced in New York at Paul, Weiss, Rifkind, Wharton & Garrison since 1950, starts writing: "I wait, or, as Red Smith once said, I sit down and think until beads of blood form on my forehead. Mostly I procrastinate."

Writing is not easy. Getting started can be especially wrenching. But procrastination rarely is the wisest course. It only makes writing harder.

"Plunge in," advises Evan A. Davis, a partner in Cleary, Gottlieb, Steen & Hamilton, and counsel to New York Governor Mario Cuomo. That sounds right.

On the other hand, maybe it depends. As William J. Jones, a corporate counsel, warned, "A long walk is a good idea, but that *should* vary with individuals. Beethoven and Dickens did extensive rewriting and editing; Mozart and Shakespeare rarely rewrote a line, but you can't tell from the final product. That's what 'counts.' I personally get in mind what I want to say and rarely rewrite. It is a great mistake to force one person's method on another."

We asked lawyers, judges, and professors how they start writing, and they described dozens of approaches, which we have grouped into a handful of categories.

Dawdlers

Thomas D. Rowe Jr., a professor at Duke Law School, reads, thinks, and then organizes: "I dither a lot to force myself to do it, and I sit down at my word processor and type, taking lots of breaks." R. Edward Townsend Jr., a litigator in Manhattan, does everything he can "to keep from starting" and then dictates "a stream-of-unconsciousness first draft," from which he creates the final product. Zick Rubin, a Boston practitioner, says: "I delay a lot and then force myself to plunge in." Rubin, who was a professor of social psychology at Brandeis University before he became a lawyer, adds: "Having more than one project helps—you start writing one thing in order to avoid writing another." William Hughes Mulligan, the well-known lawyer and judge, offered a similar approach: "I wait for a deadline I can't escape."

Scrawlers

David G. Trager, a federal judge and former dean of Brooklyn Law School, tries to get as many ideas as he can on paper "without regard to order or logic." Eric D. Green, professor at Boston University Law School, "lets it percolate. Then I blast it out and revise it later as many times as I can." Former Justice Richard Neely of the West Virginia Supreme Court, who has written several books, says: "I usually vomit a first draft onto the page to see where I am going, and then rewrite and rewrite."

Outliners and Nonoutliners

Those who plunge in usually skip the outline stage. "I envy those who use outlines and think through what they want to write," says Gerald Stern, administrator of the New York State Commission on Judicial Conduct and, for a public official, an unusually gifted writer. "I think while I write. I write quickly and in volume, and then make many changes in drafts 2, 3, 4, 5, 6, and 7." John H. Stassen, a Chicago lawyer, never writes an outline, but he does prepare "a points list." He uses that list as a springboard, starting "with the easiest point first," to ease into "the always painful process of putting words on paper. That starts the creative/analytic juices flowing."

But there are plenty of outliners, and they usually spend plenty of time redrafting. Among the most meticulous outliners is Randal R. Craft Jr., a New York City litigator. His strategy is to "outline, outline, outline. For documents whose organization is relatively simple, I outline them by making a list of the topics to be covered, and then I go back and put in the margin each topic's appropriate numerical sequence. For more complex documents, I usually use index cards for the various topics, subtopics, etc., and then, on a conference room table, I put them in various arrangements, in order to determine which arrangement appears to be the most effective. Spreading out the cards allows a broader bird's-eye view of these arrangements than computers can provide. The authorities and sources to be cited or quoted are listed on the cards. After the outline of cards is completed, I usually dictate my first draft directly from the outline, having my authorities and sources at hand for ready reference. While I dictate, I frequently pace around the room."

Perfectionists and Thinkers

A few lawyers said they aim for a polished first draft. "Generally speaking, I have written a lot of it in my head before I actually sit down and start writing," said Daniel H. Lowenstein, a professor at the University of California at Los Angeles Law School. "I tend to start at the beginning and work my way through. I am pretty compulsive about being fairly polished at the outset. For example, I almost always write my footnotes as I go along. I even write my introduction at the beginning. . . . I do not recommend this method to others. It is simply how I work."

Some lawyers emphasize thinking long and hard before writing. Justin A. Stanley, a former president of the American Bar Association, told us, "A long period of thought preceding the writing is important. Sometimes I just start writing and rewriting and rewriting. Ultimately, thought and writing must come together."

Beginners and Closers

Some lawyers work on the introduction first, others start with the conclusion, and some work on both. "Work a first paragraph to death and take it from there," advised James J. Leff, who was an experienced trial judge in Manhattan and a well-known gadfly of the court system, famous for his acerbic and literate letters to the state's administrative judges. J. Anthony Kline, a California appeals judge, starts by "stating the threshold question as succinctly as I can and then proceeding to answer it."

Still others begin by focusing on both their first and last paragraphs. Herald Price Fahringer, a flamboyant lawyer who has represented Larry Flynt and Claus von Bülow, says he tries "to write the opening and the closing first because I believe they are the most important parts of a brief or legal presentation of any substance." Similarly, Martin Garbus, who represents publishers and authors and has also written several books, drafts the first and last paragraphs and then outlines the document. Eugene R. Fidell, a Washington lawyer, writes his conclusion, then his introduction, and "then [I] settle down on the questions presented, then work up argument headings and subheadings, then write the textual parts of the argument, then go back and tinker with introduction, questions, conclusions, etc. so it all fits together."

I doubt that there are so many as a dozen professors of law in this whole country who could write an article about law, much less about anything else, and sell it, substantially as written, to a magazine of general circulation.

FRED RODELL

Strategists

George Gopen, of Duke University, selects a strategy to match the document he is drafting. For a letter, he turns on his computer and sits down. "For an article or a book chapter," he says, "I do a great deal of putting the rest of my life in order (make the phone calls, prepare the diet Coke, put on the music, etc.), do a great deal of pacing about, get intensely tense, and hope to sit down."

In their sometimes zany approaches to getting words on paper, lawyers join a distinguished group of writers. Samuel Johnson needed a "purring cat, orange peel and plenty of tea." Ernest Hemingway stood while writing, typewriter and reading board chest high opposite him. For years, Raymond Carver worked at his kitchen table, a library carrel, or in his car. In *Thinking through Writing,* Susan R. Horton compiled a splendid list of the idiosyncrasies of famous authors: Balzac wrote only at night; Emile Zola worked only in the daytime but drew the blinds because he could not write without artificial light; and Carlyle craved an atmosphere without sound. For inspiration, Schiller needed the scent of rotting apples, Stephen Spender insisted on tea, and W. H. Auden relied on coffee and tobacco. Only black ink would do for Kipling. Malcolm Lowry stood up, leaned his knuckles against a lectern, and dictated his text to his wife.[1]

The point of these stories is that there is no one correct way to begin. The most dangerous approach is not to begin at all. Procrastination may be the surest sign that you have not worked through what you wish to say. It is better just to plunge in. Yield to your quirks.

If you are unable to take the plunge, you need to figure out why. Is your block psychological or is it conceptual? A psychological block is usually the result of having too many choices or being too much of a perfectionist. A conceptual block is usually a sign of inadequate preparation.

V. A. Howard and J. H. Barton, two educational researchers at Harvard, identify the single greatest block to getting started: "the self-defeating quest to get it right the first time."[2] Establishing an unrealistic goal for a first draft can paralyze your mind. Lower your standards—temporarily. Arrange your writing schedule so that you know you can write a rough first draft and have enough time to turn it into a finished product. That will reduce the pressure on you as you start to compose.

If you still feel blocked—and you know it is psychological, not conceptual—change something about your habits: If you usually write at midday, write in the morning. If you usually dictate or write longhand, try typing. If you usually write at your desk, move to a conference room or to a library. Or try jotting down thoughts and pieces of sentences on the fly, using scraps of paper or a small pad, or keep a miniature tape recorder with you at all times. You can also trick yourself into getting started by breaking the task into small pieces and setting intermediate deadlines. Do not get bogged down in writing the introductory paragraphs—many writers leave these for last. Jump in wherever you feel most comfortable.

Donald Murray, a columnist at the *Boston Globe* who is also a journalism professor and an elder statesman among newsroom writing coaches, offers four more tips:[3]

- Pretend you are writing a letter. "Many writers, including Tom Wolfe," Murray says, "have fooled themselves into writing by starting the first draft 'Dear . . .'"
- Write the end first. "This is a technique used by John McPhee and other writers," according to Murray. If you can't start at the beginning, start at the end, Murray advises: "Once you know where you are going, you may see how to get there."
- Read a fine piece of prose. "One writer friend reads the King James Version of the Bible when he gets stuck," Murray recalls. "It is amazing how stimulating the flow of fine language can be to the writer."
- Write every day. *Nulla dies sine linea* (Never a day without writing), a saying attributed to both Horace and Pliny, "hung over Anthony Trollope's writing desk, John Updike's and mine," notes Murray. He recommends exercising the writing muscle every day, so that writing becomes "a normal, not an abnormal form of behavior."

The lawyer who procrastinates at the start may be resisting the hard work of articulating thought. The lawyer who is blocked in the middle of a writing assignment or near the conclusion may have the will to continue but not the facts. If you find that your power to compose suddenly wanes, that you are spinning out aimless and meaningless sentences, or that you are repeating yourself, you may have exhausted your knowledge of the subject. You may need to collect some additional information before you can resume writing.

But interrupting the act of composing should be your last resort. Do not put your draft down until you are sure that the block is conceptual, not psychological. Try writing yourself a memorandum that addresses the problem you are facing: "I have reached an impasse here because I can't figure out how to go from this point to that one. Perhaps if I . . ." The change of tone might reinvigorate your thinking or help you identify which information you need.

If writing yourself a memorandum does not work, the block might be caused by fatigue; a brief rest could provide the cure. Or you might be bored; a change of topic might refresh your capacity to think. Instead of finishing the section that has you stuck, move on. Ignore the unsolved problem and tackle the next one; in the meantime, a solution may sneak up on you. Or copy over a passage you've already written. "Many times," Donald Murray says, "it helps, when stuck in the middle of a piece, to copy over a part of the writing that has gone well. This helps you recover the voice and flow."

If nothing works, you're through for the day. Sleep on it.

The first machine for writing, the typewriter, came on the market in the United States in the 1870s; the second machine, the personal computer, arrived a century later. Each provoked hallelujahs in some quarters and criticism in others. The comparison is instructive, for each sparked a revolution not merely in the mechanics of composition but in the content of the documents produced.

Businessmen were initially suspicious of typewriters, but they were soon won over by the endorsements of such luminaries as Mark Twain, the first author to send his publisher a typewritten manuscript *(Tom Sawyer)*, and Lloyd George, a prominent lawyer who had learned to type during his apprenticeship and who later became the prime minister of Britain. (At that time, most secretaries were male, and clerical work was part of a legal apprenticeship.) Still, businessmen grumbled that typists, all of whom hunted for and pecked at keys with two or three or four fingers, were no faster than an accomplished office stenographer writing in longhand. Their prayers were answered in 1888, when Frank E. McGurrin, a federal court stenographer in Salt Lake City, demonstrated his system for using all ten fingers and not looking at the keyboard. In a widely publicized contest, McGurrin was judged the fastest typist in the world, and touch typing was born.[1]

Once the typewriter relieved businesses of the tedium and expense of handwriting, "verbosity was within the reach of everyone, especially lawyers," noted David Mellinkoff, the chronicler of the use and misuse of law language, in a decidedly curmudgeonly mood in his pioneering 1963 book, *The Language of the Law*. Producing words on a typewriter, he added, was "so fast, so effortless, that one inclines to lavishness, and forgetfulness."[2] And some inclined to composing reams of paper. Distressed by a 284-page brief, New York Court of Appeals Judge Matthew Jasen in 1975 rebuked the writers from the bench: "In recent years, we have witnessed great technological advances in the methods of reproduction of the written word. Too often this progress is merely viewed as a license to substitute volume for logic in an apparent attempt to overwhelm the courts, as though quantity, and not quality, was the virtue to be extolled." Jasen cited with approval a 1902 court decision that noted that prolixity was seldom seen when "every lawyer wrote his points with a pen."[3]

Gentlemen?
In re yours of the 5th inst. your to hand and in reply,
I wish to state that the judiciary expenditures of this
year, i.e. has not exceeded the fiscal year—brackets—
this procedure is problematic and with nullification
will give us a subsidiary indictment and priority.
Quotes, unquotes and quotes. Hoping this
finds you, I beg to remain as of June 9th,
Cordially, respectfully, regards.
GROUCHO MARX

In the 1980s, the same charges were levied on a new culprit: the personal computer. Mary Frances Edwards, a Washington writer, blamed word processing for the higher volume and lower quality of legal writing: "The ease of word processing has generated a barrage of paper. American lawyers bombard each other with lengthy memoranda, attachments and appendices. The miracle of word processing has also turned many lawyers into mere mechanics. . . . Due to word processing, some documents which were formerly individualized are recycled from case to case and client to client, like soft drink bottles."[4] This recycling also troubled Vivian Dempsey, who has taught legal writing at law schools in the San Francisco area: "Like the harried white rabbit in *Alice in Wonderland,* the attorney who borrows from existing documents may look at his watch and scurry off to more pressing matters instead of taking the time to tailor computer-made documents to a particular use."[5]

David S. Levine, a lawyer and critic, acknowledged that "the new technology gives us opportunities for thoughtful language and style"— but "the result tends to be prose that is both over-manicured and, as always, turgid."[6] Federal District Judge William G. Young of Boston offered a related objection: "Word processing available to lawyers assists them in raising a plethora of points. Judges feel they must deal with each of the points raised even if they are minor."

Should we blame the faulty craftsman or the tool? When computers are misused, they contribute to sprawl. Correctly used, though, they can provide extraordinary benefits. They save time, freeing more time for revisions. "A first draft produced on a word processor," says Fran Shellenberger, a law office management consultant from Maryland, "will have the quality of a second or third draft produced with machine dictation or longhand."[7]

Word processing may not work for everyone. Louis Simpson, the poet and teacher, doubted whether "Flaubert would have written prose more easily if he had owned a word processor—he complained that sometimes it took him a whole day to write a sentence."[8] But for those of us who must write more than a sentence a day, word processing has obvious advantages: we can easily reorder, rewrite, and replace text with a few keystrokes. William K. Zinsser, an elegant stylist and the author of a best-selling guide on writing, is among the many writers who have been converted from skeptic to enthusiast: "Not since the typewriter replaced the pen has a more exciting tool come along," he wrote, after his wariness of computers had dissipated. If typewriters contributed to verbosity, he thought that word processing held the promise of a cure: "The word processor can concentrate your mind on the craft of writing, revising and editing—much more powerfully than this has ever been possible, because your words are right in front of you in all their infinite possibility, waiting to be infinitely shaped. Technology, the great villain, turns out to be your friend."[9]

But law firms were slow to make friends with the first generation of electronic technology. Through the 1980s, most lawyers still composed by dictating or by writing longhand, usually on a yellow (never, never white!) pad. They discouraged their associates from using typewriters, much less word processors, often on the pretext that it was "unprofessional" for lawyers to type. (Perhaps this is the reason so many lawyers of that generation never bothered learning to type. Some female associates even confessed to hiding their typing skills because they did not wish to be mistaken for secretaries.) So offices with highly efficient terminals and computer networks often waited on associates who were penning their briefs longhand onto yellow notepads or dictating onto tapes that would be transcribed when a secretary became available.

During the 1990s, the price of high-speed desktop computers dropped dramatically, word processing software became more sophisticated, and the Internet and the lure of e-mail drew almost everyone to the keyboard. The line between computer users and non-users became and remains largely generational. Some older lawyers prefer to continue to compose as they always have; others do not know how to type or use a computer and have no desire to learn. Some non-users, though, would jump in if only their firms provided computer tutorials.

The popularity of e-mail has occasioned a new chorus of an old complaint. The old version: The typewriter saved businessmen much time but caused them to fall into "all sorts of evil practices, particularly the sin of starting a sentence without a plan for finishing it."[10] The new version: E-mail saves much time but causes people to write informally and sloppily, with no eye to proper spelling or grammar; the e-mail culture is transforming us into a nation of hurried, careless note makers.

A final twist: Now that almost everyone is at the keyboard, improvements in voice-recognition software may take some lawyers away from the keyboard and back to the lost art of dictation. For Arthur H. Christy, in practice in New York since the late 1940s, fluency in dictation has long been a badge of accomplishment, and he thought it unfortunate that younger lawyers lacked the skill: "Very few of them have the ability to dictate face to face, preferring to resort to the little black box with controls for starts and stops. Part of this may be that in the changing legal world there are fewer and fewer secretaries who take shorthand. It seems to me that if a young lawyer, particularly a litigator, can organize his thoughts, he should be able to dictate steadily without having to start and stop."

What Christy sees as a virtue, others view as a vice. More than half a century ago, Professor Edward H. ("Bull") Warren of Harvard Law School advised lawyers never to dictate anything that "calls for careful thinking." If you dictate, he said, "you are likely to get into a habit of using words of many syllables like 'formulate' or 'constituted.' If you write in long-hand you are likely to get into a habit of using words of one syllable like 'made' or 'was.'"[11]

Whether voice-recognition software will tug at lawyers now being trained on the keyboard remains to be seen. We think the trend toward composing at the keyboard is worth preserving. For those of you who are attracted by voice-recognition software, we offer this advice: Drafts composed orally will require even more rigorous editing and revisions than drafts composed at the keyboard. Although the best writing has a natural sound—as though the writer were talking to the reader—even the best oral draft will contain false starts, lapses in organization, distracting emphases, sentence fragments, missing punctuation, and other idiosyncrasies of the spoken word.

6 LESSONS FROM A WRITING AUDIT

In 1988 we conducted an experiment at a fast-growing, medium-sized corporate litigation firm on the West Coast. One of the senior partners invited us to audit the firm's writing process, to interview a cross-section of the work force (partners, associates, paralegals, secretaries, and support staff) and assess how well the firm was meeting its goal of producing high-quality documents in an efficient manner. In the course of updating this chapter, we visited another office of the same firm in 2000. The office had newer equipment, but little else had changed. We believe that our original analysis and proposals were sound—though we obviously underestimated the degree of institutional resolve that would be needed to implement our recommendations.

Field Notes

The firm annually hires a large number of associates who understand that they will be spending long hours in the office, often under intense pressure, churning out documents. Senior members of the firm say that good writing is appreciated and rewarded. Because the firm is growing so rapidly, they worry about the quality of briefs, memoranda, and other documents drafted by new associates. But the partners are too busy practicing law to devote much time to training their younger lawyers. They are too busy even to review writing samples when recruiting new lawyers. (In this, the firm resembles many other growing firms with active business practices.)

The firm falls short of its professed goals (high quality, high efficiency). It tends to have higher-priced people doing lower-priced work. For example, several associates acknowledge that they overwrite documents, expecting partners to edit and revise. Much of that editing and revising should be completed early on, by the associates themselves. A second example: one associate said he proofreads his drafts and documents because it takes too long to walk the papers to the central proofreading desk. He, and perhaps others, should be told something about the nature and value of proofreading.

Although many associates said they believe the firm values good writing, others said they think the partners are whistling in the dark. Part of the discrepancy between the partners' perception and that of the younger lawyers reflects the lack of consensus among the senior partners about what constitutes good writing. For some, "good" is shorthand for correct grammar, spelling, and capitalization; for others, the standard is a well-reasoned, tightly written document. Moreover, the partners are too busy to convey these values and standards to the associates. Whether or not the partners arrive at a consensus, they must demonstrate in every possible way their commitment to good writing. Otherwise, much of the firm's written product, at least at the draft stage, will continue to be shoddy.

Recommendations

Our writing audit concluded with a set of proposals tailored to the needs of that firm. Here, we have recast and expanded those proposals to address the problems common to many law offices.

Upgrade proofreading and establish an in-house editing office.

Law firms are publishers, and they should provide their writers (partners and associates) with the editorial services (copy editing and proofreading) that traditional publishers offer.

Lawyers are divided on the usefulness of proofreaders—those who object do so in part because they are confused about what proofreaders do. Every lawyer can benefit from having a fresh pair of trained eyes look at his or her drafts. Senior partners should discuss the proofreaders' function with all incoming lawyers and, to the extent possible, standardize the proofreaders' tasks.

In addition, law firms should consider routinely sending more drafts to copy editors, who would provide a more substantive check on written work. Some lawyers ask their office proofreaders to take on these extra responsibilities, but not all proofreaders are deft editors. In addition to identifying typographical and formatting mistakes, copy editors check for a host of writing difficulties: syntax, grammar, organization, word usage, and fact checking. (We return to the theme of the law firm as publisher in chapter 7.)

Prepare an editorial style guide and use it.

It is wasteful for highly paid lawyers to worry about the simplest considerations of editorial style: Should the *c* in "court" be capitalized? Should the number "10" be written out? How should various documents be formatted? It is also wasteful—though less expensive—to have secretaries, word processors, and proofreaders each impose a different editorial style on successive drafts of the same document.

The remedy is to prepare an editorial style guide that answers all the niggling questions peculiar to the firm's practice and sense of style. This slender guide would not duplicate the material in *The Blue Book* or the *ALWD Citation Manual.*[1] It could consist of a few pages on mechanics (punctuation, capitalization, abbreviations, treatment of numbers), a few pages on formatting (with samples), and an alphabetical list of troublesome terms (unusual proper names, Latin phrases, hyphenated compounds).

This kind of reference guide is best prepared by an editor or proofreader, after consultation with a small committee of partners who would set the firm's style policy, just as other policies at the firm are established. This group need not start from scratch; a hour or two with one of the stylebooks used by publishers (*The Chicago Manual of Style, The Associated Press Style Book,* or *Words into Type*) or businesses (*The Gregg Reference Manual* or any of several manuals published by Merriam-Webster) will suggest the general topics that should be addressed.

The firm should post its style guide on the office intranet and distribute copies to everyone who works on documents. The authors of the guide may find it necessary to reassure the attorneys that the manual is a reference tool, not a list of rules to memorize.

Start a writing newsletter.

Considering the number of memoranda that float through even the smallest law offices, most large firms could easily produce a newsletter dedicated to writing. It would include samples of fine writing within the office and cite or reprint examples of persuasive or otherwise well-crafted briefs and documents written elsewhere. It would identify by name those whose writing is worthy of praise. It would also quote examples of bad writing (though names would not be attached) and explain the error and show how to avoid it. The newsletter could be edited and produced by an in-house editor or by a partner with an interest in writing. The time that partner spends in producing the newsletter would be billed just as the managing partner's time is billed for administrative work.

Orient incoming lawyers.

Some firms take a sink-or-swim approach to newly hired lawyers, especially to their "lateral hires." These firms assume that a lawyer who has been practicing knows how to write. That assumption is faulty. Even a day spent discussing the importance of writing—the firm's expectations, how drafts are edited, what style to use, how to use proofreaders—will pay off later.

Launch a brown-bag lunch series.

Law firms can invite outsiders, such as writing specialists and judges, as well as partners or senior associates, to talk over an informal lunch about writing. Topics might include what a judge looks for in a brief, how judges read briefs, how to focus on the important topic in the fact statement, or how to avoid writer's block.

Offer regular writing workshops.

Law firms should schedule writing workshops designed primarily for newer lawyers, though everyone would benefit. Running the workshops could be entrusted to an in-house editor, a partner, or a senior associate.

A writing workshop ought not be a grammar tutorial or instruction in basic office style rules. Rather, the newer employees need to learn what the firm expects of its lawyers: to write concisely, to present an organized argument, and to answer the client's questions or solve the client's problems. Workshops should call on participants to review documents produced by other lawyers in the office, to assess writing strengths, and to employ strategies for overcoming weaknesses.

Create a quiet room for composing.

Lawyers need a quiet refuge where they can work on larger writing projects without being distracted. A composing room gives them an alternative to working at home, where they may be inaccessible during emergencies.

Reallocate the division of labor.

Efficiency and profitability require law firms to delegate work to those who cost the firm less. In many firms, however, work moves in the opposite direction: lower-paid junior associates write long-winded documents that higher-paid senior lawyers then edit and prune line by line. Some lawyers do their own proofreading, rather than leave that job to the lower-paid staff.

Law firms should require their associates to exercise good judgment: Associates should spend more of their own time composing and editing their drafts, rather than wasting the partners' expensive time on editorial chores. The partners may want to polish an associate's final draft, but they should not be reviewing drafts that are chaotic, wordy, or ungrammatical.

Review writing samples from applicants.

If associates are to be hired on paper credentials, the screening process ought to include the paper that counts: writing samples. The recruiting partner should request and review (or ask an in-house editor to review) writing samples before inviting an applicant for an interview.

Conduct a writing audit.

We encourage law offices to ask all their lawyers (or representative samples of associates and partners) to comment on the firm's writing practices. Rather than conduct interviews, as we did, the firm could distribute a questionnaire and ask for unsigned responses. The form should include the following kinds of questions:

1. How do you compose your first draft: in longhand, at a keyboard, or by dictation? How do you make revisions to that draft? Do you know how to type or use a word processing program? If not, will the firm give you lessons? Is there a piece of equipment that you would use if your firm supplied it?

2. Are you encouraged to ask questions when you receive an assignment?

3. Are page lengths assigned? If not, how do you decide how long to make a document?

4. Are you given a deadline? Do you set your own deadlines? Do you have enough time to write? Enough time to edit? If not, is the problem that the deadlines are too short or that you tend to wait until the last minute to begin writing?

5. How many times do you edit your drafts? How many times is your work edited or rewritten by others? By whom?

6. Have you ever limited the time you spent writing or editing because you felt you could not justify billing your client for more time?

7. After you turn in a document, do you see it again? Does the person who assigned it discuss the edited work with you in detail? Does anyone else offer comments?

8. Who does the editing, retyping, proofreading, and formatting of the documents you write?

9. Roughly what percentage of your time on any assignment do you devote to research, composing, and editing? Do you record the time spent on each of these activities separately?

10. Does the firm have a commitment to good writing? If so, how has it made this commitment known?

11. Describe any bottlenecks in the copy flow.

12. What do you think your writing problems are? What have you been told your writing problems are?

13. What writing reference books do you keep at your desk (e.g., dictionary, thesaurus, *The Blue Book,* stylebook, usage book)?

7 LAWYERS AS PUBLISHERS

WORDS ARE THEIR PRODUCT

Add up all the pages of the documents—memoranda, opinion letters, motions, briefs, settlement agreements, contracts, resolutions, trusts, wills—produced in a typical week by even a small law office, and the total will easily be in the thousands. Then apply a rule of thumb: 400 double-spaced pages equals one 275-page book or one issue of the *Wall Street Journal.* The math is indisputable: Every week a small law office publishes (that is, produces for distribution to outside readers) more material than a major book house or a national newspaper.

> *One might hazard the supposition that the average lawyer in the course of a lifetime does more writing than a novelist.*
> WILLIAM PROSSER

That's why we believe that law offices should take a few lessons from their counterparts in the publishing industry. A single practitioner or a small firm resembles a freelance writer or a newsletter publisher who relies on desktop publishing. Appellate lawyers often have plenty of lead time and can think of themselves as magazine writers. A big firm with lots of takeover business operates on a schedule closer to that of a major metropolitan newspaper: the lawyers do their writing on tight deadlines, often in an afternoon or overnight.

Even if all lawyers wrote seamless prose when they graduated from law school—and few do—the demands of modern law practice conspire against good writing. Lawyers live by the clock. They bill their time in units of six minutes. Yet, despite their credo that "time is money," they foolishly waste both time and money. Not even Lewis Carroll could have created a crazier system: those whose time is worth the most spend hours editing those who are paid the least.

That is how it works in many firms: Associates write long and carelessly, often checking their writing only for spelling and typographical errors. They pass their twenty-page draft along to a more senior member of the firm whose hourly rates are much higher. The senior lawyer slashes the twenty pages to ten and then edits, rewrites, and polishes those ten.

One senior partner who reviews associates' drafts told us, "If time permits, the associate does a draft, which I edit. If time does not permit, I do the major rewrite myself." A corporate partner boasted that "one of the best things I've done is to cut a 62-page summary judgment motion [prepared by an associate] to 25 pages." Few top editors at a newspaper or magazine would perform radical surgery on a story, whether or not close to deadline. Journalists build in time for editing—the most crucial stage of the writing process. Just like senior partners, top editors are paid for their judgment, and they hire assistant editors to carry out their wishes.

Lawyers approach writing differently, of course, depending on their quirks, the size and type of their practice, and the importance and complexity of the documents that they produce. Some lawyers do use their time wisely. Some who sit atop the pyramid touch only the most important documents and only at the most pivotal stages. Like first-rate editors, they multiply their effectiveness and can attend to many written matters at once. Marvin E. Frankel described his approach to writing: "In briefs for which I am responsible, I will often write a sketchy document with many blanks in order to show junior colleagues the major headings and the order of argument as I conceive it. My most competent colleagues—like many law clerks of another era—take liberties and make significant improvements, produce a reasonably polished product for me to edit and revise."

But Frankel's approach is the exception, not the norm. Too many senior-level lawyers have adopted inefficient, unproductive habits: they waste their time heavily revising the work of their juniors, and they refuse to allow anyone else in the office to lay eyes on their own writing. "I keep tight control of the master and do not let others 'polish' my work," said one senior partner at a major New York firm. Such pride of authorship has no place in law.

The central publishing function that goes unstaffed in law firms is editing. "Our single biggest problem," a partner in a large New York law firm told us, "is that people don't edit." Lawyers should edit their own work. But they also need an outsider—not the associate who researched and wrote the first draft and not the supervising partner—to edit a nearly finished document. Some lawyers would erect the attorney-client privilege as an obstacle to hiring professional editors. But that is wrong. Many people at a firm, including secretaries and proofreaders, read confidential matters although they are not lawyers. Some lawyers—especially those away from the large law factories—do rely informally on a second pair of eyes.

Many firms employ proofreaders, but copy editors bring a different set of skills to the documents they review. Proofreaders check for misspellings, dropped lines, and other typographical errors. Copy editors read for sense, meaning, consistency, and style. They also put themselves in the shoes of the intended audience—judge, client, or opposing counsel—to gauge whether the document communicates to those readers.

Copy editors at large newspapers, who have been in short supply for several years now, earn $80,000 and up, about half of what leading metropolitan law firms paid their first-year associates in 2002. Skilled copy editors would return their investment in a short period; vastly improved documents would be the daily dividend. Particularly at firms that produce more material than any single lawyer can review, a professional editor (or a small cadre of capable editors) can make sure that all documents receive scrubbing and polish before they go out the door.

That is how newspapers, magazines, and publishing houses work. Individual copy editors look at every piece. Their job is to improve the copy (and most writers, even those with large egos, bow to this function), to challenge the writer as appropriate, and, equally important, to leave a piece of clean copy alone.

Every publishing firm has its own philosophy of and approach to editing. At most book publishing houses, the top editors do little or no detailed editing. They spend their time acquiring manuscripts and looking for trends. Sometimes editors read for major gaps. Copy editors, often freelancers, review completed manuscripts line by line.

The pace at newsweeklies and newspapers is quicker. A handful of these are known as "writers'" publications; they hire talented writers and give them wide latitude. The budget is allocated mostly to writers, not editors, because it is presumed that star writers require minimal editing.

Most publications emphasize editing. At *Time* and *Newsweek,* squads of editors often homogenize the drafts of dozens of writers and reporters. Researchers gather background materials; reporters in the field put their observations and interviews into a file. A writer based in New York City then blends the materials unearthed by the researchers and filed by reporters from different locations into a single story that is subjected to several stages of editing.

At newspapers, important writing projects, in contrast to "spot" news stories, are rarely completed overnight. Skilled reporters may work for weeks or months on these stories, which may still be extensively edited or rewritten before they are printed. Stories that end up on page one in the *Los Angeles Times,* the *Washington Post,* the *New York Times,* and other first-rate papers receive special editing care, but only rarely are they totally rewritten. At the *Wall Street Journal,* front-page stories go through a special desk of editors who often heavily rewrite pieces that staff reporters have turned in as "finished." On most other sizable papers, reporters turn in stories to different "desks." A financial story is edited by editors who specialize in business news; a local story is given to a metropolitan desk. Supervising editors make sure that copy flows smoothly throughout the day and decide which stories from the different desks are the most important.

The torrent of words that flows each day at newspapers is too great for the top editors to read every article before it is published. (In contrast, at magazines, where the pace is slightly more leisurely, an editor may read every word before it appears in print—sometimes more than once. That editor reads for tone, checks for conflicts among different stories, and sees that stories have no major gaps.) At law firms, too much happens at the last minute, under tight deadlines. Firms should recognize that lawyers are not fungible and that, like journalists, they have different skills. Those with a knack for research should be assigned to research. An imaginative writer, not just any associate, ought to do most of the early drafting of an important brief. By adopting some of the conventions of publishing and journalism, law firms will inevitably improve their written product.

In borrowing procedures from the publishing industry, law firms can pick the features most congenial to their organization and working style. In general, senior partners should act as editors in chief, delegating editing functions to a new department—the copy desk.

A smoothly functioning copy desk, overseen by an office editor, would be responsible for reviewing all or a designated portion of the office's output. The desk would help set and monitor deadlines, oversee the word processing and proofreading staffs, and edit drafts before passing them on to the senior partners for final approval. Law offices that now work feverishly up to deadline would have to reorganize their timetables for researching, composing, and editing. However painful in the short run, this rescheduling would enable law firms to improve the quality of their documents in a cost-effective manner.

In the third year of law school, they ought to teach
English as a Second Language.
STEPHEN WERMIEL

Many associates (and one or two partners) we interviewed favored having a copy desk but doubted that they would use the services of an editor *before* an assignment was complete. An editor can be most helpful in the early stages, however, offering suggestions and helping to rewrite important documents when time allows. Of course, tight deadlines may leave no time for editing. But an editor can also read documents afterward to assess the writing being distributed under the firm's name and to call writers' attention to problems in their work.

In chapter 6, we mentioned other activities that could be assigned to a full-time editor: producing an occasional office newsletter on writing, assisting the recruiting partner in assessing applicants' writing samples, and offering training for new hires. All these activities will enhance a firm's written work and its image: its documents will be of higher quality and the presence of an editor will clearly signal the firm's commitment to good writing.

Kenneth A. Plevan, a partner in the New York headquarters of Skadden, Arps, Slate, Meagher & Flom, faced an emergency. He had a day to fend off a temporary restraining order against his client, a toy importer. The plaintiff had gone to federal court in Manhattan, charging trademark infringement. Only Plevan's brief could convince the judge to allow the toy importer to sell its inventory.

As he tells the story, Plevan began drafting in the routine way, rehearsing in a paragraph or two the procedural posture of the case. But as he started to write, he realized that he would surely lose his most important reader—the judge.

In writing seminars at the Skadden firm, we had suggested that lawyers borrow standard techniques from journalism: Instead of reciting facts chronologically, or opening with the narrower points and concluding with the broad proposition, they should adopt the "inverted pyramid" approach. The most important ideas of the story appear at the top and the least important at the bottom where, if the story runs too long, they can be lopped off. Above all, we had urged lawyers at the firm to pay close attention to the lead—the first paragraph or two of a document. That is where the writer needs to grab the reader, and crisp, cogent leads are as useful for lawyers as they are for journalists. Their purpose is the same: to structure the writing so that the reader is never in doubt about why the writer is writing or whether to continue reading.

The lead is a signpost, a means of orienting the reader to the path to be taken. It might consist of an anecdote or a story. It might suggest points of interest along the way, or it might simply state the destination. Well-constructed leads will tell readers how to make sense of what follows.

Ken Plevan tore up his original paragraphs and crafted a trenchant lead. In the lawsuit, Hasbro, the large toy maker, accused Skadden's client, Four Star International Trading Company, of stealing the design of its rubber dinosaurs. Plevan wanted the judge's attention immediately. He did not wait until page three to put forth an argument, as so often happens when lawyers succumb to the temptation to list a chronology or recite the procedural path of the case. He came right to the point:

> Hasbro opens its memorandum by stating that its "enormously successful 'THE TRANSFORMERS' series of toys has predictably spawned knock-offs." What is equally predictable is that Hasbro, with $300,000,000 in sales riding on this successful line of toys, will go to any length to defend its business. As we show below, however, Hasbro cannot arrogate to itself a monopoly in dinosaur-converting figures. It was, after all, the Lord, and not Hasbro, that brought the Triceratops and Brontosaurus to this earth, several hundred million years ago.

The most important reader of Plevan's brief turned out to be not the judge but the opposing counsel. So stark was the point, and so clearly made, that Hasbro backed off and settled the case on favorable terms within days.

Not all leads can be as direct as Plevan's. No immutable rules govern leads. Anecdotal leads, which have been mastered by writers at the *Wall Street Journal,* work best when the subject is sufficiently complicated that the reader must first be alerted to why the phenomenon matters. Other leads are quite straightforward, presenting the Five *W*'s (who, what, when, where, and why) and the *H* (how)—the catechism that beginning journalists have memorized for generations. Good leads can accomplish many things:

- Deliver information
- Summarize
- Pique the reader's interest
- Clarify a problem or a circumstance

The best leads deliver the relevant facts in language that is clear, logical, honest, succinct, and memorable.

Now compare Plevan's lead with this vertiginous opening paragraph of a brief that was submitted to the U.S. Court of Appeals for the Fifth Circuit (we came across this example in the *Washington Monthly*'s "memo of the month"):

> Appellee initially filed a Motion to Strike Appendices to Brief for Appellant on July 22, 1983. Appellant filed a brief in response, which Appellee replied to. Appellant has subsequently filed another brief on this motion, Appellant's Reply to Appellee's reply to Appellant's Brief in Response to Appellee's Motion to Strike Appendices to brief for Appellant (Appellant's most recent brief), to which the Appellee herein responds.

As muddled and uninstructive as this lead is, it is no aberration. Here is the beginning of a brief that Justice William Bablitch of the Wisconsin Supreme Court has recited in speeches to illustrate how poorly lawyers write:

> The state's argument is the same as the statement of the court. That is to say, that is what the court did, and that is what the court does, then the court does what the court does; and if that is what the court does, it is all right, because that is what the court does.

It takes no special learning to see that Plevan's lead outshines these two mind-benders. Plevan's is short, focused, and vivid. You do not have to read it twice to get the meaning. You can read the others over and over without enlightenment.

One of the most highly regarded contemporary legal writers and thinkers is Laurence H. Tribe, a professor at Harvard Law School. In one of the many cases he has successfully argued before the Supreme Court, he represented Grendel's Den, a Harvard Square restaurant that was seeking a liquor license. This is how he began the brief he submitted:

> At issue in this case is the validity of Massachusetts General Laws c. 138, § 16C (Section 16C), Brief of State Appellants (State Br.) 2a–3a, which delegates to certain churches and synagogues—those that, in the statute's terms, are "dedicated to divine worship," id. 2a—an ad hoc and absolute veto power over the approval of each liquor license within a 500-foot radius of the church or synagogue. Because it is providently located near

the intersection of Mt. Auburn and Boylston Streets in Cambridge, and is invested by the State with an unreviewable veto power under Section 16C, the Holy Cross Armenian Catholic Parish church (Holy Cross Church) can and does exercise absolute regulatory authority over the acquisition of liquor licenses in virtually the entire Harvard Square area.[1]

This thicket of confusing citations and unnecessary definitions could have been avoided and the lead measurably strengthened had Tribe incorporated the much more lively imagery that he buried in footnote 6, a few pages later:

> Virtually every major commercial and entertainment area in Massachusetts is within 500 feet of *some* church. At all events, the gist of Grendel's challenge to Section 16C is that it entrusts governmental power to churches. The particular *radius* of the sphere of influence thereby ceded to religious bodies—whether ten feet or ten miles—is constitutionally immaterial: the First and Fourteenth Amendments were not, after all, written with straight-edge and compass.

The buried lead is a common problem. Here is a typical example of the lawyer's failure to get to the point. What follows is the opening paragraph of a memorandum about a client's tax problem. How quickly can you spot the issue?

To: Partner
From: Third-Year Associate

Re: [No Subject Given]

INTRODUCTION

Jane Doe Smith died on July 31, 1985 (the date of death is hereinafter referred to as "DOD"). On April 31, 1986, the co-executors of her estate ("the estate") filed a federal estate tax return in which a painting by Vincent van Gogh, titled *L'Arlesienne,* (sometimes referred to herein as the "van Gogh") was stated to have a value of $2,250,000 as of January 31, 1986, the alternate valuation date (hereinafter referred to as the "AVD").* This value was based on an estate tax appraisal performed by Sotheby's Inc. ("Sotheby's"). On April 11, 1986, the Internal Revenue Service (the "Service") issued a "90-day" letter in which the Service determined that the value of the van Gogh was $5,000,000 as of the AVD. The Service's determination was based on the Service's Art Advisory Panel's valuation of the van Gogh. The Art Advisory Panel also valued the van Gogh as of the DOD at $3,500,000.

> * The date six months after death. *See* section 2032 of the Internal Revenue Code of 1986, as amended (the "Code"). The AVD, if elected by an executor, is the relevant date for valuing an estate for federal estate tax purposes. The co-executors made such an election with respect to the estate. The value of the van Gogh as of the AVD, therefore, is at issue.

The reader will search in vain for the issue in the main body of the first page. You must plow through the page to the very end, and only on reading the last sentence of the footnote will you stumble upon the point.

Many journalists spend half their writing time on the lead. Some lawyers, such as Jay Topkis, agonize over leads. "Usually I do the first paragraph of a brief many times," says Topkis. If you are like most lawyers, however, you probably spend not much more time on the beginning of a document than on the middle or end. You ought to consider spending far more time on your opening lines. The proper lead can ease your burden: If you think hard about your lead, you very likely will, in the process, figure out how to structure your document.

In composing a lead, you should avoid what Professor Marjorie Rombauer of the University of Washington at Seattle calls "mystery-style writing"—conclusions stated last, rather than first. This common failing often shows up in weak or fuzzy verbs, as though the writer were afraid to tell the reader right away the precise nature of the problem. Consider this sentence, the first in a long opening paragraph written by an associate in a memo to a partner:

> One aspect of the proposed sale of Arizona Charter Guaranty & Trust Company ("Arizona Charter") to Fidelity Life Company concerns the contract between the MAC Fund, a money market fund, and its registered investment adviser, Equitable Money Management, Inc. ("EMM"), a wholly owned subsidiary of Equitable Financial Services, Inc. ("EFS"), 80 percent of which is in turn owned by Arizona Charter.

The lead is empty. It tells the reader who has waded through the chain of ownership that an "aspect" of a sale "concerns" a contract. The writer has wasted the opportunity to say immediately how the contract affects the sale, forcing the reader instead to puzzle out a slew of connections between these corporate entities, which may or may not be relevant.

The chronological style can be equally empty. As Robert Kasanof, a New York City litigator, told us: "I remain astounded at the dependence of much litigation writing on chronological organization, which is often most difficult for the reader, coming new to the subject, to follow. Trite though it may be, I believe that a summary introduction gives the reader a gestalt which makes the arguments flow and adds persuasiveness to them. . . . A reader of legal writing is likely to be suffering from severe overload; therefore it is very worthwhile to ease the physical and logical task of following your argument."

The chronological lead is often used by lawyers who write their opening paragraph before they have thought through their problem and who do not revise that paragraph once they have solved it. Here is an example of a fact-stuffed chronological lead, followed by our suggested revision.

CHRONOLOGICAL LEAD

On November 8, 1984, Congress passed the Hazardous and Solid Waste Amendment of 1984, modifying and augmenting the Resource Conservation and Recovery Act (RCRA). Among the several changes wrought by the 1984 amendments is a new Federal regulatory system governing the installation and operation of underground storage tanks, commonly called the LUST program (for Leaking Underground Storage Tanks). The final form of this regulatory framework will be fleshed out by the EPA over the next three years as it conducts further research and institutes rule-making procedures. It is the purpose of this Memorandum to inform the client of what sorts of regulations they might expect will ultimately govern their use of underground storage tanks, and when those regulations may take effect. While perfect prediction of an agency's action is impossible, this Memorandum should allow present management to conduct informed decision-making concerning underground storage facilities.

SUGGESTED REVISION

A new federal regulatory system will govern those who operate underground storage tanks. No one can predict the substance of the final regulations, but companies must begin to plan now for EPA rule making.

In his critique of lawyers' writing, Justice Bablitch understood what many of the best journalists know: You must always engage your audience. "Effective brief writing," he said, "requires that you constantly remind yourself for whom it is you are writing. You are not writing for your client, nor to impress your client with the depth of your intellect. You are writing for the judge." Bablitch's insight applies to all leads.

Leon Friedman, a professor at Hofstra Law School and a civil rights litigator, adopts this approach: "The secret is directness: Let the judge know immediately what your position is. Recognize the time limitations that judges suffer under. If you can give him the means to decide the case in the first two minutes of reading, he will appreciate your approach."

We are not suggesting that lawyers go to journalism school. But lawyers can master good writing more quickly if they think as journalists do.

Robert M. Goldberg, who practiced in Anchorage in the 1980s, recalled how greatly influenced he was by a leading journalist a generation ago:

> The late Eddie Lahey, the Pulitzer Prize–winning reporter for the *Chicago Daily News,* told us as college journalists (Amherst Student Banquet, March 1963) that a good reporter must be able to tell a story quickly and directly. "He should be able to cover the Second Coming of Christ in under 1,000 words!" said Lahey. His comments, fueled by a month with Judge Henry Edgerton, a year with Judge David Bazelon, and 20 years on my own, have convinced me of that fundamental truth: Tell your story directly, put it in context, make it simple but interesting, and then practice what my father, former U.S. Supreme Court Justice Arthur Goldberg, calls the First Rule of Advocacy: "Sit down!"

The lead is a sales job, to lure the reader into the story. Many adopt a conversational approach. Consider the following inviting newspaper leads:

> A couple of years ago, it was so quiet here you could almost hear the marijuana grow. (From a profile of a curmudgeonly country editor in northern California.)

It's after a rainfall, when the earth smells so rich and damp and flavorful, that Fannie Glass says she most misses having some dirt to eat. (From an article on a custom practiced in some southern states.)

Roll call, the teachers agree, is the most difficult part of the day: Ho Suk Ping He, Yana Katzap, Tkkun Amongi, Azaria Badebr, Rotcheild Boruchov, Eduordo Yun. (From an article on a polyglot school in Queens.)

In dozens of cities in Europe, the U.S.'s Big Five accounting firms are doing what they can't do at home: practicing law. (From an article on the expanding international role of accounting firms.)[2]

What distinguishes these leads is how they irresistibly lure busy readers into reading on. Rene J. Cappon, an editor of the Associated Press, advises writers to think of leads "as though they cost you 10 bucks per word, each word to be engraved on stainless steel while you're sitting on a hot stove. Think economy."[3] The lead is no place for secondary detail, abstract language, or vagueness. Cramming all Five *W*'s and the *H* into the first paragraph can create congestion. Avoid throwing your readers into "cardiac arrest," as Cappon puts it, by keeping inconsequential details out of the lead and placing them deeper in the document.

Writers should also avoid straining their readers' necks with what Louis Boccardi, president and CEO of the Associated Press, calls the "tennis ball" lead. Here's the example Boccardi uses:

The U.S. Court of Appeals agreed Wednesday to review a lower court order that found the Nuclear Regulatory Commission in contempt of court for violating an order to hold open budget meetings.

"The problem here is that we treat the reader's mind like a tennis ball to be whacked back and forth across the net," Boccardi explains. "Agreed to review. Bam! Contempt of court. Bam! For violating an order. Bam! To hold open meetings. Bam! You can almost see the ball flying back and forth. It's just too much. You cure it by just stepping back and asking yourself, 'What really happened here?' "[4] In other words:

The U.S. Court of Appeals agreed Wednesday to review a contempt finding against the Nuclear Regulatory Commission for holding a closed meeting.

Lawyers' prose rarely is deathless, but it should not be deadly. No matter how complicated the facts, one reading should do. And that can be done, as this final example by Judge Learned Hand shows:

> The suit is to enjoin the performance of the picture play, "Letty Lynton," as an infringement of the plaintiffs' copyrighted play, "Dishonored Lady." The plaintiffs' title is conceded, so too the validity of the copyright; the only issue is infringement. The defendants say that they did not use the play in any way to produce the picture; the plaintiffs discredit this denial because of the negotiations between the parties for the purchase of rights in the play, and because the similarities between the two are too specific and detailed to have resulted from chance. The judge thought that, so far as the defendants had used the play, they had taken only what the law allowed, that is, those general themes, motives, or ideas in which there could be no copyright. Therefore he dismissed the bill.[5]

In five sentences, Judge Hand sets out the purpose of the suit, the facts, the issues, and the lower court's decision. No one can doubt what the case is about, and this single paragraph guides the reader through the seven pages that follow. One reading will do. No more can be asked of a lead.

9 FORM, STRUCTURE, AND ORGANIZATION

Suppose you are helping a child assemble a toy giraffe, just removed from the gift box. Out comes a longish neck and backbone, in three pieces; a head, in one; four legs, in twelve; a tail, in two. Unlike the man from Mars, who has never seen even a drawing of a giraffe and never contemplated the concept of a vertebrate, you should have an easy time of it. You know how a toy giraffe should look—you do not have to create the form from scratch—and if by chance you falter, you can stare at the picture on the box.

But for most writing projects, there is no picture on the box. Nature does not provide a ready template through which lawyers can solve their legal problems on paper. You have to decide on the shape of the head (the lead), the size of the torso (the body of the argument) and the number of limbs and their lengths (the support for the body). You also have to select and arrange the cells (words), tissues (sentences), and organs (paragraphs).

How words are arranged in phrases, clauses, and sentences is not an arbitrary matter. These arrangements are governed by grammar and semantics—the rules of construction and the rules of meaning. Sentences, in turn, are aligned in paragraphs, and paragraphs are ordered and linked to form a coherent document.

The writer has an easier time of it than nature. The living organism gestates but once, and if an unfortunate chemical accident attaches the foot to the neck, nothing apart from surgery can set the matter right. Prose composition, in contrast, can have many gestations. If a document is not structured properly at first, the writer has the luxury—and the duty—to put the head and feet and middle where they belong.

Order and Disorder

The principle of sound organization is this: Join those elements that belong together. Elements belong together for one of two reasons: (1) They are part of the same specific topic (witnesses' observations of the color of the traffic light; exceptions to the statute of limitations relevant to the case at hand) or (2) they are related topics (descriptions of the transactions establishing that the defendant violated the insider trading regulations; the international law doctrines that preclude Iran from suing the United States). You will know that you have deviated from this principle of organization when you find yourself writing the equivalent of "by the way, I forgot to mention . . ."

When composing, you will always forget to mention something. Few of us can match the mental power of the nineteenth-century American historian William H. Prescott, whose impaired eyesight forced him to memorize: "He frequently kept about sixty pages in his memory for several days, and went over the whole mass five or six times, molding and remolding the sentences at each successive turn."[1] When you do remember, especially if you are writing rapidly, you are likely to toss the thought on the page just as it comes: "By the way . . ." That's fine. But when you reread and edit your draft, you should recognize that you've attached a foot to the neck and that you must rearrange the parts.

Let's work through an example from a student brief to test the principle of organization. Here is the instructor's description of the factual setting:

> Niles Nasty, a supervisor, continually propositioned Mary Sweetly, his new executive assistant: For months he suggested at least two or three times a week that they have dinner together, that he visit at her home on the weekend to review assignments, and that she stay late at the office to discuss "developments." She politely turned down each of his overtures.
>
> In the eleventh month of a one-year probationary period, Niles told Mary that she would be promoted and given a raise, and he suggested that they go to a cocktail lounge to celebrate. She declined. He grew quite angry and told her that he carried a gun "for broads like you."

Mary complained to the company's personnel director. He refused to accept her charges, saying that it would be better to keep the matter quiet.

Mary filed a criminal complaint. She was immediately transferred to a dead-end secretarial job, three days before the end of her probationary period. Mary's three predecessors had received similar last-minute transfers. Mary was told that the transfer was temporary and that she would be reassigned to her old job once the court issued an order of protection. After the court issued the order, Mary was told that her previous position had been filled and that she could not be reevaluated for a new position until she had stayed twelve full months in any one position. Charging sexual harassment, Mary sued the company for injuries stemming from the hostile work environment, job discrimination, and the retaliatory transfer. The lower court dismissed her complaint. Mary appeals.

And here is the beginning of the student's brief:

ARGUMENT

MARY SWEETLY STATES A VALID SEXUAL HARASSMENT CLAIM BECAUSE NILES NASTY'S OFFENSIVE AND UNWELCOME BEHAVIOR CREATED A HOSTILE AND INTIMIDATING WORKING ENVIRONMENT AND TANGIBLE JOB DETRIMENT FOR WHICH THE COMPANY SHOULD BE HELD LIABLE.

1. Nasty's intertwining of his invitations with references to Mary's job suggests that Mary's submission to Nasty's advances was a condition of her employment. The modern trend within the circuit courts has been adoption of the policy of holding employers strictly liable for actions of sexual harassment by supervisors when the sexual harassment centers around threats of tangible job benefits. *Horn v. Duke Homes,* 755 F.2d 599 (7th Cir. 1985) (court stated that whatever the result under the common law of agency, Title VII [of the Civil Rights Act of 1964] demands that employers be held strictly liable in sexually harassing situations). This position of strict liability is founded upon traditional notions of agency, which mandate employer liability when the supervisor acts in an agency capacity. A strict liability rule is intended to eviscerate tangible job detriment in that it ensures compensation for victims and creates an incentive for the employer to take the strongest possible affirmative measures to prevent the hiring and retention of sexist supervisors.

2. The corporation's actions reasonably led Mary to believe that

Nasty had the authority to evaluate her performance and recommend her for promotion. The Supreme Court's recent decision in *Meritor Savings Bank v. Vinson,* 106 S.Ct. 2399 (1986), suggests that employers would be strictly liable for sexual harassment under the agency principle. Nasty was acting as an agent for the corporation while simultaneously placing conditions on Mary's economic future. A jury could reasonably find that Nasty's acts were part and parcel of his supervision of Mary, *Davis v. United States Steel Corp.,* 779 F.2d 209, 213 (4th Cir. 1985), (majority of the court held that the employee could present a case under the doctrine of respondeat superior once the offending supervisor's harassing conduct had been observed without reaction by his supervisor). Therefore, the corporation must be held liable for Nasty's threatening actions against Mary's tangible job benefits.

3. Had Nasty been a coworker rather than a supervisor, Mary could have thwarted his propositions without the risk of tangible job detriment. In *Scott v. Sears, Roebuck & Co.,* 798 F.2d 210 (7th Cir. 1986), (the court dismissed a sexual harassment claim against a coworker) the plaintiff admitted that the allegedly harassing coworker was a friend and that he had asked her out only once. The isolated threat posed to Scott's working environment and tangible job benefits by a coworker warranted the dismissal of her claim. Mary, on the other hand, was victimized by a patterned and pervasive practice of sexual harassment by a supervisor.

4. Upon the establishment of Mary's claim it is now evident that the corporation had constructive, if not actual, knowledge of the existence of the sexually hostile workplace created by Nasty, and that it took no prompt action to rectify that environment. Liability should be assessed against the corporation for the sexual harassment committed by its supervisor Nasty, *Henson v. City of Dundee,* 682 F.2d 897, 905 (11th Cir. 1982) (employer is strictly liable for actions of its supervisors that amount to sexual discrimination or sexual harassment resulting in tangible job detriment to subordinate employee). Mary's three immediate predecessors were all transferred from the department while it was under Nasty's control. Someone from the corporation's personnel department had to transfer these women. Upon that fact alone, the corporation had to have, or at the very least should have known of the offensive environment created by Nasty. Yet with that situation before it the corporation did little or nothing to remove or dissuade Nasty. The corporation could have negated its liability but chose to ignore it through three prior similar instances. The simultaneous observations and inaction on the part

of the corporation satisfies the criteria for constructive knowledge as defined by the federal courts, as well as the E.E.O.C Guidelines.

Grammatical errors, syntactical missteps, stylistic infelicities, and redundancies aside, this hodgepodge jumps from topic to topic, piling as many as seven topics into a single paragraph. Let's look at the writer's principle points, sentence by sentence:

Paragraph 1. (a) *Nature of act:* Mary's submission or refusal to submit was a condition of employment. (b) *Rule of liability:* Employers are strictly liable for sexual harassment by supervisors. (c) *Origin of rule:* The principle of strict liability stems from concepts of agency. (d) *Purpose of rule:* The rule is intended to compel employers to prevent and eliminate harassment.

Paragraph 2. (a) *Creation of agency authority:* Mary reasonably believed Niles had authority to act. (b) *Rule of liability:* Employers are strictly liable for sexual harassment by supervisors. (c) *Creation of agency:* Niles was an agent and had authority to act. (d) *Standing to sue:* An employee may sue if the company fails to react to a supervisor's actions. (e) *Rule of liability:* An employer is strictly liable if it fails to react to a supervisor's actions. (f) *Legal conclusion:* The corporation is liable.

Paragraph 3. (a) *Extent of liability:* The corporation is liable only for harassment by a supervisor, not by a coworker. (b) *Precedent:* A court dismissed a claim premised on harassment by a coworker. (c) *What happened to Mary:* Mary was harassed by her supervisor.

Paragraph 4. (a) *Notice:* The company had notice. (b) *Failure to mitigate:* The company failed to rectify. (c) *Legal conclusion:* The company should be held liable. (d) *Rule of liability:* The company is strictly liable for actions of a harassing supervisor. (e) *Notice:* The company, through its agents, must have known of the harassment. (f) *Failure to mitigate:* The company failed to rectify. (g) *Notice:* The company's activities demonstrate it had notice.

Scan this list of main points. No logical order suggests itself. In these four paragraphs, the student has jumbled many different issues: (1) whether Niles was a supervisor, (2) whether supervisors are liable, (3) whether corporations need notice, (4) how they get notice, (5) whether corporations are liable, (6) whether this corporation is liable, (7) what the standard of liability is, (8) whether an employee has standing to sue, and more.

This mishmash of ideas is hopeless. Readers expect sentences to proceed in order. When you give directions, you start with the street nearest the person you are instructing and you give the sequence of streets and turns that will lead to the desired destination. You do not say, "Well, forget about the middle streets for the moment, first let me describe a street three-quarters of the way there that may interest you; then there's a street back near you . . ." A rational sequence of thought carries the reader from the start of the journey to the end. Brief detours, if there must be any, are clearly signaled at precisely the moment they are to begin.

A different travel metaphor comes from Sir Winston Churchill, who was awarded the Nobel Prize for Literature in 1953:

> I began to see that writing, especially narrative, was not only an affair of sentences, but of paragraphs. Indeed I thought the paragraph no less important than the sentence. . . . Just as the sentence contains one idea in all its fullness, so the paragraph should embrace a distinct episode; and as sentences should follow one another in harmonious sequence, so the paragraphs must fit on to one another like the automatic couplings of railway carriages.[2]

Topic Sentences and Topic Flow

Your topics must be not only sensibly arranged but also sensibly expressed so that your readers can understand right now, right here, why you are talking about a particular point. A topic sentence is to a paragraph what a lead is to the whole document. It directs the reader's attention and announces what comes next. Consider the following sequence of topic sentences taken from a seventeen-paragraph law review article by David M. Balabanian, a San Francisco practitioner, eulogizing Justice Matthew Tobriner of the California Supreme Court.[3]

California lawyers have long played in a colorful local rite: explaining the Law of California to the World.

Lately, the frequency of such conversations has seemed to diminish.

Many of the ideas identified with our courts which seemed remarkable, even visionary, twenty, ten or five years ago, now seem commonplace, even essential.

More of California's contributions to the national jurisprudence than is generally realized (even in well-informed legal circles) came from a quiet, humble man who spent much of his long judicial career in relative public obscurity.

The scope of his work defies quick summarization.

Though time alone can adjudicate the durability and worth of his many ideas, two themes stand out:

The importance of individuality and the need to defend it against the organizational imperatives of both government and private institutions.

The substitution of reasonable expectation for fictitious agreement.

The form of his opinions was as characteristic as their content.

Another Tobriner hallmark was the absence of the passive voice.

He liked good metaphors.

Though earnest in defense of the values he held dear, he shunned the self-righteous moralizing which disfigures much liberal advocacy.

His great output required great industry.

Ever gracious and self-effacing, he resisted all temptation to adopt the eccentricities of manner or displays of choler sometimes mistaken for judicial greatness.

There are, of course, many sincere people who heartily deplore his work.

Whether, given the stasis of our legislative institutions, they ultimately could or would have struck balances more durable or popular than the courts' is unclear.

What is clear is that conflicts unresolved by the legislature have been settled by our judges in ways that once appeared unremarkable and now seem commonplace, and that one of these judges was a quiet, gentle man who sought neither controversy nor glory, got more of the former and less of the latter than he deserved, and profoundly changed the lives of us all.

From the topic sentences alone, the reader gleans the substance of the article. Each topic sentence announces a point (which is illustrated by the examples and anecdotes later in the paragraph) and moves the author's argument forward from his premise toward his conclusion.

In legal writing, the topic sentence should almost always come at the beginning of a paragraph. Writers who have mastered the art of structure, however, may experiment, placing the topic sentence in the second slot or even at the end of a paragraph in order to emphasize the details or examples that precede it. The following paragraph begins with a transition sentence that leads into the topic sentence:

> Writing is not merely a matter of words and phrases. Much more important, writing is a process by which we think our way to a solution of the problem that lies before us.

Topic sentences alone are not sufficient to provide clear, flowing paragraphs. The writer must also ensure that each sentence in the paragraph discusses the same or a closely related topic. Read the next two paragraphs for sense (the topic of each sentence is italicized):

> *An accredited law school* must graduate lawyers before the bar examination can be taken. *The bar* will not admit them to practice until they pass the exam. Only then can *they* hang out a shingle. And even then, *the finer points of law practice* will elude them; it will be many years before *they* can practice comfortably. *That experience* is not gained overnight.

> *Lawyers* must graduate from an accredited law school before they may take the bar examination. *They* may be admitted to the bar and hang out a shingle only after they pass the exam. Even then, it will be many years before *they* feel comfortable with the finer points of practicing law. *They* cannot gain that experience overnight.

Both paragraphs mean the same thing. But in the first version, the topics of the sentences are disjointed, seemingly unrelated: (1) "an accredited law school," (2) "the bar," (3) "they," (4) "the finer points of law practice," (5) "they," and (6) "that experience." The reader glides over each without seeing the connections, which are buried inside the sentences. In the second version, the topics are identical: (1) "lawyers," (2) "they," (3) "they," (4) "they." The substance is the same, but the sentences are glued together; the reader does not pause in going from one to the next. Moreover, a consistent set of topics will usually keep the sentences tighter and shorter, and there should be fewer of them.

As a writer, you select and control your topics. A muddled, disjointed, incoherent topic flow is your fault, not the fault of the material. In legal writing, you usually have five categories of topics available to you:

1. The party: the plaintiff or defendant. "*Mr. Jones* carried the radioactive isotope, contrary to the Montana code, but he failed to receive a warning from Mr. Smith that . . ." or "*Mr. Smith* failed to warn that the radioactive isotope Mr. Jones was carrying . . ."

2. The object or concept: the particular thing or concept that lies at the heart of the matter. "*The radioactive isotope* that Mr. Jones carried, contrary to the Montana code, posed a serious threat."

3. The principle: the laws and rules that govern the problem. "*The Montana code governing the handling* of radioactive isotopes forbids . . ."

4. Yourself, as a lawyer. "*I* must inform you that the Montana code . . ."

5. Your audience: the client (or judge and the opposing counsel). "*You* violated the Montana code in carrying the radioactive isotope, but . . ."

Which category you choose will depend on context and purpose. Topics should not wander indiscriminately through the paragraph. Have a reason for what you do and shape your topics to conform to it.

Purpose and Strategy

Lawyers do not write to amuse themselves but to solve some problem or meet some need. Every document a lawyer writes should reflect the purpose for which it was undertaken, yet too often lawyers seem oblivious of this cardinal principle. Problem solving requires lawyers to provide explanations, offer responses, narrate events, and prove their points.

To explain, respond, narrate, and prove, lawyers rely on the following strategies: (1) defining, (2) comparing, (3) contrasting, (4) classifying, (5) evaluating, and (6) showing cause and effect.

Lawyers who ignore their purpose and fail to select appropriate strategies write muddled, rambling, or disjointed documents. Here, for example, is the outline, or skeleton, of an office memorandum written by a first-year law student who offers a grocery list, rather than an analysis:

> [Lead] Our client is accused of larceny. The definition of larceny is unclear. The courts say different things in different cases.
>
> [Body] In Case 1, the court said . . . In Case 2, the court said . . . In Case 3, the court said . . . In Case 4, the court said . . .
>
> [Conclusion] Therefore, our client is not guilty.

Organizing the discussion around a list of cases rarely works, to the chagrin of many first-year law students, because the writer cannot connect the facts or law of the cases to the issue at hand. The writer who chooses a one-two-three organization cannot compare or contrast the holdings in order to explain the law or to reason about the client's innocence.

To structure a document intelligently, you must know what you want to do and how you can go about doing it. Suppose that your goal is to explain the law of larceny in a particular jurisdiction. To explain it, the best strategy is to classify the various definitions that the statutes and the courts have offered. A classification scheme will suggest itself when you have read enough cases. You would not begin by saying, "I have read fifty-two cases, and the first one defines larceny this way, and the second one that way, and the third . . ." Rather, you would begin by telling your reader that the courts have interpreted the larceny statutes in five ways (or six ways or seven). You would then define and describe each of these interpretations and explain the circumstances of the cases that gave rise to each interpretation. Your purpose and strategy thus will dictate the organization of your memorandum.

You would take a different approach to the same body of cases if you were writing a reply brief. Then you would probably use the same topics, and the same order of topics, that your adversary used. Your memorandum or brief would have a different shape still if your assignment was to show how a statutory amendment would affect the chances of your client's being acquitted, or if you were asked to narrate the facts, explaining what happened.

If you think out your purpose and strategy first, you should discover that your organizational and conceptual problems will help solve each other.

Formatting

Some types of formatting attract the reader's eye and illuminate the path of the argument. Two of the most effective formatting elements are headings and lists. Headings highlight the major sections of your document and inform the reader of each section's destination. In a long or complex document, the headings and subheadings mark the trail.

Lists are useful when you want to present three or more items that represent a set of some kind—for example, a series of alternatives or subcategories or steps in a sequence. A list format makes it easier for the reader to understand the number of items and to compare them. You can indent each item in the list, or place a bullet (a small circle) or other symbol before each item, or number the items.

Just as headings and lists help readers follow your structure, other elements tend to distract their attention and cause them to lose their way. The worst offenders are the long quotation, the lengthy string citation, and the ponderous footnote.

Quotations

Too many lawyers, showing off their research or hoping to decorate their arguments, load their writing with lengthy or inappropriate passages from the writings of others. These quotations interrupt the flow of thought because they are in another voice and because they do not relate precisely to the point being made.

Lawyers who use long quotations are usually thinking more about themselves than about their audience. Long quotations are often inserted out of laziness or insecurity: The writer is too tired or too uncomprehending to distill the essence of the thought. Rather than undertake that intellectual work, the lazy writer leaves it to the reader. Some valiant readers will struggle through blocks of quotations, but others skim or skip them, assuming that the writer will make the point elsewhere.

Strategic writers, in contrast, use carefully selected short quotations as ornaments to catch the reader's eye. They select the heart of a passage that bears directly on their point, and they quote only those words that sparkle—the essential phrase or sentence that is memorable, epigrammatic, or vivid in its metaphor. They also make sure that the apt quotation is aptly introduced and securely anchored to their own argument.

Chiefly I admire legal prose that eschews ostentation and so-called "scholarship." Footnotes and digression poison most legal writing. The older I get, the more I admire succinctness, and the more I despise flash.

MILTON S. GOULD

String Citations and Mis-citations

We do not know anyone who reads string citations. Many lawyers suppose they add heft and authority. Too often they are simply copied from another document, and copied by a writer who has not even bothered to read through the cases. Shirley Hufstedler, a former federal appeals judge, was one of many sitting or retired judges who complained to us of mis-citation and misuse of authorities. Salvatore A. Romano, a Washington, D.C., practitioner, views as an increasing problem the "overcitation of case law and other authorities with little or no bearing on the operative facts or issues."

Our advice: Avoid deceptive erudition. Cite only those cases that you have read. Confine your citations to the principal cases that support your point. That the courts in dozens of other cases have followed the rule you are advancing may interest the historians but not the readers of your brief.

Footnotes

The biggest interruption to the reader's train of thought is the lowly footnote. "Encountering [a footnote] is like going downstairs to answer the doorbell while making love," said Noel Coward.[4] Considerate writers reserve footnotes primarily for citations, to spare the reader's eye the strain of skipping over those alphanumeric ciphers. The pseudo-scholarly approach of tackling substantive, sometimes quite subtle, themes and topics in the fine print of footnotes is a fierce distraction. Burying an argument in a footnote, and expecting the reader to excavate it, is simply inexcusable.

When you are tempted to insert a footnote, ask yourself if the material is germane to your point. If so, find the correct place for it in your text. If not, ask yourself why you are including it at all.

It is hard to improve on Fred Rodell's acerbic dictum, offered in 1936: "If a writer does not really need footnotes and tacks them on just because they look pretty or because it is the thing to do, then he ought to be tried for willful murder of his readers' (all three of them) eyesight and patience."[5]

Length

The structure of a document depends not only on the subject but also on the length of the document. Just as a mature tree has a more complex pattern of branches than a sapling, a long document requires a more complex structure than a short one. At one firm we visited, partners told of a new associate who had drafted a brief of more than ninety pages, although he knew that the court's limit was thirty-five pages. The cost of this profligacy was measured not solely by the time the associate spent writing the draft and the partner spent reading it. The real bother was restructuring the argument to fit the page limit. Nipping a few branches was insufficient; entire limbs had to be removed.

Wordiness is a common disease that afflicts most writers. Once the words begin to flow, it is easier to continue than to stop. It is taxing to focus and limit. That requires discipline. Moreover, from our earliest school days, teachers have ingrained in us the notion that more is better. The precocious fifth-grader who writes a twenty-page paper is rewarded with an A. As adults, some writers are show-offs eager to display their research and erudition. It is painful to discard research, and all too many writers will find a way to work it in. And these days, technology indulges this urge.

You should contemplate the length of your document when you sit down to compose. Dashing headlong down the road without a notion of how far you are going is dangerous and foolish. Like runners, writers must learn to pace themselves.

Lawyers too often equate length with effort, assuming that the longer the document, the harder the writer worked on it. Paradoxically, quite the reverse is true: It takes more time to write a crisp, tight, concise piece than a loose, long, baggy one. It requires more discipline to sift through and evaluate one's research, selecting the best items and discarding the rest than to include every case and every citation.

Frustrated by long, poorly written briefs, many courts have imposed stringent page limits. Even if you are not constrained by an external page limit, you should impose your own. Consider the risks you run by writing an excessively long document:

- You risk the patience and goodwill of courts that have not set page limits.
- You risk antagonizing clients and other lay readers, few of whom

have the time or patience to read lengthy documents with care—
or even at all.

- You risk being misunderstood. The longer your document, the more complex its structure, the more likely the reader is to miss or misconstrue your argument.

- You add hours to the time it takes you to compose the document, cheating yourself of the hours you need to edit and polish it.

If any bill, answers, replication, or rejoinder, shall be found of an immoderate length, both the party and the counsel under whose hand it passeth shall be fined.
SIR FRANCIS BACON

Given these risks, why do so many lawyers write long? One theory, often advanced, is that they fear losing their case if an adversary raises a point they have omitted. Or worse, they fear being charged with incompetence or malpractice. As Justice Stanley Mosk of the California Supreme Court wrote us: "Lawyers, fearing a later charge of incompetence, and perhaps a lawsuit for legal malpractice, feel an obligation to raise every conceivable point."

But a more convincing explanation is that lawyers are indoctrinated early on to value a particular kind of thoroughness—the kind exemplified by the law review articles written by their law professors. Being arcane rarely hurts. As Professor John E. Nowak of the University of Illinois Law School argues, "The professorial style of writing, which is meant to impress deans and promotion committees, impedes any professor's ability to explain to the average reader exactly what went on in court cases."[6]

Scholarly apparatus, in the form of voluminous footnotes that wind along obscure by-ways, is thought to help. When a reporter asked Jesse H. Choper, then dean of Boalt Hall at the University of California at Berkeley, about the 1,611 footnotes in one of his law review articles, Choper deadpanned: "The numbers aren't very pertinent; it's the quality." Had he not exercised great restraint, he added, he "could have had 300 more footnotes."[7]

Some student editors of these law reviews carry with them the lessons of length as they ascend the professional ladder to judicial clerkships. Opinions have been getting longer because of "excessive reliance on and adoption of law clerks' bad habits from law reviews," said Joseph W. Bellacosa, then a judge on New York's highest court and now dean of St. John's University School of Law. Shirley Hufstedler concurred: Opinions are longer because "law clerks are doing most of the writing, and even those who are good do not know the difference between a law review note and an opinion."

I [Harlan McCugh, a senior partner with McCugh, McCugh & Moore McCughs] had an instance not long ago where a lawyer for a motion picture studio sent a one-page contract to a screenwriter I was representing. I took one look at it and became furious . . . The studio lawyer apologized and . . . promised to send over the studio's usual 170-page contract right away. As soon as I got it, we started haggling over it for three months, and I was able to charge my client my normal outrageous fee.

ART BUCHWALD

Some judges also indulge their own scholarly bent. When he was chief judge of the New York Court of Appeals, Sol Wachtler spoke of the "tendency in some courts to use a legal opinion as a research paper to display the knowledge of the writer." Moreover, judges presented with discursive briefs can demonstrate their scholarship on the cheap. Justice James Leff, a Manhattan trial judge, told us: "I do hold the opinion that when a news report says, 'In a 76-page opinion, District Court Judge X said . . . ' [it means] that he had two briefs with dozens of quotations and that he put his opinion together with scissors and magic tape." Finally, many courts either lack the judgment to exclude what is valueless or else feel compelled to answer every point to show that they are impartial and worthy of the challenge. Justice Mosk once remarked that when inundated with lengthy briefs, "courts must then discuss every conceivable point however meritless."

Thus long briefs beget long opinions, which beget long briefs. Long opinions also provide fodder for professors to chew over in long law review articles. Long law review articles provide grist for the brief and opinion writers. The circle is closed.

Some courts have tried to stem the deluge of words. The U.S. Supreme Court limits petitions for writ of certiorari to 30 pages and appellants' and appellees' briefs on the merits to 50 pages; reply briefs are limited to 20 pages. Principal briefs in the federal courts of appeals are limited to 30 pages (or 14,000 words if a proportionally spaced typeface is used, or 1,300 lines of text for a monospaced font*); motions are limited to 20 pages. The Virginia Supreme Court limits principal briefs to 50 typed or 36 printed pages, and reply briefs to 15 typed or 12 printed pages.[8] In some instances, the quality of the writing has improved. For example, after the federal district court for the Northern District of California imposed a 25-page limit for briefs, Patrick D. Mahoney, a San Francisco municipal judge, reported that the change "has forced lawyers to be much more concise, which has led to superior briefs. . . . The effect has been to eliminate repetitive arguments, to sharpen the quality of the arguments that are made, and to eliminate string citations that are of no benefit to anyone."

Page limits are a start, but lawyers circumvent them with impunity.[9] That's unfortunate. Page limitations set outer boundaries; they should not be regarded as minimum lengths or even suggested lengths. Lawyers must learn to stay well within the limits and should press the courts to sanction adversaries who exceed them.

---

* Counting words is not as straightforward a task as it might seem. In 1999 the U.S. Court of Appeals for the Seventh Circuit came close to sanctioning a lawyer for misstating the number of words in a filed brief. It turned out that the lawyer had relied on a word processing count that excluded the footnotes; *DeSilva v. DeLeonardi*, 185 F.3d 815, 1999 U.S. App. LEXIS 16794 (7th Cir. 1999). Word counts also vary among word processing programs (and versions) because some use different definitions of a "word."

The young associate who wrote the ninety-page brief is no longer employed by the law firm that was forced to cut his draft by two-thirds. He might have stayed had he known where to stop before he started. Successful journalists develop a skill in writing to space, often under a tight deadline: They tailor their materials to the inch limitation their editors impose. The most accomplished journalists assess their raw material and *tell* their editors how much space is justified, well before any word is written. Lawyers can as surely develop this skill for their writing. Lawyers must learn to tailor their materials to either a court-imposed page limit or a self-imposed limit appropriate to the purpose. Lawyers are paid for their judgment and skill in analyzing facts and presenting their analysis on their clients' behalf. A long, tangled document reflects poor judgment and constitutes poor advocacy.

Before starting to compose, you must inventory the elements of your document and estimate how many words (or pages) each will require. For example, you can oppose summary judgment in a page, by highlighting the facts at issue without extended discussion. You can summarize a case by eliminating the irrelevancies and streamlining your prose. You are not bound to your initial estimates. But by adhering to them as closely as possible, you will save yourself much time when it counts.

You will save this time by not writing extra pages in a draft and not having to cut them later. More important, you will be spared the complex task of restructuring the entire document. By their nature, lengthier documents digress more frequently than short ones, giving the former a more tangled structure that requires far more pruning. This is a plea not to omit relevant matters but to keep it short, a plea not for simplemindedness but for simplicity. Cover all the relevant matters, of course, but omit the tangents, digressions, and historical surveys.

What of the associate who is told: "Tell me everything about the Silver King Mine doctrine"? Suppose this associate locates forty-five cases on the law of eminent domain and ski resorts. To submit a memo that includes a one-or two-page summary of each case would be ludicrous. The supervising lawyer is expecting a synthesis, an analysis of doctrine, not a set of case digests. "Everything" rarely calls for equal treatment of each case, and the final brief, whoever writes it, will not contain all forty-five cases.

Even if your supervisor does say "Write up every case," you should rank them in order of importance. Group the least relevant cases together and mark them "first cut" (meaning "this is the section that can be dropped first"). Cases of marginal relevance become the "second cut," and so on. That way, a hundred-page preliminary memorandum can be collapsed into a twenty-five-page brief that includes all the most important cases.

We know that it is harder—and often takes longer—to write short. Some lawyers have told us that they do little editing because they cannot justify charging their clients for that time. Our response is that lawyers have a professional responsibility to deliver the best possible document within the deadline. That means they must do sufficient research and present that research in a polished document. Lawyers who are unstinting in research time but sparing in writing and editing must learn to better allocate their time. By writing long, flabby documents rather than short, tight ones, lawyers burden the courts, shortchange their clients, and lower standards across the profession.

10 WRONG WORDS, LONG SENTENCES, AND OTHER MISTER MEANERS

From choosing the right word to linking several paragraphs in logical sequence, the writer faces a series of choices. Anywhere along the way, a mistake will hinder understanding. Though surely the well-meaning writer commits no error with felonious intent, the cumulative impact on the reader is often fatal. Dorothy Evslin, a professor of English at a community college in Westchester County, New York, told of a student who wrote in an essay: "He was arrested for parking tickets and other mister meaners."[1] That phrase offers an apt name for the infractions that we discuss in this chapter.

These are the errors you may overlook when you are composing; you shouldn't interrupt your thinking to reword a cliché or trim a windy phrase. But you must attend to these errors during editing, when you are revising your work to meet the needs and expectations of your readers. Faulty grammar, imprecise word choice, haphazard syntax, and the other mister meaners are dangerous because they can cause your readers to stumble, to become frustrated and weary, or to misunderstand your point.

The primary purpose of editing is to make thought intelligible to the writer's audience. The rules that follow are not artificial dictates of some long-forgotten schoolteacher, but the essentials by which all writers make their thoughts clear.

Readers have too much to read and too little time in which to read it. Writers, therefore, are always competing for the reader's time. If your syntax is tangled, your grammar incorrect, your vocabulary mistaken, and your phrases a thicket, your readers will stumble and lose their way. To find your meaning, they must retrace their steps and begin again. If you force them to reread your prose too often, they will become weary of the journey and quit. When they quit, you lose.

This proposition is not speculation. Psychologists have shown that readers rushing through sentences store the points in a short-term memory register, which has a limited capacity. The longer your sentences and the more ideas they carry, the less likely that your readers will grasp, absorb, or retain your points.

Here's a simple example, from Kenneth Majer, an executive in the 1980s with Siegel & Gale. Look at the row of numerals on the next line for five seconds, then cover it over, and try to list each one.

3 8 6 1 4 0 2 9 7 5

The odds are high that you missed one or two. The odds are even higher that you could not repeat them all in the order listed. But if you glance at the row of numerals on the next line,

0 1 2 3 4 5 6 7 8 9

you'll know them all instantly and can immediately list them in the correct order. These are the same numerals that appeared above, but now there is a logical order.

Readers come to documents knowing many kinds of structure and expecting to find the appropriate one. One, as we have just seen, is the familiar arithmetical order: If you ask someone to write out the numerals conventionally, you expect them to be listed in the order given in the second row above.

Another but less obvious structure that readers know and expect is the placement of elements within a sentence. The anticipated word order is what George Gopen and Joseph Williams call the "reader expectation" of a sentence. When sentences do not conform to this expectation, the reader falters and meaning may be lost.

In interpreting the meaning of a sentence, all educated readers of English rely on rules and conventions regarding word order, sentence-verb agreement, punctuation, and the like. Sentences that do not meet these reader expectations will be misinterpreted or ignored.

In addition to satisfying these reader expectations, you need to consider the expectations of your particular audience or audiences. The principal audiences for legal writing are judges, other lawyers, clients, and other nonlawyers. Because these audiences differ in background, knowledge, and experience, they have diverse expectations when they come to a piece of legal writing. One audience will expect considerable detail; another already knows the facts. One audience will expect plain English; another will be insulted if you don't speak their jargon. We will return to the topic of audiences in chapter 12; our advice in this chapter focuses on reader expectations.

That readers expect sentences to be structured in certain ways explains why writing instructors talk of clarity and order. Obscure words, helter-skelter prose and faulty order, and sentences crowded with ideas all discourage the reader. In contrast, short sentences meticulously phrased with vivid words and images, along with frequent road maps, help direct a reader from beginning to end.

A few words about the examples we have chosen. We have culled most of them from our teaching of lawyers and students. Others were sent to us, and still others come from our reading. Occasionally, we have embroidered an example to highlight a mistake. Almost always we have changed names to mask the identities of the workshop participants and their clients. We have also compressed some of the worst and wordiest passages, lest you doze off and miss the point of the example. The worst legal writing is so long and complex that it would be self-defeating to reprint it. We wish to avoid what we call the "Ishtar syndrome," after the Warren Beatty–Dustin Hoffman movie that bombed because it portrayed two bad songwriters whose bad songs were actually sung in their entireties.

Words

Vocabulary

Referring to *Roe v. Wade,* a student wrote: "Scientists do not yet know whether life begins at contraception." The student didn't mean to be funny but, like many an unwary writer, he was oblivious to the meaning of certain words. Unlike Lewis Carroll's Humpty Dumpty (who told Alice that "when *I* use a word, it means just what I choose it to mean—neither more nor less"), lawyers cannot impose their will on words. You must double-check meanings in the dictionary. If you confuse *disinterested* with *uninterested,* or *affect* with *effect*—as many lawyers do—you should spend some time with a book that highlights common vocabulary mistakes. (We discuss some of these errors in the Usage Notes.)

> EXAMPLE: George then states that Harry's bad faith in failing to investigate his customers is exacerbated with the ease with which breaches of the license agreement could be avoided.
>
> PROBLEM: "Exacerbate" means "to increase the severity of or to aggravate, to make worse." You can't exacerbate bad faith, and you certainly can't do it with ease.
>
> SOLUTION: George then states that Harry's bad faith in failing to investigate his customers was all the worse because he could so easily have avoided breaches of the license agreement.

> EXAMPLE: The instant case is exactly analogous to S's case.
>
> PROBLEMS: The "instant" is clutter, and "analogous" denotes a relationship that, by nature, can never be exact.
>
> SOLUTION: This case is analogous to S's case.

Legalese: Latinisms, Pomposities, and Bureaucratese

After three weeks in law school, even the rawest apprentice realizes that lawyers often write in an odd style that mixes archaic words, Latinisms, jargon, and pomposities. David Mellinkoff showed that most legal jargon is fuzzy and avoidable. In *Plain English for Lawyers,* Professor Richard C. Wydick of the University of California School of Law at Davis echoed this theme: "Lawyerisms are words like *aforementioned, whereas, res gestae,* and *hereinafter.* They give writing a legal smell, but they carry little or no legal substance. When they are used in writing addressed to nonlawyers, they baffle and annoy. When used in other legal writing, they give a false sense of precision and sometimes obscure a dangerous gap in analysis." Or they can be just plain misused. Here's a gossip columnist trying to sound formal: "After her marriage Saturday to sportscaster Frank Gifford, 'The Morning Show' co-host Kathie Lee Johnson will heretofore be called Kathie Lee Gifford." Alfred E. Kahn, during his tenure as chairman of the federal Civil Aeronautics Board, gave the following advice to his staff: "Every time you are tempted to use 'herein,' 'hereinabove,' 'hereinunder,' or similarly, 'therein' and its corresponding variants, try 'here' or 'there' or 'above' or 'below' and see if it doesn't make just as much sense."[2]

Legal argot exists along a spectrum, ranging from stilted usage, such as the irksome and always unnecessary uses of *said* and *such* as adjectives, to impenetrable Latin and other foreign phrases that tempt even the best writers. James J. Kilpatrick, the syndicated columnist and usage expert, once scolded William H. Rehnquist, then associate justice of the U.S. Supreme Court, for asking whether "the power of Congress may be thought to *ex proprio vigore* apply to the power." Rehnquist could not break the habit, even when writing for a more general audience. In an otherwise flattering review of Chief Justice Rehnquist's *The Supreme Court: How It Was, How It Is,* a book noted favorably in the popular press, Professor Philip Kurland of the University of Chicago Law School complained of Rehnquist's affinity for the foreign term: "When Mr. Rehnquist describes oral argument in the Court, he writes that it 'requires controlled enthusiasm and not an impression of *fin de siècle* ennui.' Again: 'Advocacy before our Court is preeminently a *carrière ouverte aux talents* in the very best tradition of that phrase.' Some of us will not have the slightest notion what kind of ennui was peculiar to the *fin de siècle,* or what is the grand tradition of a *carrière ouverte aux talents* he has in mind. It is to be presumed that the Chief Justice was not setting an example to brief writers to indulge in such esoterica."[3]

> EXAMPLE: The pending motion for a preliminary injunction
> involves a challenge under Delaware law to an anti-takeover
> defense sometimes picturesquely described as a "street sweep."
> That sobriquet is used by cognoscenti in the esoteric field of
> corporate takeovers to refer to a rapid accumulation of a large
> block of target corporation stock.

PROBLEM: "Street sweep" may be picturesque, but the author, a judge, smudges his prose by packing together words that should rarely be used alone. As H. W. Fowler observed in his *Dictionary of Modern English Usage*, "those who run to long words are mainly the unskillful and tasteless; they confuse pomposity with dignity, flaccidity with ease, and bulk with force."[4]

EXAMPLE: Sixty days prior to expiration of the license . . .

PROBLEM: "Prior to" is clunky, unnatural, and unnecessary. Use the shorter and simpler "before." (Similarly, for "subsequent to," use "after.")

SOLUTION: Sixty days before the license expires . . .

EXAMPLE: *Under date of* February 29, 2000 . . .

SOLUTION: On February 29, 2000 . . .

EXAMPLE: *Pursuant to* the terms of the covenant, a payment of $100 must be remitted by you.

PROBLEM: "Pursuant to" is no more precise than "under," and "the terms of" adds nothing. In the main clause, the action (pay) is frozen in a noun, and the agent (you) is the object of a passive verb.

SOLUTION: Under the covenant, you must pay $100.

EXAMPLE: *Pursuant to* his authority as regional manager, plaintiff entered into a general agency contract with himself designating himself a general agent to solicit life insurance applications and memberships in the Elks.

PROBLEM: Comfortable with "pursuant to," this writer unfortunately continues unmindful that his flaccid writing obscures the point.

SOLUTION: As regional manager, the plaintiff designated himself by contract a general agent to solicit life insurance applications and memberships in the Elks.

EXAMPLE: Enclosed herewith please find . . .

PROBLEM: This is a very common, and very silly, formula.

SOLUTION: I am enclosing . . .

A close cousin to legalese, bureaucratese—or gobbledygook, the word coined by Congressman Maury Maverick in the 1940s—is a form of "government-speak" that flattens readers by rolling over them with long phrases, pompous expressions, and polysyllabic words. A simple but classic type is the police report, which speaks of "apprehending the perpetrator." Bureaucratese is intended to impress readers with the author's seriousness, and it often breaks out when a lawyer or other professional staff aide writes the remarks for a public figure. Here, for example, is John L. Lewis, speaking as the president of the United Mine Workers:

> No action has been taken by this writer or the United Mine Workers of America, as such, which would fall within the purview of the oppressive statute under which you seek to function. Without indulging in analysis, it is a logical assumption that the cavilings of the bar and bench in their attempts to explicate this infamous enactment will consume a tedious time.[5]

Sometimes even bureaucrats recoil from the airier flights of fancy floated by their subordinates. In 1990 Edward Derwinsky, secretary of veterans affairs, bemoaned such gems as "individual aerial deceleration mechanism" (parachute), "combat emplacement evacuator" (shovel), and "sea-air interface climactic disturbances" (waves).[6] But bureaucratese endures. Edward Tenner, the whimsical chronicler of "tech speak," shows how turgid and pompous phrases can replace ordinary words. For example, a dish is a "ceramic nutrient manipulation surface." A cemetery is a "biolysis center." A bartender is an "applied ethanol chemist," and a bookmaker at the racetrack is an "equine concurrent bioenergetic evaluation professional." Tech speak itself is a "postcolloquial discourse module protocol for user status enhancement"—a self-mocking explanation for this kind of pompous jargon.[7]

But bureaucratese, like legalese, has a sinister side. George Orwell warned in *1984* and in his 1946 essay "Politics and the English Language" that English could be corrupted to oppressive political ends. The euphemisms of "doublethink" and "Newspeak"—"War Is Peace"— could anesthetize the citizenry or blind it to the crimes committed in its name. When a company renames elevator operators "vertical transportation corps" and grocery stores call their baggers "career associate scanning professionals," we may laugh or wince. When the courts refer to the retarded committed to institutions as people with "minimally adequate training" or when hospitals refer to someone who died as one who "did not fully achieve his wellness potential," we cringe. But when taxes become "revenue enhancements," when women become "special interests," when a terrible fire at Three Mile Island becomes "rapid oxidation" and explosion "energetic disassembly," the joke is no longer funny.[8]

Usage

Eliminating legalisms is no guarantee of clean prose. Over the centuries, English usage has become a matter of custom, not logic. For example, knowing when to use *who* and *whom* is a sign of literacy. The lawyer who writes "the defendant became angry and often violent with whomever opposed her" violates the conventions of grammar and usage and offends both ear and eye. Usage can change, of course, and books on the subject may differ on particulars, but lawyers disregard at their peril the consensus of usage experts. Keep a comprehensive usage book on your shelf, next to your dictionary, and consult it often. (The most common usage problems are discussed in the Usage Notes.)

> EXAMPLE: Children in congregate care require the treatment setting to be comprised of a group of peers to who they can relate and with whom they can share basic values.

> PROBLEMS: "Comprise" means "include" or "contain" (the United States comprises fifty states), and therefore nothing can ever be "comprised of" anything. That usage "is always wrong," says Bryan A. Garner.[9] Here, the writer means that the setting should "consist of," "be composed of," or just plain "have." Better still, we can eliminate "the treatment setting" altogether. And note that the writer busy with "comprised of" has overlooked the inaccurate "to who."

> SOLUTION: Children in congregate care should be placed with a group of peers to whom they can relate and with whom they can share basic values.

EXAMPLE: These openings occurred due to the voluntary departure of two engineers from their positions.

PROBLEM: "Due to" means "attributable to" and should be used only to modify a noun. Here, the writer needs "owing to," "resulting from," or "because of." A quick test: The use of "due to" is correct only if the sentence makes sense when you substitute "attributable to." For example, "The delay was due to a flat tire" is fine ("The delay was attributable to a flat tire"). The misuse of "due to" is rather common, and some usage experts even allow it, but discerning readers will balk.

SOLUTION: These positions became available because two engineers quit their jobs.

EXAMPLE: The Wisconsin Supreme Court has acknowledged that when a dispute exists as to the existence of an easement . . .

PROBLEM: The unfortunate yoking of "as" and "to" has increasingly, but quite wrongly, displaced conventional prepositions. The result is a growing sterility of expression, as the far more colorful idiomatic English is washed away. For example, we often read of "the clue as to his whereabouts." "As" adds nothing; the proper expression is "clue to." In "question as to whether," eliminate "as to" altogether. We could "wonder as to his whereabouts," but we would be thinking more clearly if we "wondered where he was." Again, the use of prepositional idioms is not logical but customary.

SOLUTION 1: The Wisconsin Supreme Court has acknowledged that when there is a dispute over the existence of an easement . . .

PROBLEM: This change eliminates "as to" but introduces the troublesome "there is."

SOLUTION 2: The Wisconsin Supreme Court has acknowledged that when a dispute arises over the existence of an easement . . .

EXAMPLE: If adopted, the amendment would have barred the plaintiff's recovery where the plaintiff's negligence was equal to that of the defendant.

PROBLEM: Be wary of "where." "Where" refers to space, location, or geography; it is not a substitute for "when," "if," or "that."

In this example, the writer wanted "when" or "if" or perhaps even "because." A related misuse of "where" occurs in the expression "we note where one court said." The writer means "we note that one court said."

Overcaution and Reckless Abandon

Lawyers alternate between extreme caution and wild exaggeration. One moment, they hesitate to commit themselves even when the facts are with them—adding the qualifiers "usually," "often," "sometimes," "almost," "possibly," or "seemingly" when omitting these words would strengthen their argument. The next moment, they may blithely, even exuberantly, overstate their case. Chief Justice Edward Douglass White was famous for his overheated style. As Harvard's constitutional law professors noted years ago: "What impresses later generations in White's opinions is less their substance than their extraordinary form. He moved portentously across the thinnest ice, confident that a lifeline of adverbs—'inevitably,' 'irresistibly,' 'clearly,' and 'necessarily'—was supporting him in his progress."[10]

Few phenomena are truly "remarkable"; fewer legal points are "absolutely clear" or even just plain "clear." Likewise, "as everyone knows," "as we can plainly see," "literally," "undoubtedly," and "certainly" seldom bolster a case that has not already been made. Many lawyers use these words, and many others like them, reflexively—the hedge words because they do not want to be shown wrong, the emphatic words because they are afraid they have failed to persuade the reader. These words enfeeble rather than enhance the prose.

EXAMPLE: The situation in this case is substantially analogous to that in *Colorado Coal and Lumber* . . .

PROBLEM: If the situations are analogous, "substantially" is a meaningless emphatic. If the situations are identical, the writer shouldn't hide behind a hedge.

EXAMPLE: When addressing factual situations similar to that present in this case, courts in other jurisdictions have been virtually unanimous in holding . . .

PROBLEM: The sentence is ambiguous. It could mean that most courts which so held did so unanimously, that all courts have so held by close-to-unanimous votes, or simply that most courts have so held. Most likely, the writer meant "most courts in other jurisdictions have held," though the reader strains to reach that meaning. One imprecise word can gum up a thought.

EXAMPLE: It would seem that the options are basically three . . .

PROBLEM: Phrases such as "it would seem that" and "it would appear that" are among the most common (and worst) forms of lawyerly timidity. Whenever you are about to say "I would agree," throw caution to the wind and say "I agree." Geraldine A. Ferraro, in a letter to the *New York Times* (July 17, 1988) about her candidacy for vice-president four years earlier, wrote that cynics had dismissed her designation by Walter A. Mondale as "strictly a political move playing to the gender gap. I would agree . . . he removed gender as a disqualification for national office." That made her sound tentative. What she meant is "I agree." Ruthlessly suppress your penchant for these phrases.

SOLUTION: You have three options.

EXAMPLE: Under Illinois law, tape-recording a telephone conversation without the consent of the other parties to the conversation may constitute a criminal violation.

PROBLEMS: "May" is needlessly timid. (Can the statute be so ambiguous that the average lawyer will mistake what the legislature thinks about taping without consent?) "To the conversation" and "criminal violation" are wordy and create a chorus of jangly "-tions."

SOLUTION: Under Illinois law, tape-recording a telephone conversation without the consent of the other parties is a crime.

EXAMPLE: Since many of plaintiff's allegations of alleged illegal activity . . .

PROBLEM: "Alleged" is a legitimate word often overused and sometimes misused. In this example, "allegations of alleged" is redundant. Eliminate "alleged."

EXAMPLE: Plaintiff's failure to state the basis of her claims that Kuhn Inc. is an alleged criminal enterprise illustrates her lack of good faith in making this allegation.

PROBLEM: No need to hedge. By referring to the plaintiff's claim, the writer is not assenting to the proposition that Kuhn is a criminal enterprise and so is not conceding his adversary's position—the usual fear that prompts lawyers to overuse "alleged." The assertion here is entirely the plaintiff's. She is not claiming that Kuhn is an "alleged" criminal enterprise but that it is an actual criminal enterprise.

SOLUTION: By failing to state the basis of her claims, the plaintiff shows her lack of good faith in alleging that Kuhn is a criminal enterprise.

EXAMPLE: It is truly remarkable, but not surprising . . .

EXAMPLE: Amazingly, the G memorandum, once again, . . .

PROBLEM: Enough!

Obviousness

Another writing difficulty born of fear, conceptually sandwiched between the overly cautious and the recklessly exaggerated, is the tautology—or obviousness. Not every tautology is bad—showing that the defendant's stock sales fit squarely within the definition of insider trading is a useful, and often difficult, proposition for a prosecutor to make. But the lawyer who reminds the reader that the client wishes "to live by the statute and not break the law" is saying twice what needs to be said only once. Say what you must say, but avoid stating the obvious.

EXAMPLE: If the client does not commence litigation, it gambles that the opponents will or will not do so.

PROBLEM: That's not much of a gamble: The proposition is a certainty. The writer probably meant to say that if the client does not sue, it risks being sued.

EXAMPLE: Suffice it to say, Section 7 expressly states . . .

PROBLEM: A cousin of "needless to say" (if it is needless, why say it?), "suffice it to say" means nothing more than "this is all I want to say about the matter right now" or "when I say what I'm about to say, you'll understand what I'm saying." Rarely necessary and overworked. Purge.

EXAMPLE: The law is obvious . . .

PROBLEM: Then why do we need lawyers?

Clichés

A cliché is an overworked expression that broadcasts the writer's laziness or fatuousness. A cliché may communicate, but it does so at the risk of sending the reader to dreamland. The cliché suggests that the writer lacks the King's English; it certainly won't knock the reader's socks off, and sometimes it will just draw a blank. Most of us speak in clichés because we learned them when we were knee high to a grass-hopper, and at first blush we just grin and bear it. But in writing they tend to come a cropper. So let's get down to brass tacks and, with both feet on the ground, face the music and turn over a new leaf: Gird your loins at these wolves in sheep's clothing, give clichés the short shrift, and from now on, avoid them like the plague.

That said, clichés can sometimes be useful, precisely because they are familiar. Sparingly used, the proper cliché can make your point most clearly. In any event, you should prefer the well-worn cliché to a ludicrous refashioning. Better to say that your client was speaking "tongue in cheek" than to assert that he was speaking with "tongue rolled in mouth." Better to attribute a motive to "sour grapes" than "tart grapes." Better to say she's "squeaky clean" rather than "whiny clean." In the hands of a good writer, a cliché can be turned to considerable effect. Consider Henry Thoreau's play on "spur of the moment": "I feel the spur of the moment thrust deep into my side. The present is an inexorable rider."

EXAMPLE: In RICO's first decade on the books . . .

PROBLEM: The clause is both tautological and clichéd. By definition, a statute is "on the books."

SOLUTION: In RICO's first decade . . .

Slang

A relative of the cliché, slang ordinarily sets too low a tone for writing by lawyers.

EXAMPLE: York has no problem with fair competition.

PROBLEM: Not only is "no problem" slang, it is ambiguous. In what way is it "no problem"?

SOLUTION: York favors [*or* welcomes] fair competition.

EXAMPLE: In refusing to compel disclosure, the court stated flat out that the work product exemption . . .

PROBLEM: "Flat out" is a colloquial substitute for "flatly," "explicitly," or "unequivocally."

Throat Clearing

Wise as it is to provide the reader with a road map, some introductory phrases serve only to let the writer rev up while composing. Use them to get going, but delete them when you edit your draft.

EXAMPLE: It is interesting to note that the declaration of Miller's spy, Mr. Arthur, fails to indicate when movement of inventory from Deer Valley was observed.

PROBLEMS: To whom is it interesting? Why? If a point is inherently interesting, readers will recognize that. Moreover, this sentence obscures the point that is heralded as interesting.

SOLUTION 1: The declaration of Miller's spy, Mr. Arthur, does not indicate when he saw the movement of inventory from Deer Valley.

SOLUTION 2: Miller's spy, Mr. Arthur, did not say when he saw inventory being moved from Deer Valley.

EXAMPLE: You are undoubtedly well aware of Sect. X of the Utah statutes and the general position of the Utah courts regarding employee covenants not to compete, and I do not intend to burden you with a lengthy dissertation on the subject.

SOLUTION: I will summarize Sect. X of the Utah statutes and how Utah courts regard employee covenants not to compete.

EXAMPLE: At the outset, it is critically important to define and clarify terminology with respect to fraudulent inducement.

SOLUTION: First, we must define fraudulent inducement.

Sexist Words

Whenever possible, use gender-neutral terms to describe occupations, status, or positions. For example, "workers' compensation," not "workman's compensation"; "firefighter," not "fireman"; "business executive," "manager," or "retailer," not "businessman"; "drafter," not "draftsman." *The New York Times Manual of Style and Usage* recommends avoiding language that calls attention to the sex of an individual when sex is irrelevant: "In general references, use a neutral job title like *letter carrier* rather than *mailman,* and *police officer* rather than *policeman* or *policewoman.* "[11] Careful writers also prefer "synthetic fiber" to "manmade fiber," and they select a nongendered equivalent for such terms as "man-hours" ("staff-hours," "work," "labor").

William Safire, the language columnist of the *New York Times,* adds a cautionary note—"Hypersensitivity to sexism in language can pull the punch out of a good sentence"—and asks rhetorically: "In wiping away the undoubted masculine tilt to a thousand years of English, and in attempting to imbue our language with gender equality, are we going too far too fast?"[12]

Wordiness

Fuzzy Phrases

Lawyers tend to use many words when one will do. They say "on the grounds that" or "for the reason that" when they could say "because." They say "in the event that" or "under circumstances in which" when "if" is fine. They say "with regard to" or "concerning the matter of" when "about" is preferable. They say "has the opportunity to" or "is able to" when they mean "can." Look for these fuzzy phrases in your writing and eliminate them. When one word works, use it.

> EXAMPLE: The court's criticism of the jury charge focused on the fact that the trial court instructed the jury that it could consider . . .
>
> PROBLEM: All usage books pounce on "the fact that." Strunk and White call it "especially debilitating" and advise that it "be revised out of every sentence in which it occurs." Removing the phrase also allows us to simplify the syntax of the clause that follows.
>
> SOLUTION 1: The court's criticism of the jury charge focused on the trial court's instruction that the jury could consider . . .
>
> SOLUTION 2: The court criticized the jury charge, focusing on the trial court's instruction . . .

> EXAMPLE: In addition, in light of plaintiff's failure to make disclosure of the existence of the covenant not to sue or to abide by it . . .
>
> SOLUTION: Also, because plaintiff failed to disclose or abide by the covenant not to sue . . .

> EXAMPLE: The defendant was in a paying nexus with the plaintiff.
>
> PROBLEM: Fuzziness coupled to bureaucratese.
>
> SOLUTION: The defendant paid the plaintiff.

Noun Compounding

In German, one may glue short words into a long string—for example, *Untergrundbahnhofeingang* (underground railway station entrance). In English, however, intelligibility suffers when nouns are tightly packed.

> EXAMPLE: We had a company staff size analysis determination.
>
> PROBLEM: No aversion to verbs and prepositions can excuse a

sentence like this one. We are not sure, but possibly it means "Our company analyzed the size of its staff."

EXAMPLE: Several courts have recently been confronted with alleged interested director transactions.

SOLUTION: Several courts have recently heard cases involving directors accused of having personal interests in company transactions.

Negatives

George Orwell said it should be "possible to laugh the *not un-* formation out of existence." The cure, he suggested, is to memorize this sentence: "A not unblack dog was chasing a not unsmall rabbit across a not ungreen field." It is not unlikely that Orwell was overly optimistic. Thirty-five years later, Secretary of State Alexander M. Haig, the dean of bureaucratese, remarked: "This is not an experience I haven't been through before."[13] In their desire to hedge, lawyers, too, persist in their love of double negatives, one more element of unnecessary complexity employed in the false belief that it lends weight or elegance to an otherwise dismal style.

EXAMPLE: We are not unmindful that litigation in a foreign jurisdiction is a burdensome inconvenience for any company.

SOLUTION: We are aware that . . .

EXAMPLE: This argument would not be without some support under Iowa case law.

SOLUTION 1: This argument has some support under Iowa case law.

SOLUTION 2: Some Iowa case law supports this argument.

EXAMPLE: The vast majority of the contracts contain no provision for refund of unearned premiums to the borrower in the event of cancellation of the insurance policy engendered by prepayment of all or part of the loan.

PROBLEMS: The negative wording ("contain no provision") makes it harder for the reader to follow the thread; propositions are easier to understand when they are affirmatively stated. The windy phrases and heavy nouns also slow the reader's progress.

SOLUTION: Few contracts provided for refund of unearned premiums to the borrower if the insurance policy was canceled because all or part of the loan was prepaid.

Often, you can avoid negatives by searching for an affirmative word that strengthens the point. For example, "few" instead of "not many"; "rejected" instead of "did not accept"; "too young" instead of "not old enough"; "left" instead of "did not remain."

EXAMPLE: The witness said that although he once knew, he no longer remembered the killer's identity.

SOLUTION: The witness said that although he once knew, he had forgotten the killer's identity.

Redundancies

Lawyers tend toward redundancy because their technical language is richly endowed with repetitive phrases that once had legal consequences—"cease and desist," "rest, residue, and remainder," "null and void," and "give and grant." Many of these doublets and triplets were adopted during the Middle Ages when legal language became an amalgam of English, Latin, and French. Whether these redundancies should continue to be used in drafting is not our concern. What makes us unhappy is that this way of thinking has seeped into ordinary writing. Some Watergate witnesses repeatedly lost their memories "at this point in time." They could have drained their prose of this muck and said simply "now" or "at this point" or "at this time." Simple redundancies are easily spotted and excised: "bedraggled" rather than "bedraggled in appearance," "green" rather than "green in color." Likewise, never speak of "consensus of opinion" or a "free gift" or "final outcomes" or "completely finished."

EXAMPLE: On August 16, 2001, at the hour of 10 A.M. in the morning . . .

SOLUTION: On August 16, 2001, at 10 A.M. . . . .

EXAMPLE: After C's death, the remaining balance of the trust . . .

SOLUTION: After C's death, the balance of the trust . . .

EXAMPLE: In addition, there are no facts whatsoever to indicate . . .

SOLUTION: No facts support . . .

EXAMPLE: The subject matter area of the discussion . . .

SOLUTION: The subject of the discussion . . .

EXAMPLE: Dolly has asked us to describe the legal consequences
which would result if she were to unilaterally terminate her service contracts with the hospitals.

PROBLEMS: "Result" is redundant (a consequence is a result), and
"unilaterally terminate" is stuffy.

SOLUTION: Dolly has asked us to describe the legal consequences
of breaking her service contracts with the hospitals.

EXAMPLE: The logical corollary of her argument . . .

PROBLEM: By definition, corollaries are always logical.

SOLUTION: The corollary of her argument . . .

EXAMPLE: By encouraging spurious class action lawsuits . . .

PROBLEM: An "action" is a lawsuit.

SOLUTION: By encouraging spurious class actions . . .

EXAMPLE: The difficulty of attracting such individuals is magni-
fied by the difficult task this board has faced in the past and
will have to face in the future.

SOLUTION: Attracting such individuals is made all the more difficult by the formidable task this board faces.

Verbosity

Lawyers have always been verbose. Combat this tendency by pre-
tending that you will be paid inversely to the number of words—or
that you must pay for the words you use. Cut, cut, cut.

EXAMPLE: During the course of our phone conversations . . .

PROBLEM: A conversation, by its nature, has a course.

SOLUTION: During our phone conversations . . .

EXAMPLE: The facts of Deer Creek are apposite to the instant motion in that Heber has disputed . . .

SOLUTION: Just as in Deer Creek, Heber has disputed . . .

EXAMPLE: In *Shrager,* the plaintiff commenced an action claiming that it had . . .

PROBLEMS: No "plaintiff" exists until an action has been commenced, and there is no action without a claim.

SOLUTION: In *Shrager,* the plaintiff claimed that it had . . .

EXAMPLE: When the bulldozer became engaged as a result of the jump start, it rolled over the decedent causing her death.

PROBLEM: An entire phrase where "jump-started" would do.

SOLUTION: After the bulldozer was jump-started, it rolled over and killed the decedent.

EXAMPLE: Despite plaintiff's claims to the contrary, since plaintiff has failed to provide any factual information at all concerning the terms of the alleged oral contracts, the contract claims are so uncertain that defendants are unable to respond.

PROBLEM: Clumps of repeated words (plaintiff, claim, contract) usually signal verbosity.

SOLUTION: Because the plaintiff has failed to state the terms of the alleged oral contracts, the defendants are unable to respond to his claims.

EXAMPLE: As hereinafter indicated, we presently believe it would be in your best interests to enter into a permanent agreement to opt out of the Act, although this is a subject we should discuss in some detail.

PROBLEMS: Cloudy phrases obscure the point, and the sentence is too long.

SOLUTION: You should enter into a permanent agreement to opt out of the Act. We should discuss.

EXAMPLE: In order to sustain an allegation of fraudulent concealment, the plaintiffs must successfully allege (1) that defendants
wrongfully concealed the conspiracy, (2) that plaintiffs did not
discover the existence of the conspiracy, and (3) that plaintiffs
failed to discover the conspiracy despite the exercise of due diligence.

PROBLEM: The writer is splitting too many hairs at the end, after
being merely foolish at the beginning.

SOLUTION: To sustain an allegation of fraudulent concealment,
the plaintiffs must prove that (1) defendants wrongfully concealed the conspiracy and (2) plaintiffs did not discover the
conspiracy even though they exercised due diligence.

EXAMPLE: Her heirs, whom she predeceased and who survived
her, . . .

PROBLEM: Why split heirs? If she predeceased them, they survived her.

SOLUTION: Her surviving heirs . . .

Strings of Prepositions

A run of prepositional phrases obscures the point of the sentence or
forces the reader to absorb too many details at once. There is no need
to jam every qualification of the principal point into the same sentence.

EXAMPLE: In rejecting the argument that a large increase in senior securities entitled to dividend and liquidation priorities resulted in an alteration of the "special rights" of a class of junior
securities entitling such class of junior securities to a class vote,
the Delaware Supreme Court in *Erickson* stated . . .

PROBLEM: The reader must hurdle nine prepositional phrases, including four consecutive phrases beginning with "of," before
reaching the subject. That's too much to ask.

Many of us were taught that a preposition was something we should
never end a sentence with. If you can follow this convention without
sounding stuffy, do it. We could have said, "Many of us were taught

that we should never end a sentence with a preposition." Sometimes, however, the effort to avoid a terminal preposition sounds stilted or pompous, because the meaning of many verbs depends on the prepositions linked to them.

> EXAMPLE: That is the sort of thing the judge said he would look into.
>
> PROBLEM: To move the preposition from the end leaves you with a sentence like this: "That is the sort of thing into which the judge said he would look." One solution is to look for a different verb.
>
> SOLUTION: That is the sort of thing the judge said he would examine.

Verbs

The verb should carry the load of every sentence. The verb contains the action. It tells what the subject is doing, and it links the agent of the action and the object of the action. The stronger and sharper the verb, the clearer your meaning. Good writers avoid strings of sentences with only such verbs as "is" and "has" to prop them up.

Nominalizations

Sentences that submerge the action in nouns usually collapse of their own weight. Without active verbs, a sentence lumbers. Freezing the action of verbs in nouns is what the grammarians call *nominalization*. Donald C. Freeman, former director of training at Shearman & Sterling and at Baker & McKenzie, says that nominalization is bad because it "interrupts canonical word order": It subverts the reader's expectation that the grammatical subject of the sentence will name the person or thing doing the action, and that the verb will name that action. When the doer is not the grammatical subject, normal word order is interrupted. Moreover, the writer often must add prepositions and other phrases to sort out meaning, giving the sentence a choppy effect. At writing seminars, Freeman has offered this example:

> At the time of Abco's cashing of the check, there plainly was a dispute between the parties as to the amount owing Abco under paragraph 4(d) of the Security Agreement.

This sentence nominalizes its two actions—cashing and disputing—and puts the agents into prepositional phrases. The subjects of the two clauses should be the doers—"Abco" and "the parties." Rewritten, the sentence loses many of its prepositions and is shorter and clearer:

> When Abco cashed the check, the parties plainly disputed the amount owed Abco under paragraph 4(d) of the Security Agreement.

Nominalizing is one of the most serious afflictions of legal prose, draining a sentence of vitality. Fortunately, nominalizations are easy to spot and easy (sometimes even fun) to transform into vigorous English. Common nominalizations include "determination," "commencement," "investigation," "reliance," "failure," "formulation," and "analysis." Another type of nominalization freezes the action in adjectives—"supportive" and "violative."

> EXAMPLE: Before the commencement of the federal bankruptcy case . . .
>
> SOLUTION: Before the bankruptcy case begins . . .

> EXAMPLE: We carried out an analysis of the blood samples.
>
> PROBLEM: Note that this sentence has a verb, but a weak, empty one. Weak verbs such as "conduct," "make," "is," and "has" signal that the main action lies elsewhere in the sentence. "Analysis" casts the activity as a noun.
>
> SOLUTION: We analyzed the blood samples.

> EXAMPLE: . . . termination of the audit within seven hours after its commencement.
>
> SOLUTION: . . . ended the audit seven hours after it began.

EXAMPLE: Plaintiff's reliance on *Jeremy Ranch* for its contention that a marketing plan or system need not be explicit is misplaced.

SOLUTION: Plaintiff mistakenly relies on *Jeremy Ranch* to argue that a marketing plan or system need not be explicit.

EXAMPLE: . . . that certain practices of that company were in violation of the California labor laws.

SOLUTION: . . . that certain practices of that company violated the California labor laws.

EXAMPLE: Courts and scholars have articulated numerous formulations of the business judgment rule.

PROBLEM: "Articulated" is an overused verb; it vanishes when we eliminate the nominalization.

SOLUTION: Courts and scholars have formulated the business judgment rule in many ways.

EXAMPLE: The plaintiff suffered the loss of his right hand when it was pulled in by his operation of a meat grinder.

SOLUTION: The plaintiff lost his right hand when it was pulled into a meat grinder he was operating.

EXAMPLE: The decisions in those shopping center cases granting specific performance have placed emphasis on combinations of the following factors.

SOLUTION: The decisions granting specific performance in shopping centers emphasize combinations of the following factors.

EXAMPLE: The court displayed no reluctance in awarding to the lender its substantial damages.

PROBLEM: This sentence does not nominalize, but the bland verb "displayed" relies on the negative "no reluctance" to give it flavor. Using a more precise verb emphasizes the action.

SOLUTION 1: The court did not hesitate to award the lender substantial damages.

SOLUTION 2: The court readily awarded the lender substantial damages.

Useful Nominalizations

The sentences we have just edited were wrenched out of context to illustrate the flaccidity produced by careless nominalization. But nominalization can be put to good purpose: to provide strong links between adjacent sentences. Nouns that describe or sum up the action of a previous sentence often can serve as a tidy bridge between the two. Beyond their use as a bridge, some nominalizations have become so standard that it would be awkward to transform them into verbs. Nominalizations can also help you avoid the awkward "the fact that."

EXAMPLE: The defendant denied that he was in the room when the murder was committed. The jury looked astounded when he denied being there.

SOLUTION: The defendant denied that he was in the room when the victim was murdered. His denial astounded the jury.

EXAMPLE: No taxation without representation.

COMMENT: Better to leave unchanged than to say: "Do not tax us unless we can vote for our representatives."

EXAMPLE: The fact that the cars collided was the top news story.

SOLUTION: The collision was the top news story.

The Passive Voice

The passive voice is a construction that permits the writer to avoid naming or referring to the person or thing that takes the action. The sentence "The lease was broken" does not say who broke the lease. The action is done to the subject of the sentence. In the active voice, the writer must tell us who is doing the breaking: "The landlord broke the lease."

Lawyers overuse the passive voice, sometimes because they know no better, sometimes to avoid assigning responsibility. Criticizing this lawyerly habit, Judge Patricia M. Wald observed in a commencement address at New York Law School that the passive voice "sanitizes and institutionalizes [lawyers'] writing and often anesthetizes the reader: all views are attributable to an unknowable 'it.' 'It is said,' 'it is reported,' 'it is argued.' "[14]

The passive voice is easy to spot: The verb is always in the participial form ("broken," instead of "broke") and always follows a form of the verb "be" ("is," "was," "being," "been")—*is broken, was broken, is being broken, has been broken.* The passive verb is often followed by a "by" clause—"*The lease was broken by the landlord.* " Even if it is not, you can always mentally insert a "by" clause in the sentence.

EXAMPLE: The appointment of Noela Snowflower as trustee of the debtor was made by stipulation between Jan Albertson, counsel for the debtor, and Deborah Redford, counsel for the creditor.

PROBLEMS: Passive constructions and nominalizations clog the sentence.

SOLUTION: Jan Albertson, counsel for the debtor, and Deborah Redford, counsel for the creditor, stipulated to the appointment of Noela Snowflower as trustee of the debtor.

EXAMPLE: Plaintiff's second effort to bring before this court a six-year-old dispute by a disappointed borrower against his former lender-bank should be dismissed with prejudice.

SOLUTION: This court should dismiss with prejudice the plaintiff's second effort to bring before it a six-year-old dispute by a disappointed borrower against his former lender-bank.

EXAMPLE: Chancery Rule 19 tracks exactly Rule 19 of the Federal Rules of Civil Procedure. Accordingly, interpretations of the federal rules by the federal judiciary are given great weight by Delaware courts concerning the interpretation of their own parallel rules.

PROBLEMS: The first verb is vivid but imprecise. The second sentence winds a trail of nominalizations, passive verbs, and prepositional phrases.

SOLUTION: Chancery court Rule 19 is identical to Rule 19 of the Federal Rules of Civil Procedure. Therefore, Delaware courts have given great weight to interpretations of the federal rules by federal courts.

Overreliance on passive verbs makes writing dull and listless. But the passive voice does serve important purposes. Use the passive when:

1. The agent of the action is unknown or irrelevant.

EXAMPLE: More than fifty arsonists were convicted in this city last year.

NOTE: The point is not who convicted the arsonists (a judge, several judges, or juries), but the number of convictions.

2. The subject of a series of sentences is the object of the action expressed in the verb.

EXAMPLE: The lease is a type of contract that for centuries has been interpreted to favor landlords. It is usually drawn by lawyers who specialize in real property, and it often consists of boilerplate that has been threshed out over decades or even longer. Leases should not be signed unless you read them carefully.

NOTE: The paragraph focuses on the lease. To transform the sentences into the active voice, we would have to introduce an array of subjects, which would disrupt the flow of thought: "For centuries courts have interpreted leases to favor landlords. Lawyers who specialize in real property draw up leases, and courts and lawyers have often threshed out their boilerplate language over decades or even longer. You should not sign a lease without reading it carefully."

3. The subject of the sentence is much longer than the object.

EXAMPLE: The difficulty is known to judges, lawyers, professors, jurors, bailiffs, clerks, and others in the judicial system.

NOTE: Cast in the active voice, this sentence would be top-heavy. The eighteen-word subject would swamp the verb and the two-word object: "Judges, lawyers, professors, people who have served on juries, bailiffs, clerks, and others involved in the judicial system know the difficulty."

4. A smooth transition calls for the object of one sentence to become the subject of the next.

EXAMPLE: The police sought the murder weapons by dragging the river in a Coast Guard launch. Dragging techniques are taught to cadets every fall in classes on seamanship and navigation. By the time the cadets graduate, they know the river intimately.

NOTE: The passive "Dragging techniques are taught" affords a cleaner transition than an active construction: "The police sought the murder weapons by dragging the river in a Coast Guard launch. Every fall, classes on seamanship and navigation teach cadets the techniques of dragging."

"There Is"

"There is," "there are," and "there have been" obscure the action and numb the mind. An occasional "there is" is inoffensive, but try to reword if you overuse these impersonal constructions.

EXAMPLE: There is no case law which specifically addresses the question presented.

SOLUTION: No case law specifically addresses the question.

EXAMPLE: There is no cure for sloppy thinking but to rethink.

SOLUTION: The only cure for sloppy thinking is rethinking.

Subject-Verb Agreement

Subjects and verbs must agree—a singular subject takes a singular verb and a plural subject a plural verb. Careful counting is the key.

EXAMPLE: Neither the tennis players nor Nancy are coming over for dinner.

PROBLEM: In "or" and "nor" constructions, the verb must agree with the closest subject. Here, "Nancy" is singular, and so the verb should be "is." In contrast, if subjects are connected by "and" the verb should always be plural: "The tennis players and Nancy are coming over for dinner."

EXAMPLE: Mere recitations of the legal issue presented to the court does not constitute sufficient pleading.

PROBLEM: The subject is "recitations," a plural, not "issue," the singular object of the prepositional phrase.

SOLUTION: Mere recitations of the legal issue presented to the court do not constitute sufficient pleading.

EXAMPLE: Both the format and the design of the database as well as the selection of information included within it is solely attributable to counsel for Leroy.

PROBLEMS: The subject is plural, and "within it" is surplus.

SOLUTION: Both the format and the design of the database as well as the selection of information included are solely attributable to counsel for Leroy.

EXAMPLE: The format of the database, together with the selection of information, are solely attributable to counsel for Leroy.

PROBLEM: Clauses beginning with "as well as," "together with," "along with," and "in addition to," are not conjunctive—they are not the equivalent of "and." Therefore, the verb must be singular if the subject outside the clause is singular.

SOLUTION: The format of the database, together with the selection of information, is solely attributable to counsel for Leroy.

Split Infinitives

When a modifier is placed immediately after the "to" in the infinitive form of the verb—for example, "to rapidly walk"—the writer has split the infinitive. From time to time there have been outcries against splitting the infinitive, though there has never been an immutable rule against doing so. Careful writers avoid the split infinitive when possible. If unsplitting the infinitive creates a choppy sentence, then by all means split it. But be aware that a few remaining purists abhor every instance of the split infinitive and will think the less of you if they find any.

EXAMPLE: By demurring, defendants are only exercising their right to vigorously litigate their claims.

SOLUTION: By demurring, defendants are only exercising their right to litigate their claims vigorously.

Pronouns

"I"

Lawyers turn somersaults to avoid using the first person. "In my opinion, it is not an unjustifiable assumption" should be "I think." Some lawyers believe that writing in the first person is too informal for a court and abstain from using "I" in all their writing. But as Judge Wald said: "Too many young lawyers today are afraid to show strong feelings of any kind: the jargon in which they write illustrates all too graphically their insecurity about stating what they believe in. They rarely use a straight declarative sentence or the pronoun 'I.'"[15]

EXAMPLE: Enclosed for your consideration is a copy of a proposed trust which has been prepared pursuant to our conference of October 2.

PROBLEM: Intent on avoiding "I," the writer resorts to the passive voice.

SOLUTION: I enclose a copy of a proposed trust that I prepared after our October 2 conference.

Antecedents

Readers will misinterpret the meaning of a sentence, or give up trying to find it, when the antecedent of a pronoun—that is, the person or thing to which the pronoun refers—is ambiguous or absent. The problem of the obscure antecedent crops up often with the overused "it" and also in the lazy construction in which the writer substitutes the word "this" for a concept expressed in an earlier sentence. This difficulty also occurs in the misuse of "which."

EXAMPLE: Plaintiff does not know that Sam knew that it was his thirty-fifth wedding anniversary.

PROBLEM: Whose anniversary? The reader will never know.

EXAMPLE: Thus, even assuming *arguendo* that punching out of a part of the label had the net effect of making it resemble another label used on women's jeans, this cannot constitute a copying of a "registered" mark.

PROBLEMS: Aside from the redundant Latinism, the unnecessary "had the net effect," and the dangling modifier, the sentence is obscure because the "this" in "this cannot constitute" does not refer to anything in particular. We can fix this problem by attaching "this" to a noun.

SOLUTION: Thus, even if we assume that punching out part of the label made it resemble another label used on women's jeans, this alteration cannot constitute a copying of a "registered" mark.

EXAMPLE: Each company is precluded from expanding its production capacity by covenants with its creditor banks which prevent borrowing for capital expansion until at least 2006.

PROBLEM: Does the "which" refer to creditor banks or to the covenants? Although the sense becomes clear on second reading, you don't want to force your reader to reread and assemble a puzzle.

SOLUTION: Covenants with creditor banks preclude each company from expanding production capacity because they prevent borrowing for capital expansion until at least 2006.

EXAMPLE: The defendant looked wildly about the room, which was evident to all the jurors.

PROBLEM: What does "which" refer to? From the context, we know that it must refer to the action in the preceding clause as a whole. Although readers can sometimes deduce an antecedent, such constructions should be avoided.

SOLUTION: The defendant looked wildly about the room; his motions were evident to all the jurors.

"That" and "Which"

The distinction between the relative pronouns *that* and *which* is not universally observed, but it is worth knowing. *That* introduces a clause that defines the noun it follows. A comma never precedes *that* when used in this way. *Which,* always preceded by a comma, introduces subsidiary information. For example, "This is my house, which Jack built" expresses the thought that this is *my* house. Jack's role is secondary. "This is my house that Jack built" suggests that of the many houses I own, this is the one built by Jack. In recent decades, several usage experts have noted the tendency to use *which* in both sentences. However, *that* is a word of many meanings and uses, and the writer would err to suppose that *which* can always substitute for it.

EXAMPLE: Recently we received information which you were interested in our publication . . .

PROBLEM: This construction is illiterate because which cannot be used as a conjunction.

SOLUTION 1: Recently we received information that you were interested in our publication . . .

SOLUTION 2: Recently you told us you were interested . . .

Fused Participles

Dear Reader: Do you mind *us* reciting all these examples? or Do you mind *our* reciting all these examples? Both questions are grammatical, but the first asks whether you object to *us* (rather than someone else) giving examples, while the second asks whether you object to the recitation. The choice between the objective pronoun (us) and the possessive pronoun (our) determines the object of the sentence. In "Do you mind our reciting," the object is the clause "reciting some examples," and the pronoun that modifies that clause must be in the possessive form. In 1906 H. W. Fowler, a leading grammarian of his day, coined the term "fused participle" for the construction that wrongly couples the objective pronoun with the true object of the sentence. R. W. Burchfield, editor of the third edition of Fowler's *Modern English Usage,* replaces the term with the equally unlovable "possessive with gerund" and observes that it is "on the retreat, but its use with proper names and personal nouns and pronouns persists in good writing."[16]

EXAMPLE: Wall Street law firms should be concerned about Professor Smith exhorting their students to work elsewhere.

PROBLEM: The sentence expresses concern about Professor Smith, not about the exhortation.

SOLUTION: Wall Street law firms should be concerned about Professor Smith's exhorting their students to work elsewhere.

EXAMPLE: What the Justice feared was the Constitution of the United States becoming a shield for the criminal.[17]

PROBLEM: The Justice feared the "becoming," not the Constitution. But the possessive "Constitution of the United States'" is impossible. Many grammarians would accept the sentence as it stands.

SOLUTION 1: What the Justice feared was the Constitution's becoming a shield for the criminal.

SOLUTION 2: What the Justice feared was that the Constitution of the United States would become a shield for the criminal.

Gender

English lacks a singular pronoun that means "he or she." Resorting to indefinite pronouns such as "each," "anyone," "everybody," and "everyone" frequently causes as many problems as it solves. For example, "Anyone who fails the bar will lose their job" pairs the singular "anyone" with the plural "their." The same mismatch arises in "If a client complains, send them to the bar association." An easy solution is to rephrase the sentence in the plural: "Employees who fail the bar will lose their job" and "If clients complain, send them to the bar association."

Another approach is to write in the second person ("you"), the first person plural ("we"), or the neutral third person ("one"). Sometimes you can use the relative pronoun "who." Sometimes you can eliminate the pronoun altogether.

EXAMPLE: If a lawyer wants to write clearly, *he* should avoid fancy words.

SOLUTION 1: If you want to write clearly, you should avoid fancy words.

SOLUTION 2: If we want to write clearly, we should . . .

SOLUTION 3: To write clearly, one should . . .

SOLUTION 4: A lawyer who wants to write clearly should . . .

SOLUTION 5: When trying to write clearly, a lawyer should . . .

If none of these approaches works, you can try recasting a sentence in the passive voice and using a relative clause: "A client who complains should be sent to the bar association"; "Fancy words should be avoided by a lawyer who wants to write clearly."

As a last resort, use both the masculine and feminine singular pronouns—"he or she." Usage books increasingly accept the use of paired pronouns. In the manual of style appended to the second edition of the *Random House Dictionary of the English Language* (1987), the editors say that using both the masculine and feminine singular pronouns is the approach "most likely to produce awkwardness," but "if the pronouns do not need to be repeated too often, it may in some cases be the most satisfactory solution available."[18]

Unacceptable approaches are the attempts to create portmanteau pronouns or noun blends: "s/he," "he/she," "wo/man." These barbaric constructions have no place in any kind of writing. Another unacceptable approach is to alternate the feminine and masculine pronouns; it is confusing and artificial, sacrificing clarity to politics. We disagree with the approach that Professor Richard H. Weisberg takes in *When Lawyers Write:* "The perceptive reader will quickly note that I have chosen to use masculine nouns and pronouns in odd-numbered chapters and feminine equivalents in even-numbered chapters. This convention spares my reader the cumbersome devices proposed by writers these days to prove their good will."[19] The devices we recommend are less cumbersome and contrived.

Arranging the Components of a Sentence

In the preceding sections of this chapter, we have been concerned with the building blocks of a sentence. Next we consider how they should be arranged so that the sentence conveys its meaning most clearly.

Dangling Participles

Writers sometimes lose their way in a sentence, forgetting that a participial clause refers to the subject that follows. These clauses dangle when they are not attached to the appropriate subject. The mistake is commonly enough made, even by the best writers. For example, Emily Brontë wrote in *Wuthering Heights:* "On ascending to Isabella's room, my suspicions were confirmed." But suspicions did not ascend to the room; Nelly did. The sentence could have read: "On ascending to Isabella's room, I confirmed my suspicions."

EXAMPLE: Before addressing the specific paragraphs in the complaint, some general comments are in order.

PROBLEM: The participial clause is "addressing the specific paragraphs in the complaint." The subject of the sentence is "some general comments." The sentence tells us that "the comments address the paragraphs." This is, of course, utter nonsense. To remedy the dangling modifier, replace the subject of the sentence with a more appropriate one, or rewrite the participial clause with a subject and an active verb.

SOLUTION 1: Before addressing the specific paragraphs in the complaint, I offer these general comments.

SOLUTION 2: Before I address the specific paragraphs in the complaint, some general comments are in order.

EXAMPLE: Assuming the governor signs the bill, you can purchase the extra shares.

PROBLEM: This clause might seem to dangle, because "you" are not doing the assuming. But many grammarians say that a sentence such as this one is acceptable because every reader will understand that it is the writer doing the assuming, just as the writer might begin, "Summing up." That said, the sentence can still be tightened.

SOLUTION: If the governor signs the bill, you can buy the extra shares.

Misplaced Modifiers and Clauses

A modifier or clause wrongly placed can lead to ambiguity.

EXAMPLE: The court emphasized that unjust enrichment was involved so that whatever was taken wrongfully constituted the fund.

PROBLEM: The writer could be saying that something was "taken wrongfully" or that something "wrongfully constituted the fund." Move the modifier.

SOLUTION: The court emphasized that unjust enrichment was involved so that whatever was wrongfully taken constituted the fund.

EXAMPLE: Likewise, defendants' assertion that injunctive relief is only to be granted where trade secrets are involved is simply not the law.

PROBLEMS: Of the general problem of misplaced adverbs, *only* looms the largest and most vexing, in part because *only* sometimes must be placed idiomatically and other times logically. The one sure error is to plunk down an *only* without thinking; its placement can dramatically alter meaning. (Theodore M. Bernstein, who wrote several usage books during his tenure at the *New York Times,* used this example: "I hit him in the eye yesterday." "Only" can be put in eight different positions, and every placement means something different. Try it.) After relocating the "only," we can remove the nominalization ("defendants' assertion") and rescue the main idea ("is simply not the law") by rewording it and placing it directly after the actors and closer to the start of the sentence.

SOLUTION 1: Likewise, defendants are legally wrong in asserting that injunctive relief is to be granted only when trade secrets are involved.

SOLUTION 2: Likewise, defendants legally err in asserting that injunctive relief is to be granted only when trade secrets are at stake.

EXAMPLE: Justice White abruptly announces that the interest in "liberty" that is implicated by a decision not to bear a child that is made a few days after conception is less fundamental than a comparable decision made before conception.

SOLUTION 1: Justice White abruptly announces that the interest in "liberty" implicated by a decision made a few days after conception not to bear a child is less fundamental than a comparable decision made before conception.

SOLUTION 2: Justice White abruptly announces that the interest in "liberty" is less fundamental if a decision not to bear a child is made a few days after, rather than before, conception.

Proximity

Readers expect the subject, verb, and object of a sentence to be closely linked. No rule dictates how tight the link must be, and good writers certainly vary the rhythm of their sentences. But a sentence can become impenetrable if these major elements are too far apart.

EXAMPLE: Thus contrary to plaintiffs' assertions, this court in *Rubell* clearly ruled that any investigation of the circumstances upon which a suit that is being presently litigated is based is privileged.

PROBLEM: The syntax sunders the link between the subject "any investigation" and the verb "is privileged." The trio of "is"s ensures that no one will catch the meaning in one reading.

SOLUTION: This court in *Rubell* held privileged any investigation of circumstances upon which a pending suit is based.

EXAMPLE: Nancy Reagan, in order to exert in a more direct way her power over the president's schedule, in 1982 began in a carefully hidden manner, to determine the most propitious days on which he could travel, a series of consultations with a San Francisco astrologer, according to Donald Regan in his new book.

PROBLEMS: This sentence is fifty-three words long. Fourteen words come between the subject ("Nancy Reagan") and the verb ("began"), and sixteen words separate the verb from its object ("a series of consultations"). Windy phrasing doesn't help: "in a more direct way" (more direct than what?) and "in a carefully hidden manner" (as compared to "a carelessly hidden manner"?).

SOLUTION 1: In 1982 Nancy Reagan began secretly to consult a San Francisco astrologer, according to Donald Regan's new book. Hoping to exert more control over her husband's schedule, Mrs. Reagan asked the astrologer to determine when the president might travel most propitiously.

SOLUTION 2: According to Donald Regan's new book, Nancy Reagan decided in 1982 that she wanted to exert more influence over President Reagan's schedule. To determine the most propitious times for the president's travel, Mrs. Reagan secretly consulted a San Francisco astrologer.

Parallelism

Parallelism is a principle requiring that paired elements of a sentence have the same grammatical structure. If the predicate has two relative clauses, and one begins with "that," so should the other. If one clause uses a verb in the present tense and active voice, the other clause should not use a passive or a present participle (the form ending in "-ing").

EXAMPLE: However, as a practical matter, committees usually make recommendations to the full board rather than taking official actions of their own.

SOLUTION: However, as a practical matter, committees usually make recommendations to the full board rather than take official actions of their own.

EXAMPLE: Although the objective of the government remains legitimate, whether this method is rationally related to advancing this legitimate objective, or a punishment for carrying the AIDS virus is arguable.

SOLUTION: Although the objective of the government remains legitimate, it is arguable whether this method rationally relates to advancing this objective or punishes people who carry the AIDS virus.

Emphasis

The best advice on achieving proper emphasis within a sentence comes from Joseph M. Williams, the author of *Style: Ten Lessons in*

Clarity and Grace. Williams sets out two rules for achieving proper emphasis within a sentence. The first principle is to move from old to new: "Whenever possible, express at the beginning of a sentence ideas already stated, referred to, implied, safely assumed, familiar, predictable, less important, readily accessible. . . . Express at the end of a sentence the least predictable, the newest, the most important, the most significant information, the information you almost certainly want to emphasize."[20]

The second principle is to move from short to long. When a sentence begins with a long subject, for example, readers must hunt for the verb. A sentence is more comprehensible when the long element comes at the end.

EXAMPLE: It was worthwhile paying every penny that we did for this information.

PROBLEM: "This information" indicates that the writer has already introduced the information. Thus the information is the "old" idea; that we had to pay for it is new. Stating the old idea first will create a tighter transition between this sentence and the preceding one, and stating the new idea last will emphasize it.

SOLUTION: This information was worth every penny we paid for it.

EXAMPLE: Judges who live among the people, who understand their hopes and fears and predilections, assuming that they are learned, fearless, and upright, are who we want.

PROBLEM: The sentence is top-heavy; its subject is so long that we lose our way before we come to the predicate. Flip it around.

SOLUTION: We want learned, fearless, and upright judges who live among the people and who understand their hopes and fears and predilections.

Focus

Some sentences seem hazy or diffuse because the central point is not the topic of the sentence. Here's an example from Donald Freeman:

> Any Product received by A from C pursuant to the terms of the Agreement which fails to meet the Standards of Specifications or is damaged, defective, or not of merchantable quality, in the view of A, acting reasonably, entitles A to receive a full credit from C for such Defective Product.

This sentence misdirects readers because it starts with the "Product," even though the true topic is A's entitlement to a refund. The sentence should be recast:

> A is entitled to a full credit for any Defective Product received from C whenever the product fails to meet the Standards of Specifications under the Agreement, or is damaged, defective, or in A's reasonable view, not of merchantable quality.

This principle, that a sentence or a series of sentences should fashion the topic—the central point—into the subject, applies even to the most abstruse sentences. George Gopen has applied this principle to rewrite portions of the Uniform Commercial Code.[21] Here is a passage from the code:

> §1–102(3): The effect of provisions of this Act may be varied by agreement, except as otherwise provided in this Act and except that the obligations of good faith, diligence, reasonableness and care prescribed by this Act may not be disclaimed by agreement but the parties may by agreement determine the standards by which the performance of such obligations is to be measured if such standards are not manifestly unreasonable.

As drafted, the passage buries the actors—namely, the parties—and the action evaporates into prepositional phrases. Gopen's revision focuses on what the parties may or may not do:

> §1–102(3) [redrafted]: Parties are free to agree to vary the effects of the provisions of this Act except
>   (a) when this Act explicitly provides otherwise, and
>   (b) when this Act prescribes obligations of good faith, diligence, reasonableness, and care.
> When the obligations listed in §1–102(3)(b) are involved, parties may

agree to determine the standards by which the performance of the obligations is to be measured, as long as those standards are not manifestly unreasonable.

If your sentences are unclear, or if you are criticized for muddling your thought, look hard at your subjects and ask whether the ones you have chosen are appropriate. Check the location of the true topics of your sentence. If they are buried late in the sentence (or the paragraph), exhume them, put them where they belong, and let them resuscitate your sentence.

Transitions

Transitional words and phrases emphasize the character of the connection between sentences. You do not need to insert these transitions between every pair of sentences, because the logic of your thought, and the relation of your topics, should be strong enough to carry the reader from one sentence to the next. Occasionally, however, you can help the reader move along by pointing out certain types of connections. In the preceding sentence, "however" highlights the *contrast* (other transitions that enforce a contrast include *but, nevertheless, on the other hand, although*). Next, you can *sequence* your thoughts (using *next, first, finally, in conclusion*). Furthermore, you can indicate that one sentence *adds* to the preceding (using *furthermore, moreover, also, in addition*). That's not all. In fact, you can dramatize your point (using *in fact, as a matter of fact, indeed, even*). Or you can illustrate a point, using *for example, for instance, to illustrate*. To highlight a cause-and-effect relationship, you can insert *therefore, so, consequently,* or *as a result*.

Choose your transitions carefully. They should complement, not undercut or blur, your meaning.

EXAMPLE: The brief is due in court in three hours. However, we might get the judge to give us an extension.

PROBLEM: "However" expresses contrast, but what are the opposing thoughts here? The sentences imply but do not state a difficulty.

SOLUTION 1: The brief is due in court in three hours. However, we do not have time to finish it.

SOLUTION 2: We have only three hours left to complete the brief and six hours' work remaining. However, the judge might give us an extension.

Run-on Sentences

In a run-on sentence, the writer mistakenly joints two independent sentences into a single sentence without appropriate punctuation. The run-on sentence can never be justified.

EXAMPLE: Maritime jurisdiction under the Suits in Admiralty Act is exclusive the Federal Tort Claims Act is not applicable to this action.

PROBLEM: Two sentences here: One ends after "exclusive" and the other begins with "the Federal." A run-on sentence is always wrong. Fix this sentence with a semicolon or a period.

SOLUTION 1: Maritime jurisdiction under the Suits in Admiralty Act is exclusive; the Federal Tort Claims Act is not applicable to this action.

SOLUTION 2: Maritime jurisdiction under the Suits in Admiralty Act is exclusive. The Federal Tort Claims Act is not applicable to this action.

Sentence Length

Even if your sentence is grammatically and syntactically sound, it still may confound the reader if it is too long. For years, journalists, grammarians, and writing analysts have debated just how long is too long. Into the 1960s, tabloid newspapers would not permit sentences with more than seventeen words. Many of today's newspaper editors frown on sentences exceeding twenty-five words. Rudolf Flesch, a lifelong critic of writing problems, developed what he termed a "readability formula" that gauges the difficulty of a piece of writing by calculating the average number of words per sentence and the average number of syllables per word.[22] Under his formula, an essay written in one- and two-syllable words grouped in short sentences is highly readable; the longer the words and the longer the sentences, the lower the readability score. Thus a document whose sentences are of the form "John loves Mary" scores far higher than a document filled with sentences that resemble "Even though John is not given to a display of his deeper emotions, he allegedly has developed a profound affection for Mary, as compared to the more equable feelings he seems to have for Lucy, Fran, and, to an extent, Sue."

Relying on Flesch's work, some advocates of "plain English" recommend that writers restrict their average sentence length to twenty words or less, and limit their average word length to a syllable and a half. But common sense suggests that readability formulas alone cannot accurately measure difficulty. Consider, for example, this sparkling hundred-word sentence, the last in Lewis Carroll's *Alice's Adventures in Wonderland:*

> Lastly, she pictured to herself how this same little sister of hers would, in the aftertime, be herself a grown woman; and how she would keep, through all her riper years, the simple and loving heart of her childhood; and how she would gather about her other little children, and make *their* eyes bright and eager with many a strange tale, perhaps even with her dream of Wonderland of long ago; and how she would feel with all their simple sorrows, and find a pleasure in all their simple joys, remembering her own child life, and the happy summer days.

But a hundred-word sentence expressing a complex concept would be unreadable and unintelligible. A sentence, Justice Cardozo warned, "may be so overloaded with all its possible qualifications that it will tumble down of its own weight."[23] "One thought per sentence" is not effective when your thought is complicated; you will need two or three sentences. Under no circumstances should you include more than one complex thought in a single sentence. Jamming several thoughts in a sentence is a symptom of an occupational hazard that we call "headnote disease."[24]

Why sentence length affects the reader's understanding is one aspect of the psychology of reading:

> The sentence is the natural unit of thought, words are the artificial units. Thought operates not by words but by ideas, that is by sentences. In reading, the eye picks up one word after another until the idea is conceived and born in the mind; then the mind forgets the separate words and only the idea remains. Or, to put the matter another way, the words are the chaff out of which the mind must winnow and save the grain, which is the thought. As we read a page of print the thought passes into the memory in the form of an idea and not as a group of words. . . . The mind will readily turn back into the words the precise meaning of what has been read; but not into the same words unless they have been laboriously learned by heart. . . . The reason for short sentences in the work of a lawyer becomes at once obvious. . . . The reader is forced to break the [long] sentence up into fragments—to camp by the way, so to speak—while the mind catches up with the eye; or perhaps while it tries to catch up but fails and gives up the chase. Of course, such delay— and more particularly such failure—works disaster on the real meaning of the author.[25]

EXAMPLE: Issuers, directors, underwriters, signatories of the registration statement, and professionals, whose reports or evaluations are used in connection with the registration statement, may all be found liable for these misstatements or omissions, subject to detailed affirmative defenses of due diligence contained in 11b.

PROBLEM: At least two thoughts here. Split the sentence.

SOLUTION: Those who may be found liable for these misstatements or omissions include issuers, directors, underwriters, signatories of the registration statement, and professionals whose reports or evaluations are used in connection with the registration statement. Their liability is subject to detailed affirmative defenses of due diligence contained in 11b.

EXAMPLE: In *Chiarella,* the Supreme Court reversed the conviction under Sect. 10(b) of the Exchange Act of an employee of a financial printer who had purchased the stock of companies that were about to become the targets of tender offers after learning of the proposed tender offers from documents that the acquiring companies had submitted for printing.

PROBLEM: Every possible qualifying detail has been packed into this sentence, a sure sign of headnote disease.

SOLUTION 1: In *Chiarella,* the Supreme Court reversed the conviction of an employee of a financial printer under Sect. 10(b) of the Exchange Act. The employee had purchased the stock of companies that were about to become targets of tender offers. He bought the stocks after learning of the proposed tender offers from documents that the acquiring companies had submitted for printing.

SOLUTION 2: In *Chiarella,* the Supreme Court reversed the conviction of an employee of a financial printer under Sect. 10(b) of the Exchange Act. The employee had learned about proposed tender offers from documents submitted for printing by the acquiring companies, and he then purchased the stock of the target companies.

EXAMPLE: Appellant's failure to make an affirmative showing of injury means that he cannot prevail either on his claim that the amount of summation time he was granted was in itself inadequate or on his other allegation that the trial court's distribution of summation time between plaintiff and defendants was in some sense unfair.

SOLUTION 1: Because the appellant failed to make an affirmative showing of injury, he cannot prevail on either of his claims— that he was not given enough time to present his summation or that the trial judge unfairly allocated the time to make summations.

SOLUTION 2: Because the appellant failed affirmatively to show an injury, he must lose on both his claims: (1) that he was not given enough time to present his summation and (2) that the trial judge unfairly allocated the time to make summations.

Overly long sentences come from hurried writing and meager editing. Under the best of circumstances, lawyers spurn periods. At times, they forgo periods altogether. They inhale deeply, spit out word after word after word, and never pause for breath. Consider this 161-word

written harangue, all packaged in one sentence, from a justice of the
Utah Supreme Court:

> However, this does not mean that the Constitution of the United States,
> which in no uncertain terms says the states are supreme in this country
> and superior to the philosophy of federal protagonists who deign to
> suggest that a coterie of 3 or 5 or even 9 federal persons immune from
> public intolerance, by use of a pair of scissors and the whorl of a 10 cent
> ball-point pen, and a false sense of last-minute confessional importance,
> can in one fell swoop, shakily clip phrases out of the Constitution,
> substitute their manufactured voids with Scotch-taped rhetoric, and thus
> reverse hundreds of cases dimmed only by time and nature, but whose
> impressions indestructibly already indelibly had been linotyped on the
> minds of kids and grandkids who vowed and now would or will vow to
> defend, not only the institution of marriage and motherhood, but to
> reserve to the states a full budget of legitimate, time-tested mores inci-
> dent to that doctorate.[26]

Enough said.

Finished a draft of that brief you've been researching the past month? Good show. Have a swell dinner. Take in a movie. Lounge in the tub. Get some sleep. But don't gloat. You're only half done. Maybe not even.

Writing is like building a house. Working with a plan, you put up the superstructure—you dig a foundation, pour in concrete, erect the walls, lay the beams that carry the stress, and finally nail down the roof. Your neighbors can see the framework of your dwelling. If you're careful (and lucky), you will have anticipated unevenness in the soil and measured the boards to a sixteenth of an inch so that they fit. If you haven't been quite so meticulous, you'll saw off the ends of boards that stick out. But you would not yet invite your neighbors to tea. Much remains to be done: sanding, plastering, papering, painting—and you'll need running water, electricity, windows, and doors. Structure is important, but the details make your house livable.

> *There's no such thing as good writing—there's only good rewriting.*
> LOUIS D. BRANDEIS

It is editing that gives coherence to the structure of a writer's thoughts. By the time you've completed a draft, you have "solved" the conceptual problem, but that solution is not likely cast in the form in which it will communicate your points most sharply and effectively to your audience. The shaping work—the editing that will take your structure and make it talk to others—lies before you.

Editing should not be an afterthought. It is not a cursory inspection to ensure that you've spelled the names of your client and the judge properly. The paragraphs may seem to make sense to your exhausted eye, but you have much to do before you can be certain that you are seeing how others will see your writing the first time they read it. That certainty comes from editing. Editing is as crucial to the final product as the draft itself, and you need to spend nearly as much time editing as you did composing.

How you edit is important. There is an order to editing, just as there is an order to finishing your house. You cannot do all the tasks at once and you should not do them wildly out of sequence. You would not paint your house before you sanded it, and if you hope to show off your handiwork, you would apply a primer and several coats of high-gloss paint. Of course, you don't have to go to all this trouble to live in your house—*you* can live in an unfinished structure. If a portion of a wall protrudes, you can learn to walk around it, even laugh about it, tell your neighbors you like the eccentricity. But you can take no such comfort in your unfinished writing. You do not write only for yourself. Others will live in, or die by, your words.

Seductive as your own words on paper may be, you must resist the feelings that your finished draft arouses in you. Abandon sentimentality; the joy will come from scraping, sanding, and burnishing, not from papering over the beam that doesn't fit.

In the memoirs of literary writers who reflect on their craft, the loudest theme is revision. Raymond Carver regularly wrote twenty to thirty drafts of each of his short stories. Philip Roth, a prolific novelist, says he once spent six months of eight-hour days and emerged with one page: "I often have to write 100 pages or more before there's a paragraph that's alive. Okay, I say to myself, that's your beginning, start there; that's the first paragraph of the book. I'll go over the first six months of work and underline in red a paragraph, a sentence, sometimes no more than a phrase, that has some life in it."[1] Ernest Hemingway always rewrote what he had written the day before, only then adding his daily allotment of 400 or 500 new words.

These are professional writers, you protest—that's all they do. True, lawyers have many responsibilities in addition to writing, but other obligations do not excuse lawyers from reserving time for their writing. Many busy lawyers spend the time, and it shows.

John Kenneth Galbraith said that the air of spontaneity in his writing began to appear only during the fifth or sixth revision.[2] Judge Richard A. Posner, one of the most widely admired jurists in the country, wrote us: "I do much self-editing, sometimes going through as many as twenty drafts (though ten is the most in all but a tiny handful of cases) until I am satisfied. Much of the editing is designed to simplify the product and give it a casual, colloquial, and spontaneous appearance. I admit to hypocrisy in working so hard to give the appearance of effortlessness!"

Editing is difficult, and it takes time. Lawyers who assert that they are so squeezed for time that they must routinely file a document minutes after it is drafted are shortchanging their clients, irritating the judges, and deceiving themselves. If you can honestly say you have no time to edit, then you misunderstand the nature of writing.

Even if you are on a tight schedule, you can create time for editing by setting a false deadline. Plan to finish your draft some hours, days, or weeks before you must submit the document. For example, if on Monday you are assigned a brief due Friday afternoon, plan to complete your draft no later than Wednesday afternoon. Put it aside until Thursday morning, and then begin to edit.

You should not begin editing the instant you have completed your draft. To read your own words dispassionately, you must distance yourself and forget what you thought you meant by them. In editing, you must stand outside yourself and read from the perspective of a stranger. That means you should lay the draft aside at least overnight and even, if you have planned well, a day or two.

Every document should be edited for structure, length, clarity, and continuity. The final step is to proofread the document. We discuss the four editing passes in the sequence that we find most comfortable, but you may find that a slightly different order works better for you.

Editing for Structure

Experienced writers generally begin by reviewing the structure of the draft. Read through the entire document once or twice. Then reread the first and last paragraphs. Ask these questions:

- Have you written a lead that provides a road map?
- Does your concluding paragraph show that you've reached your destination?
- Does every paragraph make only a single point?
- Is every concept discussed in a single place in the draft or is the discussion scattered?
- Do the transitions work effectively to connect your points?

You can answer these questions readily enough by writing in the margin what topics each paragraph discusses. Use only a word or two. You will quickly discover whether your paragraphs wander and how well they are connected. If a topic is split among several unconnected paragraphs, it is time to restructure. Bring each piece of the topic together and rewrite. If the transition between topics is too abrupt, you must find a way to connect them or else you must reorder the topics. A paragraph that begins "in an unrelated development" or "moving along now to the next point" marks a breakdown in the flow and order of topics. Ask yourself why one point ought to follow another, and then tell your reader.

Even though you may have already rewritten your lead several times, you cannot be certain that it carries the load it should until you have rethought its relation to the rest of the document. And if you have hastily written out only one draft, without having revised as you progressed, rewriting the lead is imperative. Your original vision of how your argument would unfold may have been mistaken—it often is. Not until you have finished composing the entire document—that is, solved your problem—can you clearly see the entire course, from start to finish. Only then can you have the confidence and perspective to rewrite the lead in a form and style that will best serve the reader.

Editing for Length

Once assured that the structure is sound, you must trim ruthlessly. Most drafts are too long. Either they exceed a court-mandated page limit or the lawyer left nothing out in a desire to be as comprehensive as possible. The length of your draft should never be a guide to the length of your final effort. You can surely shed more than a quarter of your words without destroying the substance.

Cutting takes time. Many people mistakenly equate length with effort: A long paper, they falsely assume, takes more time to write than a short one. In fact, it is harder work to cut—while preserving all salient points—than it is to write long initially. "It takes enormous amounts of time to make legal writing short, simple, concise, and clear," says Richard Emery, a New York City lawyer whose words and phrases are frequently quoted in local newspapers. "Long briefs are generally the result of not enough work on the finished product."

Cutting must be done in two steps—in the loose jargon of our age, the editor must take a "macro" chop and a "micro" slice. The macro chopping excises unnecessary substantive discussion. The micro slice removes clutter, verbiage, obviousness, windy phrases, and redundancies. Does every case you cite require a forty-line description of the facts? Can you more concisely summarize the holdings in your principal body of cases? Must you list every precedent governing the conditions for ruling in your favor? Many judges think not, and many join Judge Joseph W. Bellacosa, formerly of the New York Court of Appeals, in complaining about string citations and "cut-and-paste quotation montages posing as briefs or legal writing."

Brevity is a virtue twice over. A short paper saves the busy reader time. A short work also dramatically enhances your prospects of being understood. As Robert Kasanof of New York put it: "Ordinary legal writing is often so choked with the desire not to leave out anything which comes to the writer's mind that the objective of the writing is often lost."

Editing for Clarity

To improve the clarity of your draft, use the principles discussed in the previous chapter. You may find it helpful to move category by category.

For instance, read through your document once, looking just for nom-inalizations. Wear blinders to every other problem. After you check for and remove nominalizations in one or two documents, you will discover that you can spot and remedy them quickly—in far less time than had you been trying to correct every mistake in every sentence on a single pass. Then go on to root out unnecessary passives, then flabby phrases, then throat-clearing openings, then excessive use of "there is," then dangling and misplaced modifiers, and so on. To guard against sen-tences that are too long, check to see that you have at least one sentence-ending period in every two or three lines of text. If not, your sentences are probably too long. Split them up, rewriting as you do.

Over time, you will find fewer of these kinds of errors in your writ-ing. Editing will make you more aware of these mistakes, and you will become less likely to commit them when you're composing.

Editing for Continuity

By now you will have read through your document many times. It may not look much like the first draft. You have rewritten your sentences, shifted paragraphs, and condensed or omitted arguments. No matter how you have made your edits—in colored pen, with scissors and tape, or on the computer—you need to produce a clean copy for this fourth editing pass.

Now read through the document once again, to make a final check for continuity. Ask yourself whether the transitions make sense, whether first references fully identify a case or person, and whether the sentences and paragraphs—now quite different from the ones you had at the beginning of your editing—are logically ordered.

Proofreading

The final step is to proofread your document. Proofreading comprises three distinct tasks: checking for misspellings and typographical errors, fixing punctuation, and ensuring consistency in capitalization and other matters of editorial style. Proofreading is essential—you do not go to court with your shirttails hanging out, and your final copy should be just as well dressed as you are.

Exactness in the use of words is the basis of all serious thinking. . . . Words are clumsy tools, and it is very easy to cut one's fingers with them, and they need the closest attention and handling. But they are the only tools we have, and imagination itself cannot work without them.

JUSTICE FELIX FRANKFURTER

Checking for Spelling and Typographical Errors

In 1987 a group of New York lawyers protesting an action of a bar association committee began a letter this way: "The Executive Committee of the Association of the Bar of the City of New York, again implementing its own recently adopted procedure, has authorized a special committee to review and evaluate the qualifications of Judge Douglas Ginsberg for appointment to the United States Supreme Court." Although the issue became moot when Judge Ginsburg withdrew from consideration, he did not withdraw the "u" from his name.

Bad spelling almost cost Daniel Manion a spot on the U.S. Court of Appeals for the Seventh Circuit in Chicago in 1986. A graduate of Indiana University School of Law, Manion had difficulty with words like "defiately" (definitely?), "verbatum" (verbatim), and "comperable" (comparable). His secretary eventually took responsibility for mistakes that, she said, "happen at the end of a very demanding day." In an editorial, the *Wall Street Journal* suggested Manion buy his overworked secretary a spell-checker for her word processor.[3] But his secretary's chivalry hardly exonerates Manion, who was responsible for briefs that he signed and who should have proofread them before submitting them.

The row over Manion prompted Daniel Seligman, then *Fortune* magazine's "contrarian," to point out spelling mistakes he had spotted in opinions of the Supreme Court: In one of Chief Justice Warren Burger's opinions, "resistant" came out "resistent"; Justice Brennan rendered "chastise" as "chastize"; "defendants" often became "defendents."[4] A vast number of lawyers misspell "accommodate." That group includes Wallace Stevens, who was trained as a lawyer and spent a double career as poet and insurance executive.[5]

Many people, not just lawyers, say they just can't spell, never could, and aren't likely so deep into their careers to master the admittedly illogical system of English spelling. They shrug, or they buy spell-checking programs for their word processors. As a check against typographical errors introduced by tired fingers, a spell-checker is a useful but by no means faultless device. It will flag inversions of letters ("hte" for "the"), extra letters ("pleeadings"), and many muddled words. But spell-checkers will not spot words wrongly used, such as the commonly confused "there," "their," and "they're." And they will never find a dropped word or line, words typed out of order, verbs in the wrong tense, or inverted dates and numbers. If you cannot spell, you must hire someone who can, someone who will patiently read proof for all the errors that can sandbag an otherwise well-crafted document.

Checking for Bad Punctuation

Punctuation seems to many lawyers a niggling afterthought, scarcely worth the effort. In rare instances, that attitude can be legally fatal. Theodore Bernstein recalled the Michigan Constitution, which some years ago legalized slavery by misplacing a comma.[6] Section 8 of Article 2 said: "Neither slavery nor involuntary servitude, unless for the punishment of crime, shall ever be tolerated in this state." That sentence says that criminals may be punished by making them slaves. The mistake discovered, the comma was moved from its position after "servitude" to its appropriate place after "slavery."

The courts should feel obliged to make themselves
intelligible to the men on the street or the subway.
JEROME FRANK

In most instances, punctuation can mean the difference between a graceful document and a clumsy one. But somehow the pernicious notion arose that punctuation does not count in the law, that, as a nineteenth-century Massachusetts judge put it in a phrase adopted by the Supreme Court, "punctuation is no part of the statute." Mellinkoff rightly called this dictum a "snatch of concise nonsense."[7]

Punctuation can make all the difference, as the fight over the 1984 Republican platform nicely illustrated. The original draft spoke out against "any attempts to increase taxes which would harm the recovery." That was a position against some but not all taxes—against only those taxes that would be harmful. The Republican right wing, insisting on holding President Reagan to his vow never to raise taxes, protested and won a comma: "any attempts to increase taxes, which would harm the recovery." Thus it was asserted that *all* taxes would damage economic recovery.

You can find punctuation rules in many usage books; here we catalogue only the most prevalent errors and difficulties.

COMMAS

With appositives. Use commas before and after appositives, words or phrases that re-identify the noun or pronoun to which they are attached. Too many lawyers will throw in a comma at the beginning and omit one at the end.

> EXAMPLE: The newest appointee to the bench, Judge Sarah Jones was confirmed last week.
>
> PROBLEM: "Judge Sarah Jones" is an appositive, a name that identifies who the newest appointee is. The appositive string must have commas at both ends.
>
> SOLUTION: The newest appointee to the bench, Judge Sarah Jones, was confirmed last week.

With nonrestrictive clauses. Place commas before and after nonrestrictive clauses, which contain information parenthetical to the main thought.

> EXAMPLE: The Supreme Court, in a fit of pique at the rising number of Fair Labor Standard cases said yesterday that . . .
>
> PROBLEM: The clause "in a fit of pique . . . cases" is a nonrestrictive clause, and it must have commas at both ends.
>
> SOLUTION: The Supreme Court, in a fit of pique at the rising number of Fair Labor Standard cases, said yesterday that . . .

In a series. We are of two minds about the serial comma, the comma that some writers place before the *and* or *or* in a series of three or more elements. One of us, who insists that his way is clearer and more logical, stoutly urges that the serial comma be used: "She took her umbrella, newspaper, suntan lotion, and high spirits to the beach." The other insists that his way saves a bit of space and is no less logical (because the *and* or *or* announces the final element) and just as stoutly urges that the serial comma be dropped: "She took her umbrella, newspaper, suntan lotion and high spirits to the beach." We refused to settle the issue with a coin toss and agreed to air our difference. Whichever choice you make, be consistent.

After most opening phrases. Under this heading, we could spin out lots of variations, but we won't. As in the preceding sentence (and this one too!), a comma follows an adverbial phrase that begins a sentence.

With conjunctions and disjunctions. Also separate the clauses of a sentence connected by conjunctions and disjunctions *(and, but, or, neither, nor, so).* But do not set off conjunctions and disjunctions by themselves when they start a sentence.

With dependent clauses. Set off dependent clauses that follow the main clause if they add parenthetical information. In the last sentence, "if they add parenthetical information" is not parenthetical; it is, in the technical language, a restrictive dependent clause, necessary to the thought, and takes no comma. A nonrestrictive dependent clause occurs in the next sentence and requires a comma: These rules really are very simple, even though they may take some time to learn.

With dates and states. Place a comma before and after the year when you write the full date: "On June 1, 2001, we finished the manuscript." Likewise, place a comma before and after the name of a state when you name both the city and the state: "We arrived in Park City, Utah, the day before the big parade."

A final comma-related problem is the "comma splice," the term grammarians use to describe two independent sentences that are wrongly joined by a comma.

> EXAMPLE: The ITA in all cases to date has determined that the PRC has a state-controlled economy, however, it has in some cases also determined that Yugoslavia has a state-controlled economy.

> PROBLEMS: A comma splice. The "however" marks the start of a new sentence, and therefore a period or a semicolon is needed after "economy." Also, the last four words of the sentence are redundant.

> SOLUTION 1: The ITA in all cases to date has determined that the PRC has a state economy; however, it has in some cases determined that Yugoslavia has a state-controlled economy.

> SOLUTION 2: The ITA in all cases to date has determined that the PRC has a state economy. However, it has in some cases determined that Yugoslavia has a state-controlled economy.

QUOTATION MARKS

In American usage, the comma and the period are always placed inside closing quotation marks. The most common misuse of quotation marks in lawyers' writing occurs in the indented quotation. When you indent a long quotation to set it off from the text, do not place quotation marks at the beginning or end of the passage. The indenting signals that the passage is a quotation; the marks are redundant.

COLONS

Setting off a series or announcing a connected thought, the colon usually is simple enough to use: Words, phrases, or entire sentences can follow the colon. But in setting up a series preceded by a verb, you should not place a colon after *is, was,* or *were:* "The major components were fire, earth, air, and water." Use a colon, however, to attach a list to a complete sentence: "He rattled off the places they had visited: Beijing, Paris, Durban, Caracas, and Carbondale."

APOSTROPHES

More and more, apostrophes are less and less. Students and young lawyers all seem to have missed the same day in school when the apostrophe was handed out. Apostrophes are used in possessive constructions and in contractions. The possessive form of nouns must contain an apostrophe: John's coat, Mary's lamb, the town's regret, for pity's sake, the court's ruling, the next move was Sophie's. To form the possessive of a singular noun ending in *s*, some style manuals recommend *'s* (James's cat), but others do not (James' cat). Plural nouns take an apostrophe alone: the birds' flight. With the exception of *one's,* the personal possessive pronouns do not contain apostrophes: *yours, his, hers, its, ours, theirs.*

In a contraction, the apostrophe sits in the place of the dropped letter: *hadn't, won't, isn't, it's.* The misuse of *it's* and *its* is widespread—and unforgivable. *It's* is a contraction for "it is" or "it has." *Its* is a possessive pronoun. If you were absent the day that the apostrophe was handed out in elementary school, take a moment now to commit this simple point to memory.

Checking for Consistency in Editorial Style

The final proofreading task is to check for consistency in editorial style. Editorial style is a matter of custom or preference, not logic. Some firms, offices, and courts impose a style book—*The Blue Book,* for example. Some use more general works: *The United States Government Printing Office Style Manual, The New York Times Manual of Style and*

Usage, or *The Chicago Manual of Style.* But a law office will find only parts of these general references tailored to the lawyer's needs.

For the sake of consistency, an office should have a set of general rules governing such matters as capitalization, use of honorifics, abbreviations, spelling out of numbers, and citation forms. We have a memorandum from a senior partner of a law firm who chastised associates who capitalized "court." He told them to capitalize only when referring to the Supreme Court or the court for whom the document is being written. When memoranda circulate in firms about such niggling points, it is time the office recognize the need for an in-house style guide.

A style guide should focus on matters relevant to your daily practice. Too often, legal stylebooks wander, providing all sorts of obscure information that most lawyers will never need and which, in any event, can be found more easily in dictionaries or usage books. For example, *The Texas Law Review Manual on Style* listed as a spelling aid three hundred words ending in "ible" or "able"—including *coctible, marcesible,* and *thurible.**

The sensible office should borrow the best suggestions and most relevant items from existing style books and publish its own, just as it publishes a telephone directory. No longer would partners need to circulate condescending memos addressing a few items at a time, and secretaries, typists, and proofreaders could enforce a firmwide consistency.

Editing in Steps

To illustrate the principles discussed in this chapter, we offer four passages that we edit in a series of steps.

---

* *Coctible* is an obsolete term for "may be cooked"; *marcesible* means "liable to wither or fade"; and a *thurible* is a container for burning incense (and the "ible" is part of the root, not a suffix). These words don't belong in stylebooks, and they don't belong in your briefs.

EXAMPLE: On Friday, September 5, Judge Earp entered a temporary restraining order against defendants to prevent them from
"chopping down the tree" before this matter could be heard by
this court and after his characterization of certain "self-help"
"brute force" conduct in which defendants had engaged—specifically, unilaterally seizing what plaintiff's counsel conceded was
corporate property as security for an alleged indebtedness from
plaintiff—as "law of the jungle."

This sentence is too long and requires several readings to interpret—
primarily because the clauses are misplaced. First step: Break it apart
and rearrange the clauses.

EDIT 1: On Friday, September 5, Judge Earp entered a temporary
restraining order against defendants to prevent them from
"chopping down the tree" before this matter could be heard by
this court. The judge did so after his characterization of certain
"self-help" "brute force" conduct in which defendants had engaged as "law of the jungle." He was referring to the unilateral
seizing of what plaintiff's counsel conceded was corporate property as security for an alleged indebtedness from plaintiff.

Next, we focus on the verbs. In sentence 1, we convert the passive
"could be heard" to the active voice, and we eliminate the redundant
"against defendants to prevent them" by placing the object ("defendants") of the infinitive ("to prevent") where it belongs. In sentence 2,
we rewrite the nominalization ("characterization") and move the critical
clause " 'law of the jungle' " directly next to the verb it modifies. In
sentence 3, we rewrite the flat nominalization ("alleged indebtedness")
and eliminate the overworked "alleged" by using "claimed."

EDIT 2: On Friday, September 5, Judge Earp entered a temporary
restraining order to prevent defendants from "chopping down
the tree" before this court could hear the matter. He characterized as "law of the jungle" defendants' "self-help" "brute force"
conduct. Judge Earp was referring to defendants' seizing of
what plaintiff's counsel conceded was corporate property as security for a debt they claimed plaintiff owed them.

We now make a pass for fine-tuning. Although "temporary restraining order" is a term of art, we rewrite the nominalization. At the end of sentence 1, "the matter" is imprecise—the court will hear argument—and for the sake of idiom, we add "the" before "defendants" and "plaintiff." Sentence 2 is still awkward and redundant: the "self-help" and "brute force" dilute the effect of "'law of the jungle,'" and we can replace "defendants" with "their." In sentence 3, the counsel's concession is irrelevant.

EDIT 3: On Friday, September 5, Judge Earp temporarily restrained the defendants from "chopping down the tree" before this court could hear argument. He characterized their conduct as following the "law of the jungle." Judge Earp was referring to defendants' seizing of corporate property as security for a debt they claimed the plaintiff owed them.

Our next example follows a similar course. In edit 1 we break a labyrinthine sentence into simpler sentences. In edit 2 we focus on the verbs.

EXAMPLE: Paragraph 51 (2) of the stipulation implies that religion is not an important facet of a child's life and that in-religion placement will not result in any higher quality care. Yet this is contrary to the Legislature's determination that the placement of a child with an authorized agency under the control of persons of the same religious faith as that of the child is the best method of instilling in that child a moral and ethical value system in accordance with that child's religious heritage when the State is acting *in loco parentis.*

EDIT 1: Paragraph 51 (2) of the stipulation implies that religion is not an important facet of a child's life and that the child will not benefit from being placed in a family of the same religion. Yet this is contrary to law. The Legislature has determined that placing a child with an authorized agency controlled by persons of the same religious affiliation as the child will best instill in that child a moral and ethical value system that accords with that child's religious heritage.

EDIT 2: Paragraph 51 (2) of the stipulation undervalues the importance of religion in a child's life and implies that the child will not benefit from being placed in a family of the same religion. The stipulation ignores the law. The Legislature has determined that a child should be placed with an authorized agency controlled by persons of the same religious affiliation as the child. Those persons will best instill ethics and morals that conform to the child's heritage.

ALTERNATIVE: ... The Legislature has determined that to best instill ethics and morals that conform to a child's heritage, the child should be placed with an authorized agency controlled by persons of the same religious affiliation as the child.

Note, too, that we eliminated vacuous phrasing ("ethical and moral value system") and the tautological *in loco parentis* (when the state places children, it must be acting *in loco parentis*).

Our third example is a fund-raising letter that was sent to members of the Harvard Law School class of 1980.[8] The letter begins, "Dear Classmate":

What impact do you have on the Harvard Law School?

- You make it financially possible for one of the 1,273 students who need financial aid to attend the Law School.
- You guarantee that the Law School expends the highest quality clinical education program, while other schools cut back their clinical education programs due to costs.
- You continue innovations in legal education, including smaller and multifaculty classes for first-year students.

It is true that current students benefit every day from alumni support. We also benefitted from the support of alumni when we were students. Tuition, $11,400 this year, covers only 60% of the cost of educating current students.

Your gift does make a difference to the Law School. I hope that you will join me in making sure that we can continue to make it possible for every qualified student to attend the Law School, without regard to financial circumstances. I hope you will help us maintain the Law School's reputation for advances in legal education.

Please send your gift by June 15th to assure that it is credited in this fiscal year. Please accept my thanks for your gift to the Law School.

This letter is stuffed with redundancies, stray words, and pompous phrases; it sounds as if it had been dictated from a cellphone. We count the repetitions that we will fix: "financially possible" and "financial aid"; "highest quality clinical education program" and "clinical education program"; "students benefit" and "we also benefitted" (the preferred spelling is "benefited"); "making sure that we can continue to make it possible." We note the throat-clearing ("It is true that") and the infelicitous words and phrases ("guarantee," "expends," "continue innovations," "due to costs," "maintain reputation for advances"). After some tidying up and rewording, we have:

How do your contributions help the Harvard Law School?

- You enable one of 1,273 financially needy students to attend the school.
- You help the Law School retain its high-quality clinical education program. (Other schools have been forced to reduce support for their clinics.)
- You sustain innovation in legal education, including small classes and team-taught classes for first-year students.

Students benefit every day from alumni support, just as we did when we were students. Tuition, $11,400 this year, covers only 60 percent of the cost of educating each student.

Your gift makes a difference to the Law School. I hope you will join me to assure a place for every qualified student, regardless of financial need. Help us maintain the Law School's leadership in legal education.

Please send your gift by June 15 so that it can be credited in this fiscal year. Thank you.

Our final example is an excerpt from Chief Justice Burger's 1974 opinion in *United States v. Nixon.*[9] In that case, the Supreme Court, by a vote of 8–0, held that President Nixon had to surrender his Watergate tapes to the United States special prosecutor. The case was heard and decided in extraordinary circumstances; the Court issued its opinion sixteen days after hearing argument.

EXAMPLE: This presumptive privilege [executive privilege] must
be considered in light of our historic commitment to the rule of
law. This is nowhere more profoundly manifest than in our
view that "the twofold aim [of criminal justice] is that guilt
shall not escape or innocence suffer." We have elected to employ an adversary system of criminal justice in which the parties
contest all issues before a court of law. The need to develop all
relevant facts in the adversary system is both fundamental and
comprehensive. The ends of criminal justice would be defeated
if judgments were to be founded on a partial or speculative presentation of the facts. The very integrity of the judicial system
and public confidence in the system depend on full disclosure
of all the facts, within the framework of the rules of evidence.
To ensure that justice is done, it is imperative to the function
of courts that compulsory process be available for the production of evidence needed either by the prosecution or by the defense.

In this case we must weigh the importance of the general
privilege of confidentiality of presidential communications in
performance of his responsibilities against the inroads of such a
privilege on the fair administration of criminal justice. The interest in preserving confidentiality is weighty indeed and entitled to great respect. However, we cannot conclude that advisers
will be moved to temper the candor of their remarks by the in-
frequent occasions of disclosure because of the possibility that
such conversations will be called for in the context of a criminal
prosecution. On the other hand, the allowance of the privilege
to withhold evidence that is demonstrably relevant in a criminal
trial would cut deeply into the guarantees of due process of law
and gravely impair the basic function of the courts. A President's acknowledged need for confidentiality in the communications of his office is general in nature, whereas the constitutional need for production of relevant evidence in a criminal
proceeding is specific and central to the fair adjudication of a
particular criminal case in the administration of justice. Without access to specific facts a criminal case may be totally frustrated. The President's broad interest in confidentiality of communications will not be vitiated by disclosure of a limited
number of conversations preliminarily shown to have some

bearing on the pending criminal cases. . . . The generalized assertion of privilege must yield to the demonstrated, specific need for evidence in a pending criminal trial.

EDIT 1: This presumptive privilege must be considered in light of our historic commitment to the rule of law, a commitment most profoundly manifest in our view that "the twofold aim [of criminal justice] is that guilt shall not escape or innocence suffer." In our adversary system of criminal justice, the parties must develop all relevant facts and contest all issues before a court of law. If courts were to reach judgment without all the facts, the ends of criminal justice would be defeated. Integrity of the judicial system and public confidence in it depend on the fullest disclosure of facts consistent with the rules of evidence. To ensure that justice is done, courts must be able to compel witnesses to produce evidence needed by either the prosecution or the defense.

In this case we must balance an interest in ensuring that presidential communications remain private against the court's need for disclosure. We must choose between a policy of disclosure that could imperil the President's capacity to carry out his responsibilities of office and a policy of preserving confidentiality that could impair the court's ability to reach sound judgment.

The interest in preserving confidentiality is entitled to great respect. However, we cannot conclude that the President's advisers will become less candid because in a criminal prosecution a court might infrequently require them to testify about their conversations. And were we to bar such evidence in criminal trials in which it is demonstrably relevant, we would undercut the guarantee of due process of law and gravely impair the courts' basic function. A President's acknowledged need for confidentiality in the communications of his office is general, whereas the court's need for relevant evidence in a criminal proceeding is specific. If the parties do not have access to specific facts, the case may be totally frustrated. When a limited number of conversations have been shown preliminarily to have some bearing on a criminal case, their disclosure will not vitiate the President's broad interest in keeping his communications confidential. . . . The generalized assertion of privilege must yield to

The Presidents' claim to an absolute executive privilege depends on the strength of our historic commitment to the rule of law, a commitment most profoundly shown in our view that "the twofold aim [of criminal justice] is that guilt shall not escape or innocence suffer." In our system adversaries contest all issues must develop all relevant facts and to

The ends of criminal justice would be defeated if courts reached judgments without all the facts. The very integrity of the judicial system and public confidence in it depend on the fullest disclosure of facts, consistent with the rules of evidence. justice requires that courts be empowered to compel witnesses to produce evidence needed by party.

In this case we must balance two interests: weigh the importance of the Privacy of presidential communications and the courts need for disclosure. We must choose between a policy of disclosure that could imperil the Presidents capacity to carry out his responsibilities and a policy of preserving confidentiality that could hinder a court from reaching a sound judgment. ¶ We respect the strong interest in preserving confidentiality. However, we cannot conclude that the President's advisers will become more reticent because a court might infrequently require them to testify in a prosecution about their conversations and barring privilege to withhold evidence that such demonstrably relevant evidence in a criminal trial would undercut the guarantees of due process of law and gravely impair the function the courts A President's need for confidentiality is general whereas the court's need for relevant evidence in a prosecution is specific Without access to specific the parties may be totally frustrated and justice thwarted. When preliminarily general claim of confidentiality a few conversations have been shown to bearing on a prosecution, their disclosure will not jeopardize The generalized assertion of privilege must yield to the demonstrated, specific need for

173

the demonstrated, specific need for evidence in a pending criminal trial.

EDIT 2: The President's claim to an absolute executive privilege depends on the strength of our historic commitment to "the rule of law," a commitment most profoundly shown in our view that "the twofold aim [of criminal justice] is that guilt shall not escape or innocence suffer." In our system, adversaries must develop all relevant facts and contest all issues. If courts reached judgments without all the facts, criminal justice would be defeated. Integrity of the judicial system and public confidence in it depend on the fullest disclosure of facts consistent with the rules of evidence. Justice requires that courts be empowered to compel witnesses to produce evidence needed by either party.

In this case we must balance two interests: privacy of presidential communications and the court's need for disclosure. We must choose between a policy of disclosure that could imperil the President's ability to carry out his responsibilities and a policy of preserving confidentiality that could hinder a court from reaching a sound judgment.

We respect the strong interest in preserving confidentiality. However, we cannot conclude that the President's advisers will become more reticent because a court might infrequently require them to testify in a prosecution about their conversations. And barring such demonstrably relevant evidence in criminal trials would undercut the guarantee of due process of law and gravely impair the courts' function. A President's need for confidentiality is general, whereas the courts' need for relevant evidence in a prosecution is specific. Without access to specifics, the parties may be totally frustrated and justice thwarted. When a few conversations have preliminarily been shown to bear on a prosecution, their disclosure will not jeopardize the President's general claim of confidentiality. . . . The generalized assertion of privilege must yield to the demonstrated, specific need for evidence in a pending criminal trial.

We spent more than an hour editing this passage. In edit 1 we untangled the sentences but left most of the verbiage undisturbed. In edit

2 we hunted down redundant and windy phrases; for all the changes we made, we discussed and discarded many more. After two rounds of editing, we had cut the original (405 words) by about 25 percent (to 297 words). (We reproduce a handwritten version so that you can follow our trail.)

In both edits, we strove to preserve the court's tone. Had we chosen to alter the tone and sharply simplify the passage, we would have a 77-word summary, a little more than one-sixth of the original.

> SUMMARY: The President asserts that presidential advisers will not be candid if they know that their conversations might be disclosed in court. His position is entitled to respect. But his claim is general and cannot outweigh a court's need for specific information that, at least preliminarily, has been shown to be relevant to the pending prosecution. Without all the facts, our adversary system of criminal justice could not work. Public confidence and judicial integrity depend on full disclosure.

Only the clock can tell you when to stop editing. "We must check our writing right up to the moment of deadline," wrote James J. Kilpatrick, who called this advice "perhaps the most important of all" for writers. We endorse his call for rigorous editing and proofreading, as we do so much else in his admirable book *The Writer's Art*. But just a few pages later, Kilpatrick misstates the title of Theodore Bernstein's book on outmoded rules of English usage, transforming *Miss Thistlebottom's Hobgoblins* into *Miss Throttlebottom's Hobgoblins*.[10] Bernstein said he gave the book this peculiar name in part because he believed "that a title so hard to pronounce and so hard to remember will be difficult to forget."

No matter how diligently we may edit, errors, like stubborn weeds in a garden, infest our prose. The only remedy: Edit again.

Until now, we have shown how to write acceptable prose—prose more serviceable than that of most lawyers. Apply our principles and you will produce sturdy prose. For most purposes, sustained clarity is sufficient; you will be considered an able writer. But writing is more than clarity and concision. Many would-be painters are adept at drawing; they can draft a cloud or a human form that is technically acceptable. Their finished works, however, are not judged solely by technique but by more subtle considerations of style, feeling, and composition. So tone, voice, and style mark an essay as more than technically proficient. They enable a lawyer to transcend the mundane and make a piece of writing memorable.

> *I admire Holmes above all legal writers, followed by Robert Jackson and Learned Hand. Of course writing of their quality cannot be taught, but if only lawyers would strive to write clearly and simply, avoiding legal jargon, exaggeration, and polemic, improvement would be vast.*
>
> JUDGE RICHARD A. POSNER

Throughout our history, a few judges and lawyers have enriched our culture with their words. In writing about free speech, Justice Louis D. Brandeis could have said that "societies that suppress free speech have succumbed to irrational fears and caused harm that they later, knowing more, might have regretted." Instead, he said: "Men feared witches, and burned women."

Too often, though, lawyers don't know the difference between prose that soars and prose that sinks. We have no formula for making prose memorable—indeed, to transcend composition that is merely serviceable the writer must forgo formulaic thought and expression. Memorable prose is writing that surprises through its freshness, writing that eschews cliché, bombast, triviality, artificiality, hollow embellishment, and many other affectations that mark the writer as tin-eared and callow. In what follows we hope to persuade by example. We present illustrations of prose that misses, and end by offering examples that instruct, entertain, and sing.

Style That Fails

Here is a paragraph lifted from a brief submitted to us as an example of "good" lawyerly writing. In this passage, the lawyer is discussing a statute that permits a child's out-of-court statements to be admitted in evidence:

> Despite the facial clarity of the plain words of the above statute, the litigant fares no better than the scholar in searching for a definition of "corroboration." The statute implies that the term is not only susceptible to definition, but indeed, demands that such a definition be expressed in functional operation if the statute is to represent more than precatory words. Absent definition, the statute is a right without a remedy, a tiger without fangs—an osmotic membrane masquerading as a shield for abused children.

The tangled images alone are enough to trip the reader. To show that the legislature has botched the statute, the lawyer should be understated, cool, direct, and should not resort to bombast and purple phrases. Garish images are not the obvious alternative to the gray run of legal prose; just because this kind of language differs from the ordinary does not make it effective.

"Even good writers become infected with the bug of ostentation when they write for courts," said Milton Gould, a New York trial lawyer who was also a noted storyteller. "The older I get, the more I admire succinctness, and the more I despise flash." Scott F. Turow, a lawyer and best-selling novelist, told us that the legal writer should strive for "lucidity and quiet persuasiveness."

Evan Thomas, an editor at *Newsweek* who spent a summer in the 1970s as an associate at a large law firm in New York, recalls: "The young lawyers wrote this dense, turgid, overanalyzed convoluted stuff, while many of the older lawyers wrote so simply and clearly that their prose could go on a sports page. For all their verbiage, the young lawyers never got to the point, while the old guys zeroed right in."

Many lawyers are so immersed in the plodding prose of the workaday world that they confuse an ornate, oily, and overdone tone with good writing. Or they are beguiled by simple or nonlegal expressions and think that even the pedestrian phrase shines. At one firm we visited, a young associate told us breathlessly that a partner had coined a perfectly marvelous phrase that was, unfortunately, now being rather overused in the firm's briefs—it was that good. The phrase: "strikingly similar."

Stuffiness even infects some lawyers' nonlegal writing. Here is the first paragraph of a fund-raising letter to 30,000 Harvard Law School alumni:

> In preparation for Year 33 of the Annual Giving campaign of the Harvard Law School Fund serious consideration was given as to the amount that should be set for this year's goal. Last year contributions to the Fund from alumni and friends were $3,524,600, a new record amount both overall and in alumni gifts, yet we were $75,400 short of our $3.6 million objective. The setting of this year's goal at $4 million, therefore, represents a formidable challenge.

Burdened by heavy nouns, we slog through the anonymity of the passive construction to find unsociable sentences. That is a strange way to induce people to part with their money, a lot of money, a redundant amount of money, a "new record amount"! This opening paragraph wholly misses its audience; it dwells on the woes of the fund's officers, not on the concerns of the potential givers.

In a more serious matter, a Wisconsin lawyer misjudged his audience in writing a snide open letter to the judges of the state court of appeals, who had affirmed a decision to commit his client to a mental institution. Here's how he began:

> You are probably quite smug about your decision in this case. You were
> presented with an issue which was admittedly not clear cut and which
> had a potential impact on a fairly large segment of persons who had
> been committed under the Wisconsin insanity law. So what did you do?
> You *think* you managed to avoid deciding the case altogether. Sorry I
> can't congratulate you on this clever evasion of a precedential statutory
> interpretation. This may come as something of a shock, but you *didn't*
> avoid an interpretation of the insanity law with a major impact on this
> state.[1]

This lawyer misconstrued the meaning of informality. A respectful, colloquial tone might have caught the judges' sympathy; instead, this snide, taunting tone irritated the Wisconsin Supreme Court, which dismissed his petition and noted:

> At a minimum, defense counsel violated a cardinal rule of effective ap-
> pellate legal writing. The rule is: "*Avoid disparaging lower courts or op-
> posing parties.*" At a maximum, some language in the petition may have
> gone beyond the realm of permissibly zealous advocacy.

Similarly, when judges depart from their sober tone, they often lose control of their language and write opinions memorable only for their silliness, immaturity, or hyperbole. In 1930 Judge M. M. Logan of the Kentucky Court of Appeals dissented from a majority opinion that upheld the dominion of a surface owner over caves that lay beneath his land:

> Let us give thought to the petitioner Edwards, his rights and his pre-
> dicament, if that is done to him which the circuit judge has directed to
> be done. Edwards owns this cave through right of discovery, exploration,
> development, advertising, exhibition, and conquest. Men fought their
> way through eternal darkness, into the mysterious and abysmal depths
> of the bowels of a groaning world to discover the theretofore unseen
> splendors of unknown natural scenic wonders. They were conquerors
> of fear, although now and then one of them, as did Floyd Collins, paid
> with his life, for his hardihood in adventuring into the regions where

Charon with his boat had never before seen any but the spirits of the departed. They let themselves down by flimsy ropes into pits that seemed bottomless; they clung to scanty handholds as they skirted the brinks of precipices while the flickering flare of their flaming flambeaux disclosed no bottom to the yawning gulf beneath them; they waded through rushing torrents, not knowing what awaited them on the farther side; they climbed slippery steeps to find other levels; they wounded their bodies on stalagmites and stalactites and other curious and weird formations; they found chambers, star-studded and filled with scintillating light reflected by a phantasmagoria revealing phantoms, and tapestry woven by the toiling gods in the dominion of Erebus. . . . They knew nothing, and cared less, of who owned the surface above; they were in another world where no law forbade their footsteps. They created an underground kingdom where Gulliver's people may have lived or where Ayesha may have found the revolving column of fire in which to bathe meant eternal youth.[2]

Here is the unintentionally hilarious opening paragraph of an opinion by Justice Frank A. Carlin of the City Court of New York in 1941:

This case presents the ordinary man—that problem child of the law—in a most bizarre setting. As a lonely chauffeur in defendant's employ he became in a trice the protagonist in a breath-bating drama with a denouement almost tragic. It appears that a man, whose identity would be indelicate to divulge, was feloniously relieved of his portable goods by two nondescript highwaymen in an alley near 26th Street and Third Avenue, Manhattan; they induced him to relinquish his possessions by a strong argument ad hominem couched in the convincing cant of the criminal and pressed at the point of a most persuasive pistol. Laden with their loot, but not thereby impeded, they took an abrupt departure, and he, shuffling off the coil of that discretion which enmeshed him in the alley, quickly gave chase through 26th Street toward 2d Avenue, whither they were resorting "with expedition swift as thought" for most obvious reasons. Somewhere on thoroughfare of escape they indulged the stratagem of separation ostensibly to disconcert their pursuer and allay the ardor of his pursuit. He then centered on for capture the man with the pistol, whom he saw board the defendant's taxicab which quickly veered south toward 25th Street on 2d Avenue, where he saw the chauffeur jump out while the cab still in motion, continued toward 24th Street; after the chauffeur relieved himself of the cumbersome burden of his fare the latter also is said to have similarly departed from the cab before it reached 24th Street.[3]

Lest anyone suppose these grand flourishes belong to an age past, let us sample two opinions written in the mid-1980s. First, an opinion by Justice Bruce Wright of the Supreme Court in Manhattan, concerning a property dispute between a dentist and an assistant who became his lover and then jilted him for another man. This is how Justice Wright begins:

> Two young people, cohabiting without the ceremony of a wedding, lived for a time in blissful harmony and trust, confident in the fragile balustrade of an imagined future and its longevity. They plighted a troth without ritual. Wrapped in the drama of their mutual pulse, they were ill-starred. Passionate pilgrims, they had no seer to caution their fall from the grace of doomed affection, or warn that love places its victims on emotional welfare rolls.[4]

Now the prose begins to gallop:

> As with the Trojan War, where the heroes of Homer squabbled, some of the symmetry of tragedy crept into the relationship of the parties. Ill-starred lovers have from time immemorial stumbled gloriously among the snares of their own drums. Troilus sighed for the infidelity of Cressida. Pyramus and Thisbe had their midsummer night's mésalliance, as did Othello and Desdemona. There are precedents a-plenty for bitterness and the scathed spirit. . . . Palinurus, wounded by betrayal, wept that, "The object of loving is to end love." Savaged by the treason of uxorial cuckoldry, he felt, in the words of a poet that "Life goes on, but I don't remember why."

And then, in an abrupt order, Justice Wright denied a motion for a preliminary injunction, allowing the case to proceed to trial. That's a lot of erudition to waste on a preliminary motion.

Judge Richard Curry of the Cook County Circuit Court ruled on the Chicago Cubs' request to install lights in Wrigley Field:

> Baseball, "the national pastime"—the thing of which young boys dream and old boys fantasize—the subject of songs, poems, satire, ballads and

verse—the occupation of heroes and bums—the grist for the columnist and the gambler—the avocation of the bystander and the theatre for the grandstander—the ballast for the summer months and the leaven for the winter months—the theme which accommodates both nostalgia and expectation—a game that can be played as work, witnessed as fun and memorialized as history—a diversion which has developed its own lexicon with words such as "bush"; "choke", "whiff"; "balk" (and in Chicago) Hey! Hey! . . . In as much as this case is in the domain of "everybody's business" its issue should be deliberately stated in a manner most likely to attract and hold maximum attention. Perhaps something like this:

> Do those who schedule play time for the games of our national pastime have the right to interfere with bedtime by starting the game at nighttime, instead of the customary daytime?[5]

Blithely misspelling his way through sixty-two pages of a little law and a lot of lore, Judge Curry winds up:

> ". . . YOU'RE OUT!"
> Yes, you're out. O . . . U . . . T. The Cubs are out. The inning is over. The contest is lost. Now it's time for the box score, summary and the wrap up. Have you ever heard a postmortem on a sporting event when some "intangible" wasn't cited as an element in the victory or the defeat? Well we have one in this case also. The Cubs lost, of course, for all of the reasons stated above but, in addition thereto, they should have had a better scouting report before coming to Court. Everyone around the courthouse is familiar with "Justice" with her robes flowing, her blindfold and her scales. What the Cubs' "book" on her failed to note is that she is a southpaw. *Justice is a Southpaw* and the Cubs just don't hit lefties!!!
> ". . . AT THE OLD BALLGAME".

Judge Curry's opinion is so overspiced (or overcooked) and his sarcasm so heavy-handed that the plaintiff could justifiably cry foul. (See what happens when you read too much overheated prose.)

Judge Curry evidently meant to be funny. But self-conscious humor by those who cannot control it is puerile. Even lawyers and judges who are genuinely talented and funny writers should restrain themselves. As

Justice Benjamin N. Cardozo said in 1925 in his famous essay "Law and Literature": "Flashes of humor are not unknown, yet the form of opinion which aims at humor from beginning to end is a perilous adventure, which can be justified only by success, and even then is likely to find its critics almost as many as its eulogists." And as Judge George Rose Smith of the Arkansas Supreme Court noted in the 1960s: "Judicial humor is neither judicial nor humorous. A lawsuit is a serious matter to those concerned in it. For a judge to take advantage of his criticism-insulated, retaliation-proof position to display his wit is contemptible, like hitting a man when he's down."[6]

Probably the worst form of judicial humor is doggerel. In a suit filed by a seaman against a shipowner to recover lost wages, Edward R. Becker, U.S. district judge in Philadelphia, explained why he resorted to verse:

> The motion now before us
> has stirred up a terrible fuss.
> And what is considerably worse,
> it has spawned some preposterous doggerel verse.
>
> Plaintiff's counsel, whose name is Harry Lore,
> read defendant's brief and found it a bore.
> Instead of a reply brief, he acted pretty quick
> and responded with a clever limerick:
>
> Not to be outdone, the defense took the time
> to reply with their own clever rhyme.
>
> Overwhelmed by this outburst of pure creativity,
> we determined to show an equal proclivity,
> Hence this opinion in the form of verse,
> even if not of the calibre of Saint-John Perse.[7]

A Michigan appeals judge, J. H. Gillis, in upholding a lower-court ruling that denied damages to the owner of a tree rammed by an automobile, began his opinion:

> We thought that we would never see
> A suit to compensate a tree.[8]

These examples are dreadful. But even good doggerel (think Ogden Nash) and light verse (Joyce Kilmer) are inappropriate in legal writing.

Style That Works

Humor can have its place if it emerges from substance rather than form. A pro se plaintiff sought damages in Judge Gerald J. Weber's court against "Satan and His Staff" for placing "deliberate obstacles in his path." Judge Weber, of the Western District of Pennsylvania, could have dismissed the case peremptorily or responded with a derisive opinion. Instead, he chose to treat the plaintiff with dignity, and the opinion that resulted is dry and understated. Here is a portion of Judge Weber's solution:

> We question whether plaintiff may obtain personal jurisdiction over the defendant in this judicial district. The complaint contains no allegations of residence in this district. While the official reports disclose no case where this defendant appeared as defendant there is an unofficial account of a trial in New Hampshire where this defendant filed an account of mortgage foreclosure as plaintiff. The defendant in that action was represented by the preeminent advocate of that day, and raised the defense that the plaintiff was a foreign prince with no standing to sue in an American Court. This defense was overcome by overwhelming evidence to the contrary. Whether or not this would raise an estoppel in the present case we are unable to determine at this time.[9]

Judge Weber is funny with a straight face. Wry humor is difficult for even the best stand-up comics, who can call on body and facial expressions; it's far more difficult for a writer, especially one writing in the legal tradition. Nevertheless, wit deftly used elevates a passage to make it memorable. Here's Judge Frank R. Easterbrook of the U.S. Court of Appeals for the Seventh Circuit in Chicago:

> Morton Goldsmith was the head of a chain of clinics and pharmacies, many flying the banner of Drug Industry Consultants, Inc. (DIC). Between 1981 and 1984 DIC's clinics and pharmacies, and those of associated enterprises, prescribed and sold large quantities of codeine-based

cough syrups to addicts. The clinics were selective. To be a patient, you had to have a Medicaid card. Not necessarily yours; anyone's would do. The Medicaid card was the key to DIC's profits.[10]

Self-deprecating wit helped Supreme Court Justice Robert H. Jackson blunt the embarrassment of disavowing a position he had taken as attorney general a few years earlier. In an elegant paragraph into which he skillfully wove quotations, Jackson wrote what has become almost the standard apology for judges who must retract or lawyers who must backtrack:

> I concur in the judgment and opinion of the Court. But since it is contrary to an opinion which, as Attorney General, I rendered in 1940, I owe some word of explanation. I am entitled to say of that opinion what any discriminating reader must think of it—that it was as foggy as the statute the Attorney General was asked to interpret. . . . Precedent, however, is not lacking for ways by which a judge may recede from a prior opinion that has proven untenable and perhaps misled others. See Chief Justice Taney recanting views he had pressed upon the Court as Attorney General of Maryland. Baron Bramwell extricated himself from a somewhat similar embarrassment by saying, "The matter does not appear to me now as it appears to have appeared to me then." And Mr. Justice Story, accounting for his contradiction of his own former position, quite properly put the matter: "My own error, however, can furnish no ground for its being adopted by this Court. . . ." Perhaps Dr. Johnson really went to the heart of the matter when he explained a blunder in his dictionary—"Ignorance, sir, ignorance." But an escape less self-depreciating was taken by Lord Westbury, who, it is said, rebuffed a barrister's reliance upon an earlier opinion of his Lordship: "I can only say that I am amazed that a man of my intelligence should have been guilty of such an opinion." If there are other ways of gracefully and good naturedly surrendering former views to a better considered position, I invoke them all.[11]

Jackson adroitly adapts his tone to solve the problem he faced: how to apologize for errors while retaining his dignity and authority. The reader, after all, might suppose that if he was wrong once, as he admits, he might be wrong even now. Jackson's tone disarms the reader. A man who confesses his mistakes, without false humility or obsequious servility, is absolved of blame. In invoking great men of the past who had confessed to similar errors in similar ways, in acknowledging the fallibility of mature adults, Jackson manages to amuse the reader without detracting from his solemn message: Trust me now.

Some years later, to justify his own repudiation of an earlier opinion, California Justice Stanley Mosk quoted Jackson's statement and appended to it a memorable line from Supreme Court Justice Felix Frankfurter, who had also had occasion to change his mind: "Wisdom too often never comes, and so one ought not to reject it merely because it comes late."[12]

Tone is bottled in no formula. The appropriate tone depends on your audience and your sense of self: reserved or casual, solemn or whimsical, serious or ironic, sober or sarcastic, genuine or sycophantic. As a lawyer, you always have a serious purpose, but your tone need not be somber. (Think of Mark Twain, whose tone was always comic, his purpose usually serious.) A trivial quarrel need not be dismissed by a joke. Nor does a case with large stakes compel a solemn tone. Here is how U.S. District Judge William C. Conner in Manhattan deflated the pretensions of two powerful corporations:

> The lawsuit represents a major battle in an endless war between two titans of the over-the-counter ("OTC") drug industry, in which each accuses the other of falsity in its advertising claims of efficacy and safety. Small nations have fought for their very survival with less resources and resourcefulness than these antagonists have brought to their epic struggle for commercial primacy in the OTC analgesic field.[13]

Tone is embedded in every piece of writing. Formality and dullness are tones as much as a cool wit. You cannot escape tone; you can only hope to strike the proper one for your purpose. The choice lies not simply between the dull and the extravagant. Tone, like style, ranges across a spectrum between these extremes.

Much of this book has been concerned with questions of style: long sentences or short, fancy words or plain, active voice or passive, direct statements or oblique comments. The spare style is often identified with Ernest Hemingway, an author who started as a journalist and whom many legal writing specialists suggest emulating. This advice angers others, who say that what Hemingway did is not what lawyers ought to do.[14]

Hemingway deserves better. His name has come to stand for two distinct propositions: (1) Lawyers should (or should not) write in a spare style, and (2) lawyers should (or should not) narrate stories about people rather than expound abstract concepts. The debate is oversimplified and jumbled. It disserves Hemingway, and lawyers, to suppose that questions of style and storytelling are either-or propositions.

We advocate a spare style, but we are not suggesting that lawyers imitate Hemingway. Lawyers must at times discuss abstract principles, but they must remember that the best way to engage their audience is to tell stories. Reflecting on hundreds of petitions for certiorari that he read each year while at the *Wall Street Journal,* Stephen Wermiel said: "It strikes me that lawyers feel no need to make their cases sound interesting. And I think that is a serious error. . . . The justices need to have their interest captured just as much as I do."

Here's Judge John R. Brown, a widely admired judge of the U.S. Court of Appeals for the Fifth Circuit, telling a story, as he began an opinion about a collision on a navigable waterway:

> It was a dark and stormy night.* A patchy, low-lying fog covered the murky waters of the river and obscured the banks. Ships, passing in the night, were but phantoms, vague outlines disappearing into the mist. Ships' whistles, echoing across the dark expanse, seemed like mournful cries from another world. Then suddenly, looming out of the darkness, another ship appeared. The distance was too small; time too short; before anyone could do more than cry out, the unthinkable occurred. The ships collided. The tug, helpless, drifted downriver. Floundering like some giant behemoth wounded in battle, the tanker came to ground and impaled itself on some voracious underwater obstruction. And still the whistles, echoing, seemed like cries from another world.[15]

The style of this passage is too flamboyant for some tastes, but it transports readers to the site of the accident, allowing them to see and hear

---

* Brown's "dark and stormy night" repeats the opening line of Edward George Bulwer-Lytton's novel *Paul Clifford* (1830), a line that has spawned an annual parody contest.

the collision. This description is more evocative than a flat "Two vessels, one large and one small, were involved in a waterway collision on an evening of inclement weather."

Another judge, Donald Burnett, of the Idaho Court of Appeals, affected the taut, matter-of-fact style favored by some mystery writers, what might be called an "opinion *noir*":

> It was a shotgun blast in the early morning that killed Merardo Rodriguez. As he lay on the floor of his house, his wife placed a pillow beneath his head and watched him die.[16]

This style—direct, immediate, forceful—can also be effective in non-narrative writing. Note, for example, the understatement and economy used by Judge Joseph R. Nolan of the Massachusetts Supreme Judicial Court in his dissent from the majority's decision to permit life-support equipment to be turned off:

> In the forum of ethics, despite the opinion's high-blown language to the contrary, the court today has endorsed euthanasia and suicide. Suicide is direct self-destruction and is intrinsically evil. No set of circumstances can make it moral. Paul Brophy will die as a direct result of the cessation of feeding. The ethical principle of double effect is totally inapplicable here. This death by dehydration and starvation has been approved by the court. He will not die from the aneurysm which precipitated loss of consciousness, the surgery which was performed, the brain damage that followed or the insertion of the G-tube. He will die as a direct result of the refusal to feed him. He will starve to death.[17]

Dismissing his colleagues' rhetoric as "high-blown," Judge Nolan uses plain words (suicide, evil, die, starve), relatively simple syntax, and stark contrasts ("will die" vs. "will not die").

As these examples suggest, eloquence comes more from simplicity than from a profusion of lush and overblown words. Long words and dandified phrases deaden rather than enlighten. At the end of a remarkable commencement address at Yale Law School in 1979, Professor Leon S. Lipson gave a four-minute exhortation composed entirely of one-syllable words. Here is an excerpt:

On this day, or soon, you will take leave of this yard, these halls, and us. We wish you well. As your Sage for a Day, coaxed to preach if not to teach, I ought to send you on your way with great store of wise and shrewd saws, short sharp tools that I should put in your hands for you to wield so as to carve a good and full life from the wild lush fields of the law.

But I know that you did not wait to hear this from me, or till now. You made haste to shop for those tools as soon as you came here. In the past three years, or—as it may be—two or one, you have learned some facts and some law; you have made some friends, young and not so young and not so old and old, learned from them and they from you; in class and in your rooms, with your friends or by your own lone selves, you have picked a few books to bits, page by page, case by case, line by line. Your brains are stocked with rules clear or dim, with thoughts keen or dull, some of them your own; you have heard much of rights and wrongs, of courts and boards and jails, of new ways to tax the rich or help the poor or plead to a charge or bust the trusts or split the stock or cut the pie, and why not to; your ears are cocked to catch (if not to heed) the still small voice of truth, and your eyes are strained to spy out a star to steer by.

As you lead your life in the law, we hope you will do good, grow wise, and thrive. In the years to come, think of us now and then. Come back to see us when you can, and more than once if you can. Let us hear from you words of your feats of skill and works of art. . . .

As you grow more and more skilled in *what* you do, and as you ask *why* you do what you do, we trust that on the whole we here shall prove to have meant much more to you: more as the time goes on, and not least when you have no thought of us at all, for, will you nill you, you will bear—all the rest of your life—the stamp, or brand, or blaze, of the Yale Law School.[18]

Professor Lipson's talk is notable as a tour de force, rather than for any single line. But sometimes one memorable line can elevate an otherwise mundane brief. A single sentence in legal discourse can recast or transform the debate. Irwin Rochman, a defense lawyer serving as a special state prosecutor in New York, once spent several hours composing a single sentence. The name Attica, he wrote, "should be a symbol not only of riot and death, but also of the capacity of our system of criminal justice to redress its own wrong."[19] Rochman had two goals:

to persuade a judge to dismiss the remaining indictments stemming from the prison uprising in 1971 and, secondarily, to have the *New York Times* choose his sentence as its quotation of the day. He was doubly successful.

> *The power of clear statement is the great power*
> *at the bar.*
> DANIEL WEBSTER

Every lawyer should strive for one original, memorable sentence in every brief—one sentence that the judge will borrow, one sentence that will be quoted by journalists. This kind of writing is difficult, for the most memorable sentences always sound as though they were composed effortlessly.[20]

> The criminal is to go free because the constable has blundered.
> —*Justice Benjamin N. Cardozo*

> The most stringent protection of free speech would not protect a man in falsely shouting fire in a theater and causing a panic. [This is one of the most widely quoted and *misquoted* pieces of jurisprudence; "falsely" is frequently omitted, changing Holmes's meaning entirely.]
> —*Justice Oliver Wendell Holmes*

> A sign that says "men only" looks very different on a bathroom door than a courthouse door. [On the standard of review in equal-protection cases.]
> —*Justice Thurgood Marshall*

The power of these sentences lies in their earthiness. Here are no words of art, no foreign terms, no polysyllabic tongue twisters. The words are plain, homespun, evocative. They state a truth that is as easy for the reader to grasp as it is straightforward for the writer to express.

Writing a memorable line is a skill that all writers should strive to attain. In preparation, a writer must read widely and well. "In my view good writing requires more than mental skills; it requires exposure to the substance of human experience in history and literature and in general science," Milton S. Gould told us. On this count, lawyers whose undergraduate reading was limited to textbooks in economics or the sciences are at a disadvantage.

The best way to prepare for the law is to come to the study of law as a well-read person. Thus alone can one acquire the capacity to use the English language on paper and in speech and with the habits of clear thinking which only a truly liberal education can give.

JUSTICE FELIX FRANKFURTER

To gauge how widely law students and lawyers read, we have, in workshops over the years, presented passages from great literature. One of these is a brilliant, evocative paragraph by Loren Eiseley, the finest American science writer of his time. The short excerpt from *Darwin's Century* discusses the discovery of geological time that prepared the way for the theory of evolution:

> Like the fabulous western isles the idea [of evolution] would be coasted at first through dangerous intellectual waters. It would be termed a phantom, a figment of man's restless imagination. It would be labeled like a sea monster "blasphemous," "illusory," and "godless." Finally it would lie there under the lifting fog-wisps which had so long obscured the human vision, a country of wraiths and changelings among whom was to be counted man himself. Time such as humanity had never dreamed before lay across that world. It was a land where water wore away the shapes of mountains, and the great bones and carapaces of vanished beasts lay hoar and rime-frosted in deep crevices and canyons.[21]

Almost all the law students and young lawyers turn up their noses, complaining that the passage is too abstract. So immersed are these people in their professional literature that they have little capacity to be moved by a style alien to them. Eiseley paints a vivid, image-laden picture about a highly abstract concept; the paragraph is a model of its kind. Our complaint, in turn, is that their taste in reading is far too narrow—too narrow to prepare them to be good writers, and too narrow to prepare them for their professional responsibilities.

> *[Lawyers possess] a peculiar Cant and Jargon of their*
> *own, that no other Mortal can understand.*
>
> JONATHAN SWIFT

A sustained reading habit can help any writer compose powerful and memorable sentences and paragraphs—elegant expression is not reserved for novelists and essayists. Over the years, gifted advocates and judges have set forth great thoughts in single sentences or clusters of sentences.[22]

We must never forget that it is a *constitution* we are expounding.
—*Chief Justice John Marshall*

Our Constitution is color-blind, and neither knows nor tolerates classes among citizens.　　　　　　　　　　—*Justice John Marshall Harlan*

[W]hen men have realized that time has upset many fighting faiths, they may come to believe even more than they believe the very foundations of their own conduct that the ultimate good desired is better reached by free trade in ideas—that the best test of truth is the power of the thought to get itself accepted in the competition of the market, and that truth is the only ground upon which their wishes safely can be carried out.
　　Every idea is an incitement. . . . Eloquence may set fire to reason.
—*Justice Oliver Wendell Holmes*

Immunities that are valid against the federal government by force of the specific pledges of particular amendments have been found to be implicit in the concept of ordered liberty, and thus, through the Fourteenth Amendment, become valid as against the states.
—*Justice Benjamin N. Cardozo*

Anticipation as such cannot invalidate a copyright. Borrowed the work must indeed not be, for a plagiarist is not himself pro tanto an "author"; but if by some magic a man who had never known it were to compose anew Keats's Ode on a Grecian Urn, he would be an "author," and, if he copyrighted it, others might not copy that poem, though they might of course copy Keats's.   —*Judge Learned Hand*

[If] there is any fixed star in our constitutional constellation, it is that no official, high or petty, can prescribe what shall be orthodox in politics, nationalism, religion, or other matters of opinion or force citizens to confess by word or act their faith therein.

If it is interstate commerce that feels the pinch, it does not matter how local the operation which applies the squeeze.

We are not final because we are infallible, but we are infallible only because we are final.   —*Justice Robert H. Jackson*

Legislators represent people, not trees or acres. Legislators are elected by voters, not farms or cities or economic interests.
                                            —*Chief Justice Earl Warren*

We deal with a right of privacy older than the Bill of Rights. [Marriage] is a coming together for better or worse, hopefully enduring, and intimate to the degree of being sacred. It is an association that promotes a way of life, not causes; a harmony in living, not political faiths; a bilateral loyalty, not commercial or social projects. Yet it is an association for as noble a purpose as any involved in our prior decisions.
                                            —*Justice William O. Douglas*

These passages are concise and vivid, and they offer fresh ways of looking at commonplace issues. Search the vocabularies of these writers: You will not need a dictionary to understand the thought, nor a thesaurus to sharpen the image. Words are not wasted, nor sentences prolonged. Most illustrate the abstraction with a concrete and unexpected image—what could better evoke the power of an idea than the fire that eloquence might ignite; what could better describe the ideals of equality than the homespun picture of a color-blind constitution?

These passages are among the most memorable words of the best writers in our legal tradition. Of these, Holmes and Brandeis endure. Anthony Lewis, who spent more than forty years at the *New York Times* and is widely regarded as one of the best contemporary writers about law, puts them at the top of his list: "No one today comes close." He calls Brandeis's concurring opinion in *Whitney v. California* the "greatest single piece of legal writing I know." Read the following central passage from that opinion slowly. Look at the words Brandeis chose, particularly the verbs. Notice how the topics connect, and how precisely the longer sentences are structured. Above all, consider the reasonable, measured tone: Justice Brandeis is not braying, he is persuading.

> Those who won our independence believed that the final end of the State was to make men free to develop their faculties; and that in its government the deliberative forces should prevail over the arbitrary. They valued liberty both as an end and as a means. They believed liberty to be the secret of happiness and courage to be the secret of liberty. They believed that freedom to think as you will and to speak as you think are means indispensable to the discovery and spread of political truth; that without free speech and assembly discussion would be futile; that with them, discussion affords ordinarily adequate protection against the dissemination of noxious doctrine; that the greatest menace to freedom is an inert people; that public discussion is a public duty; and that this should be a fundamental principle of the American government. They recognized the risks to which all human institutions are subject. But they knew that order cannot be secured merely through fear of punishment for its infraction; that it is hazardous to discourage thought, hope and imagination; that fear breeds repression; that repression breeds hate; that hate menaces stable government; that the path of safety lies in the opportunity to discuss freely supposed grievances and proposed remedies; and that the fitting remedy for evil counsels is good ones. Believing in the power of reason as applied through public discussion, they eschewed silence coerced by law—the argument of force in its worst form. Recognizing the occasional tyrannies of governing majorities, they amended the Constitution so that free speech and assembly should be guaranteed.
>
> Fear of serious injury alone cannot justify suppression of free speech and assembly. Men feared witches and burned women. It is the function of speech to free men from the bondage of irrational fears. To justify suppression of free speech there must be reasonable ground to fear that serious evil will result if free speech is practiced. There must be reasonable ground to believe that the evil to be prevented is a serious one. Every denunciation of existing law tends in some measure to increase the probability that there will be violation of it. Condonation of a breach enhances the probability. Expressions of approval add to the probability. Propagation of the criminal state of mind by teaching syndicalism increases it. Advocacy of lawbreaking heightens it still further. But even

advocacy of violation, however reprehensible morally, is not a justification for denying free speech where the advocacy falls short of incitement and there is nothing to indicate that the advocacy would be immediately acted on. The wide difference between advocacy and incitement, between preparation and attempt, between assembling and conspiracy, must be borne in mind. . . .

Those who won our independence by revolution were not cowards. They did not fear political change. They did not exalt order at the cost of liberty. To courageous, self-reliant men, with confidence in the power of free and fearless reasoning applied through the processes of popular government, no danger flowing from speech can be deemed clear and present, unless the incidence of the evil apprehended is so imminent that it may befall before there is opportunity for full discussion. If there be time to expose through discussion the falsehood and fallacies, to avert the evil by the processes of education, the remedy to be applied is more speech, not enforced silence. Only an emergency can justify repression. Such must be the rule if authority is to be reconciled with freedom. Such, in my opinion, is the command of the Constitution.[23]

Next consider Holmes's dissent in *United States v. Schwimmer,* which Lewis says is "close to poetry in its density." Like Brandeis, Holmes uses short, familiar words and connects his thoughts without wasteful transitions or windy phrases. He, too, speaks in a mild manner that strengthens the force of his argument. He is not being disagreeable; how can one disagree with him? Of course, in time, no one did: This dissenting opinion is now the well-established majority view.

The applicant seems to be a woman of superior character and intelligence, obviously more than ordinarily desirable as a citizen of the United States. It is agreed that she is qualified for citizenship except so far as the views set forth in a statement of facts "may show that the applicant is not attached to the principles of the Constitution of the United States and well disposed to the good order and happiness of the same, and except in so far as the same may show that she cannot take the oath of allegiance without a mental reservation." The views referred to are an extreme opinion in favor of pacifism and a statement that she would not bear arms to defend the Constitution. So far as the adequacy of her oath is concerned, I hardly can see how that is affected by the statement, inasmuch as she is a woman over fifty years of age, and would not be allowed to bear arms if she wanted to. And as to the opinion the whole examination of the applicant shows that she holds none of the now-dreaded creeds, but thoroughly believes in organized government and prefers that of the United States to any other in the world. Surely it cannot show lack of attachment to the principles of the Constitution that she thinks that it can be improved. I suppose that most intelligent people think that it might be. Her particular improvement looking to the abolition of war seems to me not materially different in its bearing on this case from a wish to establish cabinet government as in England, or a single house, or one term of seven years for the President. To touch a more burning question, only a judge mad with partisanship would exclude because the applicant thought that the 18th Amendment should be repealed.

Of course, the fear is that if a war came the applicant would exert activities such as were dealt with in Schenck v. United States. But that seems to me unfounded. Her position and motives are wholly different from those of Schenck. She is an optimist and states in strong and, I do not doubt, sincere words her belief that war will disappear and that the impending destiny of mankind is to unite in peaceful leagues. I do not share that optimism nor do I think that a philosophic view of the world would regard war as absurd. But most people who have known it regard it with horror, as a last resort, and, even if not yet ready for cosmopolitan efforts, would welcome any practicable combinations that would increase the power on the side of peace. The notion that the applicant's optimistic anticipations would make her a worse citizen is sufficiently answered by her examination, which seems to me a better argument for her admission than any that I can offer. Some of her answers might excite popular prejudice, but if there is any principle of the Constitution that more imperatively calls for attachment than any other it is the principle of free thought—not free thought for those who agree with us but for freedom for the thought that we hate. I think that we should adhere to that principle with regard to admission into, as well as to life within, this country. And, recurring to the opinion that bars this applicant's way, I would suggest that the Quakers have done their share to make the country what it is, that many citizens agree with the applicant's belief, and that I had not supposed hitherto that we regretted our inability to expel them because they believe more than some of us do in the teachings of the Sermon on the Mount.[24]

Judges such as Holmes and Brandeis are staples of literary excellence, known to everyone and studied by everyone. There is always a time lag before contemporary writing, of any age, is admitted to the canon. It's hard to be an icon when you are alive. Moreover, the number of lawyers writing today is vastly greater than in any age past, and it is therefore more difficult for a consensus to emerge about who the best modern writers are.

> *Whene'er you speak, remember every cause*
> *Stands not on eloquence, but stands on laws:*
> *Pregnant in matter, in expression brief,*
> *Let every sentence stand with bold belief;*
> *On trifling points not time or talents waste,*
> *A sad offense to learning and to taste;*
> *Nor deal with pompous phrase, nor e'er suppose*
> *Poetic flights belong to reasoning prose.*
>
> JUSTICE JOSEPH STORY

But some contemporary writing stands out. Several judges called our attention to *United States of America v. Janet Leslie Cooper Byrnes,* a 1981 opinion of the Second Circuit. The author of the opinion was William Hughes Mulligan, a leading wit and toastmaster of the New York bar. *United States v. Byrnes* was his last opinion before leaving the bench for private practice. Mulligan, too, sent the opinion along, with this caveat: "Fairly amusing, though inelegant, and maybe overdone." This is how he began:

Who knows what evil lurks in the hearts of men? Although the public is generally aware of the sordid trafficking of drugs and aliens across our borders, this litigation alerts us to a nefarious practice hitherto unsuspected even by this rather calloused bench—rare bird smuggling. The appeal is therefore accurately designated as *rara avis.* While Canadian geese have been regularly crossing, exiting, reentering and departing our borders with impunity, and apparently without documentation, to enjoy more salubrious climes, those unwilling or unable to make the flight either because of inadequate wing spans, lack of fuel or fear of buck shot, have become prey to unscrupulous traffickers who put them in crates and ship them to American ports of entry with fraudulent documentation in violation of a host of federal statutes. The traffic has been egregious enough to warrant the empaneling of a special grand jury in 1979 in the Northern District of New York to conduct a broad investigation of these activities. Even the services of the Royal Canadian Mounted Police were mustered to aid the inquiry.[25]

After a trial, a California woman was convicted of falsely testifying about her role in bringing into this country, with spurious entry papers, four trumpeter swans and two red-breasted geese. Judge Mulligan had a good time describing what happened at the grand jury and at trial. Like Will Rogers, he wryly commented on the facts as he led the reader along. For example:

> No birds have been indicted and there is no indication in the record that they were even aware of, much less participated in, the criminal activity unearthed by the grand jury. They were at least as innocent as the horses whose jockeys were bribed to discourage their best efforts at Pocono Downs. . . .
>
> The trumpeter swan makes a noise described by a trial witness, Cherie Perie, as "*weird*." The appellant, on the other hand, in her grand jury testimony, stated that the male trumpeter during courtship "struts around with his neck and head held high and makes this marvelous little trumpeting sound." . . . *De gustibus.* The mute apparently courts in silence.

After a further learned discussion of birds and precedents, here is how Judge Mulligan ended:

> The judgment of conviction is affirmed, justice has triumphed and this is my swan song.

And ours.

NOTES

PREFACE

1. *Legal Education and Professional Development—An Educational Continuum,* Report of the Task Force on Law Schools and the Profession: Narrowing the Gap (Chicago: American Bar Association, Section of Legal Education and Admissions to the Bar, July 1992).

2. *Columbia University Law School News,* February 2001, p. 7.

1. DOES BAD WRITING REALLY MATTER?

1. *Manhattan Lawyer,* November 3–9, 1987, p. 9.

2. George D. Gopen, "The State of Legal Writing: *Res Ipsa Loquitur,*" 86 *Michigan L. Rev.* 333, 342–43 (November 1987).

2. DON'T MAKE IT LIKE IT WAS

1. All the examples in this paragraph come from David Mellinkoff, *The Language of the Law* (Boston: Little, Brown, 1963): Fortescue, p. v; the plaintiff with his head in the pleadings, p. 191; Hale, p. 190; Bacon, p. 193.

2. Jonathan Swift, *Gulliver's Travels,* in *The Writings of Jonathan Swift,* eds. Robert A. Greenberg and William Bowman Piper (New York: W. W. Norton, 1973), p. 217; Jeremy Bentham, *Works* (1843); quoted in Mellinkoff, *Language of the Law,* p. 262; Henry Fielding, *Tim Vinegar* (1739); quoted in Mellinkoff, ibid., p. 193.

3. Thomas Jefferson's letter to Joseph C. Cabell, September 9, 1817, quoted in Mellinkoff, *Language of the Law,* p. 253.

4. Urban A. Lavery, "The Language of the Law," 7 *A.B.A.J.* 277, 283 (1921); Karl N. Llewellyn, "On What Is Wrong with So-Called Legal Education," 35 *Columbia L. Rev.* 651, 660 (1935); Fred Rodell, "Goodbye to Law Reviews," 23

Virginia L. Rev. 38 (1936); William L. Prosser, "English as She Is Wrote," 7 *J. Leg. Ed.* 155, 156 (1954) [first published in 28 *English J.* 38 (1939)]—with the excerpt from the final exam at 158.

5. Arthur T. Vanderbilt, "A Report on Prelegal Education," 25 *N.Y.U.L. Rev.* 199, 209 (1950).

6. William Warren, "Fifty-Second Annual Meeting A.A.L.L.," 52 *L. Library J.* 341 (1959).

7. Carl McGowan, "Law and the Use of Language," 47 *A.B.A.J.* 897, 900 (1961).

8. Warren E. Buffett, preface to *A Plain English Handbook: How to Create Clear SEC Disclosure Documents* (Office of Investor Education and Assistance, Securities and Exchange Commission, August, 1998), p. 1; Arthur Levitt, introduction to *A Plain English Handbook,* p. 3.

9. Lawrence M. Friedman, "Law and Its Language," 33 *George Washington L. Rev.* 563, 567, 568 (1964).

10. Robert W. Benson, "The End of Legalese: The Game Is Over," 13 *R. L. & Soc. Change* 519, 522 (1984–85).

11. Norbert Wiener, *The Human Use of Human Beings* (Garden City, N.Y.: Doubleday Anchor Books, 1954), p. 107.

12. *Brown v. Board of Education* II, 349 U.S. 294 (1955).

13. The complete recall notice: "A defect which involves the possible failure of a frame support plate may exist on your vehicle. This plate (front suspension pivot bar support plate) connects a portion of the front suspension to the vehicle frame, and its failure could affect vehicle directional control, particularly during heavy brake application. In addition, your vehicle may require adjustment service to the hood secondary catch system. The secondary catch may be misaligned so that the hood may not be adequately restrained to prevent hood fly-up in the event the primary latch is inadvertently left unengaged. Sudden hood fly-up beyond the secondary catch while driving could impair driver visibility. In certain circumstances, occurrence of either of the above conditions could result in vehicle crash without prior warning."

14. Mellinkoff, *Language of the Law,* pp. 315, 321.

15. Steven Stark, "Why Lawyers Can't Write," 97 *Harv. L. Rev.* 1389 (1984); Fred Rodell, *Woe Unto You, Lawyers* (1939; reprint, New York: Berkley, 1961), pp. 16, 17.

16. Friedman, "Law and Its Language," p. 564.

17. Mark Matthewson, "Verbatim," *Student Lawyer,* January 1988, p. 7.

18. Oliver Wendell Holmes, "The Path of the Law," 10 *Harv. L. Rev.* 457, 469 (1897).

19. Friedman, "Law and Its Language," p. 571.

20. Peter Lubin, "Happy Hereinafter," *The New Republic,* April 11, 1988, p. 14.

21. Mellinkoff, *Language of the Law,* p. 403; his comments about the typewriter are on p. 261.

22. Carl McGowan, "Lawyers and the Uses of Language," 47 *A.B.A.J.* 900 (1961).

23. Stark, "Why Lawyers Can't Write," p. 1389.

24. Richard Hyland, "In Defense of Legal Writing," 134 *Univ. of Pennsylvania L. Rev.* 599, 608 (1986).

25. "The Writing Gap," *Yale Alumni Magazine,* January 1976, p. 16.

26. A. Bartlett Giamatti, "Sentimentality," *Yale Alumni Magazine,* January 1976, pp. 17–19.

27. Jacques Barzun, "English As She's Not Taught," reprinted in *On Writing, Editing, and Publishing* (Chicago: University of Chicago Press, 1971), p. 19.

28. Jacob Bronowski and Bruce Mazlish, *The Western Intellectual Tradition* (New York: Harper Torchbooks, 1962), p. 192.

29. Kathleen M. Carrick and Donald J. Dunn, "Legal Writing: An Evaluation of the Textbook Literature," 30 *New York Law School L. Rev.* 645, 653–54 (1985).

30. Robert A. Leflar, "Some Observations Concerning Judicial Opinions," 61 *Columbia L. Rev.* 810, 815–16 (1961).

31. Rodell, *Woe Unto You, Lawyers,* p. 11.

32. Arthur T. Vanderbilt, "A Report on Prelegal Education," 25 *N.Y.U.L. Rev.* 199, 209 (1950).

33. McGowan, "Lawyers and the Uses of Language," p. 901.

34. George Orwell, "Politics and the English Language," reprinted in *In Front of Your Nose, The Collected Essays* (New York: Harcourt Brace Jovanovich, 1968), vol. 4.

35. See *Code of Professional Responsibility* DR 7–106(C) (4): A lawyer shall not "assert his personal opinion as to the justness of a cause. . . . [or] as to the culpability of a civil litigant."

36. Compare John T. Noonan Jr., *Persons and Masks of the Law* (New York: Farrar, Straus & Giroux, 1976), p. xi: "The responsibility [of lawyers] comes in the response to other persons; it is the greater the more one is conscious that he or she—not some imagined entity—is acting, and the more one is conscious that the action affects not a hypothetical A but a real Helen Palsgraf."

37. Hyland, "In Defense of Legal Writing," p. 620.

38. Friedman, "Law and Its Language," p. 572.

39. Hyland, "In Defense of Legal Writing," p. 625; Richard K. Sherwin, *When Law Goes Pop* (Chicago: University of Chicago Press, 2000), p. 6.

40. In the 1960s Marshall McLuhan's aphorism "the medium is the message" encapsulated the notion, the *reductio ad absurdum* of modern communications theory, that content is meaningless. See J. Ben Lieberman, "McLuhanacy," in Gerald Emanuel Stearn, ed., *McLuhan: Hot & Cool* (New York: Signet, 1967), p. 217.

3. TEN STEPS TO WRITING

1. Susan R. Horton, *Thinking through Writing* (Baltimore: Johns Hopkins University Press, 1982), pp. 156–57.
2. Friedrich von Schiller, quoted in James L. Adams, *Conceptual Blockbusting*, 2d ed. (New York: W. W. Norton, 1980), p. 119.
3. Oliver Wendell Holmes, quoted in Catherine Drinker Bowen, *Yankee from Olympus* (Boston: Little, Brown, 1944), p. 324.
4. John Kenneth Galbraith, *The New Industrial State* (Boston: Houghton Mifflin, 1967), pp. viii–ix.

4. OF DAWDLERS AND SCRAWLERS

1. Susan R. Horton, *Thinking through Writing*, pp. 6–7.
2. V. A. Howard and J. H. Barton, *Thinking on Paper* (New York: William Morrow, 1986), p. 22.
3. Donald H. Murray, *Writing for Your Readers* (Chester, Conn.: Globe Pequot Press, 1983), pp. 143–45.

5. THE MECHANICS OF GETTING IT DOWN

1. Our sketch of the history of typing is drawn from Bruce Bliven Jr., *The Wonderful Writing Machine* (New York: Random House, 1954), p. 62 (on Twain), p. 79 (George), pp. 103–4 (market), and pp. 113–15 (McGurrin).
2. David Mellinkoff, *The Language of the Law*, p. 261.
3. Judge Matthew Jasen's rebuke appears in *Slater v. Gallman*, 377 N.Y.S. 2d 448, 38 N.Y.2d 1,339 N.E.2d 863 (1975); the decision he cited is *Stevens v. O'Neill*, 169 N.Y. 375 (1902).
4. Mary Edwards, unpublished manuscript in authors' files.

5. Vivian Dempsey, "The Dangers of Junk Documents," *California Lawyer*, October 1987, p. 4.

6. David S. Levine, " 'My Client Has Discussed Your Proposal to Fill the Drainage Ditch with His Partners': Legal Language" in *The State of Language*, edited by Leonard Michaels and Christopher Ricks (Berkeley: University of California Press, 1980), p. 406.

7. Fran Shellenberger, "Who Should Type?" *Word Progress*, American Bar Association Section of Economics of Law Practice, Winter 1988, p. 20.

8. Louis Simpson, quoted in the *New York Times Book Review*, January 3, 1988, p. 12.

9. William K. Zinsser, *On Writing Well*, 3d ed. (New York: Harper & Row, 1988), pp. 205, 214.

10. Bliven, *Wonderful Writing Machine*, p. 133. Bliven offers the following example of such a sin: "We are pleased to forward to you the merchandise referred to in your valued order of the 21st except that, on account of unforeseen difficulties in the supply of materials, we have substituted light blue for navy hoping that this will not inconvenience you rather than cause further delay which, as you know, we are as anxious to avoid as you are in view of our pleasure during these past months of being of service to your esteemed organization as well as personally."

11. Edward H. Warren, *Spartan Education* (Boston: Houghton Mifflin, 1942), p. 31.

6. LESSONS FROM A WRITING AUDIT

1. The venerable *Blue Book* is under assault, and for good reason. Over its seventeen revision cycles, the *Uniform System of Citation*, as it is formally titled, has become anything but uniform; succeeding editors from the Harvard, Yale, Columbia, and Pennsylvania Law Reviews have altered its rules from edition to edition so that those who have relied on it the longest are most imperiled in their use of it. Challenging it is the *ALWD Citation Manual, a Professional System of Citation,* written by Darby Dickerson of Stetson University Law School under the auspices of the Association of Legal Writing Directors, an organization representing most American law schools. The rules in the *ALWD Manual* system are more likely to be familiar to generations of law review editors and to remain stable over time.

8. WRITING THE LEAD

1. *Larkin v. Grendel's Den, Inc.*, 459 U.S. 116 (1982), Brief of Appellee.
2. *Wall Street Journal*, August 20, 1985; *New York Times*, February 13, 1984; *New York Times*, April 26, 1986; *Wall Street Journal*, May 31, 2000.
3. Rene J. Cappon, *The Word* (New York: Associated Press, 1982), p. 31.
4. Louis Boccardi, quoted in Cappon, ibid., p. 46.
5. *Sheldon v. Metro-Goldwyn Pictures Corp.*, 81 F.2d 49 (2d Cir. 1936).

9. FORM, STRUCTURE, AND ORGANIZATION

1. Allan Nevins, *The Gateway to History*, rev. ed. (New York: Anchor Books, 1962), p. 376.
2. Winston Churchill, *A Roving Commission* (New York: Scribner's, 1941), pp. 211–12.
3. David M. Balabanian, "Justice Was More Than His Title," 70 *California L. Rev.* 878 (1982).
4. Noel Coward, quoted in G. W. Bowersock, "The Art of the Footnote," 53 *American Scholar* 54 (1984).
5. Fred Rodell, "Goodbye to Law Reviews," 23 *Virginia L. Rev.* 38 (1936), p. 41.
6. John E. Nowak, "Woe unto You, Law Reviews!" 27 *Arizona L. Rev.* 317, 323 (1985).
7. Paul M. Barrett, "To Read This Story in Full, Don't Forget to See the Footnotes," *Wall Street Journal*, May 10, 1988, p. 1.
8. U.S. Supreme Court page limits: U.S.Sup.Ct. Rule 33.1.g; U.S. Courts of Appeals page limits for briefs: F.R.A.P. Rule 32(a)(7); U.S. Courts of Appeals page limits for motions: F.R.A.P. Rule 28(d)(2); Virginia Supreme Court page limits: Virginia Supreme Court Rule 5:26(a).
9. For a rare suggestion that failure to abide by the rules might disqualify a brief, see *Caniglia v. Caniglia*, 2 NCA 185, 1993 Neb. App. LEXIS 29: "We note that the appellee's brief is not in compliance with [the Nebraska court rules]. . . . We caution that the failure of a party to submit a brief which complies with our own rules may result in our treating the case as one in which no brief has been filed by that party."

10. WRONG WORDS, LONG SENTENCES, AND OTHER MISTER MEANERS

1. Dorothy Evslin, "In the Write Spirit," *New York Times,* January 16, 1987, p. 27.

2. Richard C. Wydick, *Plain English for Lawyers,* 2d ed. (Durham: Carolina Academic Press, 1985), p. 53; Lisa Faye Kaplan, "Hot Stuff!" New Rochelle, N.Y.: *Standard-Star,* October 22, 1986; Alfred E. Kahn, memorandum of June 16, 1977, "The Style of Board Orders and Chairman's Letters."

3. James J. Kilpatrick, quoted in Ronald Goldfarb, "My Secretary, Hereinafter Referred to as Cuddles . . . ," *Barrister,* Summer 1978, p. 43; Philip Kurland, *New York Times Book Review,* September 20, 1987, p. 3.

4. H. W. Fowler, *A Dictionary of Modern English Usage,* p. 342.

5. John L. Lewis, quoted in Rudolf Flesch, *The Art of Readable Writing* (New York: Harper & Row, 1949), p. 208.

6. "Asides," *Wall Street Journal,* June 22, 1990, p. A8.

7. Edward Tenner, "Cognitive Input Device in the Form of a Randomly Accessible Instantaneous-Read-Out Batch-Processed Pigment-Saturated Luminous-Cellulose Hard-Copy Output Matrix," *Discover,* May 1986, pp. 58–59.

8. "Career associate scanning professionals" and "wellness potential" are cited in "Could you, er, say that again?" *U.S. News & World Report,* April 20, 1987, p. 71; "minimally adequate training" appears in *Youngberg v. Romeo,* 457 U.S. 307 (1982); the euphemisms for the fire and explosion at Three Mile Island come from Joanne Lipman, "In Times of Trouble, Candor Is Often the First Casualty," *Wall Street Journal,* December 15, 1986.

9. Bryan A. Garner, *A Dictionary of Modern American Usage* (New York: Oxford University Press, 1998), p. 143.

10. Paul A. Freund, Arthur E. Sutherland, Mark DeWolfe Howe, and Ernest J. Brown, *Constitutional Law, Cases and Other Problems,* 2d ed. (Boston: Little, Brown, 1961), 2: lxiii.

11. Allan M. Siegal and William G. Connolly, *The New York Times Manual of Style and Usage,* rev. ed. (New York: Times Books, 1999), p. 204.

12. William Safire, *The New York Times Magazine,* May 16, 1999, p. 30.

13. George Orwell, "Politics and the English Language," reprinted in *In Front of Your Nose, The Collected Essays* (New York: Harcourt Brace Jovanovich, 1968), 4:138n; Alexander Haig, quoted in the *New York Times,* January 29, 1987, p. A10.

14. Patricia M. Wald, commencement address to the class of 1988, New York Law School, June 12, 1988, Lincoln Center, New York.

15. Ibid.

16. R. W. Burchfield, ed., *The New Fowler's Modern English Usage* (New York: Oxford University Press, 1996), p. 610.

17. The example is taken from Wilson Follett, *Modern American Usage* (Hill & Wang, 1966), p. 158.

18. *Random House Dictionary of the English Language* (New York: Random House, 1987), p. 2470.

19. Richard H. Weisberg, *When Lawyers Write* (Boston: Little, Brown, 1987), p. xxi.

20. Joseph M. Williams, *Style: Ten Lessons in Clarity and Grace,* 2d ed. (Glenview, Ill.: Scott, Foresman, 1985), pp. 33–34.

21. Handout distributed at the Legal Writing Institute, University of Puget Sound Law School, Tacoma, Washington, August 5, 1988.

22. Rudolf Flesch, *How to Write Plain English: A Book for Lawyers and Consumers* (New York: Harper & Row, 1979), pp. 22–23.

23. Benjamin N. Cardozo, "Law and Literature," 52 *Harv. L. Rev.* 471, 474 (1939) [reprinted from 14 *Yale Review* 699 (July 1925)] and *Law and Literature* (New York: Harcourt Brace, 1931), pp. 7–8.

24. Jethro K. Lieberman, "To Reach and Teach the Public, Write Better," in Robert S. Peck and Charles J. White, eds., *Understanding the Law: A Handbook on Educating the Public* (Chicago: American Bar Association, 1983), p. 25.

25. Urban A. Lavery, "The Language of the Law," 8 *A.B.A.J.* 269, 272 (1922).

26. *In re Ann Goalen,* 30 Utah 2d 27, 30, 512 P.2d 1028, 1029–30 (1973). Our thanks to Professor Stephen A. Newman of New York Law School for referring us to this example.

11. REVISING YOUR PROSE

1. In George Plimpton, ed., *Writers at Work: The Paris Review Interviews,* 7th series (New York: Viking, 1986), p. 271.

2. John Kenneth Galbraith, "Writing, Typing, and Economics," *Atlantic Monthly,* March 1978, p. 103.

3. *Wall Street Journal,* editorial, June 2, 1986.

4. Daniel Seligman, "Rotten Writing in High Places," *Fortune,* August 18, 1986, p. 77.

5. Holly Stevens, *The Letters of Wallace Stevens* (New York: Alfred A. Knopf, 1981), p. 37 (journal entry of June 15, 1900).

6. Theodore M. Bernstein, *Dos, Don'ts & Maybes of English Usage* (New York: Times Books, 1977), p. 42.

7. *Hammock v. Farmers Loan & Trust Co.,* 105 U.S. 77, 84 (1891). David Mellinkoff, *The Language of the Law,* p. 251.

8. Our thanks to Erika S. Fine for sending us this example.

9. *United States v. Nixon,* 418 U.S. 683 (1974).

10. Kilpatrick, *The Writer's Art* (Kansas City: Andrews, McMeel & Parker, 1984), pp. 138 and 145.

12. MAKING YOUR WRITING MEMORABLE

1. Our thanks to Christopher G. Wren for referring us to *State v. Rossmanith,* 146 Wis.2d 89, 430 N.W.2d 93 (1988).

2. *Edwards v. Sims,* 24 S.W.2d 619, 622–23 (Ct. App. Ky. 1930).

3. *Cordas v. Peerless Transportation Co.,* 27 N.Y.S.2d 198 (City Ct., N.Y. County, 1941).

4. *Goldin v. Artache,* New York Law Journal, August 26, 1986.

5. *Chicago National League Ball Club, Inc. v. Thompson,* No. 84 Ch11384 (Circuit Court, Cook County, 1985), *affirmed,* 108 Ill.2d 357, 483 N.E.2d 1245 (1985). Our thanks to George J. Siedel for calling our attention to this opinion.

6. Benjamin N. Cardozo, "Law and Literature," 52 *Harv. L. Rev.* (1939), p. 483; George Rose Smith, "Primer of Opinion Writing for Four New Judges," 21 *Arkansas L. Rev.* 197, 210 (1967).

7. *Mackensworth v. American Trading Transportation Co.,* 367 F.Supp. 373 (E.D. Pa. 1973).

8. *Fisher v. Lowe,* 122 Mich. App. 418, 333 N.W. 2d 167 (1983).

9. *United States ex rel. Mayo v. Satan and His Staff,* 54 F.R.D. 282, 283 (W.D. Pa. 1971). Our thanks to Adam Kasanof for calling this opinion to our attention.

10. *United States v. Sblendoriio,* 830 F.2d 1382, 1384 (7th Cir. 1987).

11. *McGrath v. Kristensen,* 340 U.S. 162, 177–78 (1950) (concurring) (citations omitted).

12. *Henslee v. Union Planters National Bank & Trust Co.,* 335 U.S. 595, 599 (1949) (Frankfurter, dissenting).

13. *American Home Products Corp. v. Johnson & Johnson,* 654 F.Supp. 568 (S.D.N.Y. 1987).

14. For an example of the pro-Hemingway faction, see Steven Stark, "Why Lawyers Can't Write," 97 *Harv. L. Rev.* 1389 (1984); for an anti-Hemingway view, see Richard Hyland, "In Defense of Legal Writing," 134 *Univ. of Pennsylvania L. Rev.* 612, 621 (1986).

15. *Allied Chemical Corp. v. Hess Tankship Co. of Delaware,* 661 F.2d 1044, 1046–47 (5th Cir. 1981).

16. *State v. Baker,* 103 Idaho 43, 644 P.2d 365 (Idaho App. 1982).

17. *Brophy v. New England Sinai Hospital, Inc.,* 398 Mass. 417, 497 N.E.2d 626, 640 (1986).

18. *Yale Law Report* No. 1, Fall 1979, pp. 3–4. We thank Simon H. Rifkind for calling this address to our attention.

19. *New York Times,* February 27, 1976, p. 1.

20. Cardozo, *People v. Defore,* 242 N.Y. 13, 21 (1926) (dissenting). Holmes, *Schenck v. United States,* 249 U.S. 47, 52 (1919). Marshall, *Cleburne v. Cleburne Living Center,* 473 U.S. 432, 468–69 (1985) (concurring in part and dissenting in part).

21. Loren Eiseley, *Darwin's Century* (Garden City, N.Y.: Doubleday Anchor, 1961), p. 2.

22. Marshall, *McCulloch v. Maryland,* 4 Wheat. 316, 407 (1819). Harlan (quoting a phrase from the brief by Albion Tourgee, the losing plaintiff's lawyer), *Plessy v. Ferguson,* 163 U.S. 537, 559 (1896) (dissenting). Holmes, *Abrams v. United States,* 250 U.S. 616, 630 (1919) (dissenting); *Gitlow v. New York,* 268 U.S. 652, 673 (1925) (dissenting). Cardozo: *Palko v. Connecticut,* 302 U.S. 319, 325 (1937). Hand, *Sheldon v. Metro-Goldwyn Pictures Corp.,* 81 F.2d 49, 54 (2d Cir. 1936). Jackson, *Board of Education v. Barnette,* 319 U.S. 624, 642 (1943); *United States v. Women's Sportswear Manufacturers Assn.,* 336 U.S. 460, 464 (1949); *Brown v. Allen,* 344 U.S. 443, 540 (1953). Warren, *Reynolds v. Sims,* 377 U.S. 533, 562 (1964). Douglas, *Griswold v. Connecticut,* 381 U.S. 479, 486 (1965).

23. *Whitney v. California,* 274 U.S. 357 (1927) (concurring).

24. *United States v. Schwimmer,* 279 U.S. 644, 653–55 (1929) (dissenting).

25. *United States v. Byrnes,* 644 F.2d 107 (2d Cir. 1981).

These usage notes offer pointers on the errors in grammar, syntax, diction, and spelling that appear most often in legal writing. The entries are drawn from usage books, from lawyers' memoranda on usage and style, and from our observations and those of our colleagues.

abbreviations Do not use abbreviations in text other than personal titles, such as Mr., Ms., Prof., and Dr., and commonly recognized initials, such as SEC.

absolute words Certain adjectives do not allow comparison or qualification. They are either-or words: Either their quality is present or it is not, and so they can't be modified by "partly" or "very" or "most" or "a little bit." Some examples: complete, equal, essential, eternal, fatal, final, identical, imperative, indispensable, perfect, pregnant, total, unanimous, unique, universal, virgin.

absolve from *or* of

abstain from

accede to

accessory after, before, *or* to

accommodate to *or* with: Note the spelling: two *c*'s and two *m*'s.

accord in *or* to

accordance with

accountable for *or* to

accuse of

acquiesce in

adapt. *See* **adopt**.

adept at *or* in

adhere to

admit of, into, *or* to: *Admit to* usually connotes guilt; do not use in place of "stated," "said," or "acknowledged."

adopt, adapt *Adopt* means "to take on as one's own, to espouse"; *adapt* means "to adjust, to make fit."

advantage of *or* over

adversarial Dictionaries did not recognize this word until 1969. The proper phrase is "adversary system," not "adversarial system."

advise of *or* about

affect, effect The verb *affect* means "to influence"; the noun *affect* is a psychological term that describes mood. The noun *effect* means "result" or "consequence"; the verb *effect* means "to bring about" or "to accomplish."

affinity between *or* with

aforementioned Avoid. *See* **lawyerisms**.

aggravate, irritate *Aggravate* means "to make worse, enhance, enlarge"; *irritate* means "to arouse, annoy, inflame." For example: "He was irritated that she kept him waiting in the rain. Her sarcasm aggravated his hostile mood."

all, not all "All members of the band are not here yet" means that no member of the band has arrived. When the meaning is "some members of the band are still absent," the sentence should read "Not all members of the band are here yet."

all ready, already *All ready* means "fully prepared" (they were all ready to go); it is inappropriate in formal writing. *Already* means "now, by this or that time, previously, before, so soon."

all right Colloquial, inappropriate in formal writing. Note the spelling (*alright* is incorrect).

alleged *Allege* is a serviceable verb ("the plaintiffs allege that the defendant injured them"). But the adjective *alleged* and the adverb *allegedly* are overworked and misused. For example: "The first grand jury to consider the case declined to indict Goetz for attempted murder, charging him only with alleged gun possession." Obviously, Goetz was charged with *actual* gun possession; alleged possession of a gun is no crime. Also in error: "There is no question [that Ray Luca] was based on Mr. Spilotro's alleged life as perceived by law enforcement authorities." "The Bible doesn't say 'Thou Shalt Not Commit Alleged Adultery,'" *Winners & Sinners,* a bulletin on usage once published by the *New York Times,* advised its readers. "The weasel words *alleged* and *allegedly* turn up too often, giving our columns an unwelcome precinct-house odor. Why do they appear? Maybe because it's thought—mistakenly—that they shelter us from libel or editorializing. We're no less safe, and we're easier to read, if we say what we mean, in everyday English." See also p. 117.

allude, elude To *allude* is "to refer to something indirectly, to hint at"; to *elude* is "to avoid detection or capture or memory."

allusion, illusion *Allusion* denotes a hinting at or indirect reference to; *illusion* is a deceptive appearance. One may "allude to" something (there is no verb "illude"), and something may be "illusory" (there is no adjective "allusory").

already. *See* **all ready.**

also *Also* must be near the word it is to modify. "He also is the bearer of bad news" is not the same as "He is also the bearer of bad news."

alternate, alternative The meanings of these two distinct words are beginning to bleed at the edges. The verb *alternate* means "to go back and forth between two positions, by turns"; the noun *alternate* means "a substitute" (as an alternate, he rarely plays); the adjective *alternate* means "every other" (on alternate Mondays) or "in turn"; *alternately* describes an arrangement in which two groups are in alternation (like children seated boy, girl, boy, girl). In contrast, *alternative* refers to a choice (alternative sources of energy; alternative school). "Alternate Dispute Resolution" is a misnomer (the participants do not alternate between mediation and court); the correct term is "Alternative Dispute Resolution" (the system gives people an alternative to court).

amenable to

amend, emend *Amend* means "to make formal changes in" (amend the Constitution); *emend* is "to correct a mistake."

among, between Purists insist that *between* refers to two people or things; *among* to three or more. But many usage books agree that when contracts are negotiated among many parties, each considered as an individual, "between" is preferable: "The nine players struck a deal between themselves before approaching the owner."

and/or Avoid this ambiguous shorthand. Decide whether your mean *and* or *or,* and use that word. If neither conjunction works, rewrite the sentence. For example, instead of "The staff will meet Monday and/or Thursday," write "The staff will meet Monday and Thursday" (two meetings), "The staff will meet Monday or Thursday" (one meeting), or "The staff will meet Monday and, if needed, Thursday as well." See David Mellinkoff, *The Language of the Law* (Boston: Little, Brown, 1963), pp. 306–18.

antipathy against, to, between, *or* for

anxiety about *or* for

appreciation of *or* for

apprehensive of *or* for

arguendo Pomposity. Avoid. *Arguendo* means "for the sake of argument"; say that.

as *As* can be mishandled in many ways. Don't use it as a substitute for "because": "Because [*not* as] he arrived late last night, I did not see him until this morning." "Regarded as" does not require "being": "She is regarded as [*not* as being] the best dancer in the world." Delete the surplus "as" in, for example, "The class elected Sheila as president." *See also* **like, as.**

as . . . as The correct expressions are *as much as* or *as large as* (*never* as much than). The constructions "they have four times as high a risk than others" and "they charged three times as much for tourists than for residents" are ungrammatical.

    A distinction that has all but disappeared calls for *as . . . as* in affirmative expressions (Mike is as quick as Lindy), and *so . . . as* in negative expressions (Mike is not so quick as Lindy). Nowadays, *as . . . as* may be used either affirmatively or negatively.

    The phrase "as good or better than" should be written "as good as or better than."

as of yet *Yet* suffices: "She hasn't posted bail yet [*not* as of yet]."

as such Ordinarily awkward and inappropriate.

as to Do not use *as to* as a global substitute for the idiomatic preposition that follows a noun: clue to (*not* clue as to), debate over (*not* debate as to), issue of (*not* issue as to). *See also* **prepositions.**

aspire to, after, *or* toward

assent to

assumption of

attest to

attorney Remember that *attorney* and *lawyer* are not synonyms; see David Mellinkoff, *The Language of the Law* (Boston: Little, Brown, 1963), p. 80.

averse to

awhile, a while *Awhile* is an adverb (She waited awhile); *while* is a noun (She waited for a while).

badly Misused to mean "bad" in the expression "I feel badly." Verbs such as "feel," "appear," and "look" take an adjective, not an adverb.

based on Be careful not to dangle this modifier. The meaning of "Based on the clue in the motel, we drove directly to the airport," is the "we" (not the driving) are "based on the clue." Another example: "Axel and Hal allege in their complaint that First Bank breached the January 15 agreement. Based on this so-called breach, they seek damages in excess of $10 million." The second sentence implies that Axel and Hal, rather than their suit, are based on the breach. Rewrite to avoid the dangler (Axel and Hal claim that First Bank breached the January 15 agreement. Basing their suit on this so-called breach, they seek damages) or delete the phrase (Axel and Hal claim that First Bank breached the January 15 agreement. They seek damages of more than $10 million).

being Do not use *being* as a substitute for "because": "He missed the speech because [*not* being that] the plane was late." And delete *being* after "regarded as": "She is regarded as [*not* as being] the best dancer in the world."

between. *See* **among.**

between you and I Never! The preposition *between* requires pronouns in the objective case. Always and only "between you and me."

candid about

canvas, canvass *Canvas* is a cloth, used for sails and paintings. *Canvass* means "to examine systematically" or "to solicit, to question," as in a poll.

capable of

capital, capitol *Capital* is the city that is the seat of a government; *capitol* is the building.

Cardozo, Benjamin Note the correct spelling of his surname.

careless about, in, *or* of

case Change "It is often the case that lawyers are long-winded" to "Lawyers are often long-winded."

certainly Certainly overused; to be avoided. If something is certain, explain how or why it is certain, rather than merely asserting that it is.

character Correctly used to refer to a person's moral qualities or to a role in a play. Omit as a prop for an adjective: change "a speech of an inspiring character" to "an inspiring speech."

choose among *or* between

claim Restrict to the sense in which a plaintiff makes a claim in a complaint; do not use as a substitute for "assert," "insist," or "declare."

clue to

commence Use "begin."

completely Avoid [*not* Avoid completely]. *See* **emphatics.**

comprise *Comprise* means "to embrace or include": "The law firm comprises sixty partners and twenty associates." The alternative wording is

"The law firm is composed of [*or* consists of] sixty partners." A summary: The whole comprises the parts. The parts are comprised in the whole. The whole is composed of its parts. The parts compose [*or* constitute] the whole. Note that "comprised of" is nonstandard, although it is seen more and more.

concur in *or* with

confident of

contemptuous of

continuous, continual *Continuous* refers to an uninterrupted occurrence over time (a continuous vigil); *continual* means repeated at intervals (the continual banging of the shutters).

contractions Do not use contractions (isn't, don't, can't) in briefs or court memoranda.

convince of (*not* to)

correlation between *or* of

correspond to *or* with

criterion, criteria *Criterion* is singular, *criteria* plural. Do not follow the error made by the Supreme Court: "No consideration of the second or third criteria is necessary if a statute does not have a clearly secular purpose." 472 U.S. at 56.

curriculum *Curriculum* is singular, *curricula* plural.

data By etymology, a plural noun, although increasingly used as a singular. *See also* **plurals**.

de minimis If you must use this phrase, note the correct spelling.

debate over *or* about

deem Many lawyers love this word, for no apparent reason. As chairman of the Civil Aeronautics Board, Alfred E. Kahn wrote this memo to staff: "I once asked a young lawyer who wanted us to say 'we deem it inappropriate' to try that kind of language out on his children—and if they did not drive him out of the room with their derisive laughter, to disown them." Say, rather, "it is inappropriate."

delusion, illusion A *delusion* is a false belief; an *illusion* is a false perception.

dicta *Dicta* is a plural noun; the singular is *dictum. See also* **plurals**.

differ with, on, *or* from

different Omit this overworked modifier in sentences such as "We called on a dozen different people."

different from Purists insist that only *different from* is correct: "Frogs are different from [*not* than] toads."

differentiate among, between, *or* from

disappointed in *or* with

discreet, discrete *Discreet* means "judicious, circumspect, prudent, modest in approach or manner, unobtrusive"; *discrete* means "separate, disconnected, discontinuous."

disinterested, uninterested *Disinterested* means "not personally engaged in, impartial"; *uninterested* means "not interested, not caring, indifferent."

dissatisfied with

double negatives. See p. 123.

due to *Due to* is a prepositional phrase that modifies a noun: "Our loss was due to our injuries." It is equivalent to "attributable to," and it should not be used as a substitute for "owing to" or "because of."

educated about, for, *or* in

effect. *See* **affect.**

either-or words. *See* **absolute words.**

elude. *See* **allude.**

emend. *See* **amend.**

emphatics Opposite of hedge words, equally undesirable. Avoid trite and hackneyed phrases (well settled) and dogmatic intensifiers (clearly, plainly, without doubt, completely, flagrant, surely, certainly, indeed, obviously, beyond question). The bare adjective "false" is stronger than "completely untrue."

enormity Does not mean "extremely large, immense." *Enormity* has a moral connotation and means "a monstrous wrong."

equally as Redundant. Change "I was entitled to the reward equally as much as him" to "I was entitled to the reward equally with him" or "I was entitled to the reward as much as he." Change "Sam is equally as tall as George" to "Sam is as tall as George."

equivalent in *or* to

essential in, of, to, *or* for

etc. *Etc.* means "and so forth" or "and other things," and so "and etc." is always incorrect. This Latin abbreviation (for *et cetera*) should be used sparingly and never at the end of a list introduced by "for example" or "including."

evoke, invoke *Evoke* means "to draw out or elicit" (he tried to evoke her sympathy); *invoke* means "to call into use" (she invoked her right not to incriminate herself).

fact that A barbarism; avoid. For "owing to the fact that," substitute "because." For "in spite of the fact that," use "although" or "despite." Often, the phrase needs no replacement: "I was unaware of the fact that I was late" means "I was unaware I was late." Trim "The fact that he had not succeeded did not deter him" to "His failure did not deter him" or "He was not deterred even though he failed."

factor A legitimate term of art in commerce, but do not use it as a filler. Revise "Word processing is an important factor in getting out work" to read "Word processing is important to getting out work."

farther, further *Farther* refers to physical distance; *further* can refer to distance, but it has the additional sense of "additional," "more," "to a greater extent": a further [*not* farther] consideration.

fewer. *See* **less.**

first person. *See* **I.**

flagrant Avoid; *see* **emphatics.**

flaunt, flout *Flaunt* means "to show off ostentatiously." *Flout* means "to mock, to treat with contempt or disrespect, to disobey." Thus, "Flouting the laws of the city, some young people flaunted their nudity."

forbid to (*never* from)

foregoing Avoid it.

forthwith Avoid this silly lawyerism.

fortuitous, fortunate *Fortuitous* means "coincidental" or "accidental"; *fortunate* means "lucky."

free from, of, *or* in

gamut, gantlet, gauntlet. *See* **running the gamut.**

garnishee A noun (the garnishee protested); the verb is *garnish* (plaintiff seeks to garnish the wages).

gift A noun, not a verb. Avoid the redundant "free gift"—all gifts are free.

graduate from Older usage books insist on the form "she was graduated from law school," but "she graduated from law school" is now considered acceptable. Do not drop the preposition: "she graduated law school" is colloquial.

he/she. See p. 140.

hedge words Early on, lawyers learn to avoid speaking directly. They say "It would seem that it is raining out" when what they mean is "look, it's pouring." Avoid unnecessary qualifiers. See also p. 117.

herein Avoid. *See* **lawyerisms.**

hereinafter Avoid. *See* **lawyerisms.**

heretofore Avoid. *See* **lawyerisms**.

herewith Unnecessary. Adds nothing to the meaning of "I have completed and am returning to you herewith the questionnaire."

hint at

historic, historical *Historic* means "momentous" (a historic occasion); *historical* means "pertaining to history" (a historical account).

honorifics, titles Social or courtesy titles should be used sparingly. For example, write "Emily Jones," not "Ms. Emily Jones"; reserve the title for the second mention, with the surname alone ("Ms. Jones"). Be consistent: Don't refer to her sometimes as "Jones" and sometimes as "Ms. Jones," and if you refer to women as "Ms." use "Mr." for the men. In contrast, professional honorifics and titles—Dr., Professor, Senator, Judge—should precede any use of the full name or surname.

hopefully An adverb meaning "full of hope" (Hopefully, he awaited his wife's return). Often misused to mean "I hope," "we hope," or "it is to be hoped that." This sentence is incorrect: "Hopefully, it will stop raining so we can go out for a walk."

however When used to mean "in whatever manner," *however* is not set off by commas: "However you get to town, call me as soon as you arrive." When used to mean "but," *however* must be set off by a pair of commas: "The cat, however, had climbed down the tree." When used to join two sentences, *however* must be preceded by a semicolon and followed by a comma: "She agreed to meet him at ten o'clock; however, she was not there when he arrived." Place the word wherever it best conveys the contrast you are making. See also p. 163.

I When you mean "I," write "I." Avoid circumlocutions (the present author), passive constructions (it would seem), and prepositional phrases (in my opinion). See also p. 136.

I do not think "I do not think this proposition is true" puts the matter backwards. Instead, write "I think this proposition is false" or, better still, "This proposition is false."

identical with

if, whether After "say," "know," "ask," and "doubt," use *whether* rather than *if.* "I do not know whether this total is correct."

illusion. *See* **allusion**.

immensity. *See* **enormity**.

impact Do not use *impact* as a verb (only teeth are impacted). For "the breach of contract impacted on their plans," substitute "the breach of contract had an impact on their plans" or "the breach of contract ruined their plans."

impervious to

imply, infer *Imply* is what you do when you make a statement from which someone else will *infer* your meaning. "From the prints in the mud, she inferred that the fugitives were riding camels." "She was nervous about accusing the Senator directly, but she implied that he had cheated on his income taxes."

importantly The usage books disagree, but more prefer the introductory phrase "more important" to "more importantly." Reserve *importantly* to denote self-importance, as in "he walked about the room importantly."

impress into, upon, *or* with

improvement in, of, *or* upon

in terms of Flabby, wooden, useless. "It was a favorable case in terms of precedent" means "It was a favorable precedent."

in the event that Can always be reduced to "if."

incentive to *or* for

inconsistent with

incredible, incredulous *Incredible* means "unbelievable"; *incredulous* means "skeptical" or "unbelieving."

infer. *See* **imply**.

input Not a verb. If you must use this word, write "We need your input"—not "Please input your thoughts."

inquire into *or* of

inquiry into

insight into

instant case "This case" is preferable.

intended for Omit the redundant "for" in expressions such as "The secretary intended *for* those procedures to be the principal mechanism."

inter alia Use "among other things" or, better, don't use either the Latin or the English phrase; it is rarely necessary.

interest in

interface Not a verb, and the noun is best restricted to technical discussions of physics or computer technology.

interment, internment *Interment* means "burial"; *internment* refers to imprisonment or confinement, usually during wartime.

invoke. *See* **evoke.**

involved A weak verb that imparts little or no information. Edit "The *Yarrow* case involved a claim by an auctioneer for recovery of his expected commission" to read "In the *Yarrow* case, an auctioneer tried to recover his expected commission."

irony Not a synonym for "coincidence." *Irony* refers to an outcome contrary to what was generally expected or to a meaning contrary to the obvious meaning of the person making the utterance.

irritate. *See* **aggravate.**

it would seem that Avoid this hedge. For "It would seem that he is correct," substitute "He is correct."

its, it's Without the apostrophe, the word is a possessive pronoun (its origins); with the apostrophe the word is a contraction for "it is" (it's amazing) or "it has" (it's been raining).

judgment Note the spelling: no *e* between the *g* and the *m*.

kind Verbose when used to prop up an adjective. "A speech of a scintillating kind" is "a scintillating speech."

late Think carefully before you use "the late" to refer to a person. "The bill was signed by the late President Johnson" is illogical (he wasn't dead when he signed it). The term is generally not useful.

lawyerisms Avoid archaic flourishes: whereas, wherein, aforementioned, forthwith, heretofore, hereinafter, thereunto appertaining. Spurn rhetorical formulas (goes to the question of), and delete or translate musty Latin phrases *(arguendo, inter alia, supra).* Banish inflated substitutes for *the, this,* and *that:* Write "the statement," "this statement," or "that statement," not "said statement," "same statement," or "such statement."

In his last official act as general counsel of the U.S. Department of Commerce, Homer E. Moyer Jr. issued a memorandum on plain English and said this: "*Avoid legalisms.* Latin phrases, abbreviations, and other legalisms are the badges of legal writing. However, they are commonly redundant, usually pretentious, and invariably unnecessary. When legalisms punctuate a paragraph, readability suffers. Like lavish capitalization, frequent exclamation marks, and underscoring for emphasis, legalisms serve as crutches when plain English would nicely suffice. The addition of 'supra,' 'arguendo,' or 'inter alia' rarely amplifies a thought. Even more dispensable are 'therein,' 'hereinafter,' 'provided, however,' and similar rhetorical baggage. In almost all instances, 'herewith' is redundant, as in 'a copy is enclosed herewith.'"

Justice George Rose Smith of the Arkansas Supreme Court has said no lawyer should ever use these terms: "said" (in the sense of "aforesaid"): "I can do with another piece of that pie, dear; said pie is the best you've ever made"); "same" (similar sense: "I've mislaid my car keys; have you seen same?"); "such" (similar sense: "Sharon Kay stubbed her toe this afternoon, but such toe is all right now"); "hereinafter called" ("You'll get a kick out of what happened today to my secretary, hereinafter called Cuddles"); and *inter alia* ("it supplies information needed only by fools").

lay, lie *Lay* is a transitive verb (except as a nautical term: "laying about") that means "to put." Present tense is *lay* ("watch as I now lay the book on the table"); past tense, *laid* ("he laid the book on the table"); present participle, *laying* ("they are laying the new carpet"); past participle, *laid* ("he has already laid his plans"). *Lie* is an intransitive verb. Present tense is *lie* ("the dogs lie about in the kitchen"); past tense, *lay* ("yesterday she lay on the bed in pain"); present participle, *lying* ("the dogs are lying on the floor"); past participle, *lain* ("the dogs had lain there for hours").

lead, led *Lead* is the present tense of "to lead"; *led* is the past tense and the past participle (he led them, he has led them). All the nouns—whether pronounced with a long *e* (follow her lead) or a short *e* (made of lead)—are spelled the same way.

less, fewer *Less* refers to amount or quantity, *fewer* to number. "She has less space in her house than you have. Her house has fewer rooms."

lie. *See* lay.

like, as *Like* connects nouns and pronouns; *as* connects phrases and clauses. "She is just like her mother," but "She visited her mother as she did long ago."

like, such as In a series, *like* means "similar to but not an example of." Thus "Prodigies like Mozart are rare" is not about Mozart but about prodigies who resemble him. In contrast, "Athletes such as Smith should be ashamed of themselves" includes Smith in the gallery of those who should feel ashamed.

literally Overused and misused. *Literally* does not mean "figuratively." "We worked so hard we literally died" is nonsense.

loan *Loan* is a noun, the thing lent. The verb is *lend*.

masterful, masterly *Masterful* means "domineering, imperious, vigorous, powerful." *Masterly* means "possessing the skill or knowledge of a master."

mastery of *or* over

means of, to, *or* for

meddle in *or* with

media *Media* is plural, *medium* singular. *See also* **plurals**.

minister to

minuscule Note the spelling: think of "minus" (not "mini").

mirandize Jargon used by police officers, meaning "to read suspects their rights." Avoid.

mistrustful of

mitigate, militate *Mitigate* means "to make less severe" or "to soften" (The judge mitigated her sentence, reducing it to two years). *Militate* means "to weigh heavily" or "to have a substantial effect" (The budget deficit militated against increased spending).

motive for

Ms. *See* **honorifics, titles.**

nature Verbose. For "a speech of a compelling nature," substitute "a compelling speech."

negatives. See p. 123.

neither . . . nor The pair is "neither . . . nor" (*not* neither . . . or).

noisome, noisy *Noisome* means "disgusting, foul smelling"; *noisy* refers to sound.

nominalization. See p. 128.

not only . . . but also "Not only" must be followed by "but" or "but also," and each part of the pair must be correctly placed. For example: "Mr. Ciseros not only fails to cite a single authority in support of his contention, he fails to distinguish the authorities cited by defendants" should be changed to "Mr. Ciseros fails not only to cite a single authority to support his contention but also to distinguish the authorities whom defendants cite."

null and void Often redundant.

parameter This mathematical term does not mean "perimeter" or "limit"; it refers to a specifically defined type of variable—one that lawyers rarely encounter.

pass muster The expression means "to measure up"; the past tense is *passed muster* (note the spelling).

passive voice. See p. 131.

per se Not necessary per se; useful mainly to antitrust and libel lawyers.

peradventure Overused, as in "beyond peradventure."

plagiarism Note the spelling.

plainly. *See* **emphatics.**

pleased at, by, *or* with

plurals Although a few usage experts disagree, *data, media,* and *dicta* are plural nouns and require a plural verb ("the data are missing"). Collective nouns—*jury, staff, couple, class, management, team, company*—may be plural or singular, depending on the meaning: "The jury is dismissed" and "The jury are expected to observe this policy." The same is true of *all, what,* and *none:* "All was lost" and "All are well." *The number* is singular ("the number of variants is large"), but *a number* is plural ("a number of judges object"). One thing is certain about these uncertain words: They cannot be both singular and plural at once: "When the judge excuses them, the jury stand [*not* stands] up to leave."

pomposities Always prefer the short common word to the polysyllable. "Prefatory to our lunching together" means "before lunch." Here's a short list of words to avoid (and their replacements): ameliorate (improve), approximately (about), commence (begin), endeavor (try), finalize (end), implement (carry out), initiate (begin), proliferation (spread), purchase (buy), remuneration (pay), underprivileged (poor). See also p. 110.

portentous, pretentious *Portentous* means "momentous"; *pretentious* means "full of pretense, ostentatious." Note the spellings: "portentious" is not a word.

pre- The prefix is redundant in *preplanned, prearranged, pre-recorded,* and *pre-screened.* It is usually redundant in *preexisting* (a preexisting commitment), although *preexisting condition* arises in discussions of medical insurance.

precipitate, precipitous As an adjective, *precipitate* means "speeding headlong, moving rapidly and heedlessly, lacking deliberation." *Precipitous* means "extremely steep"; it describes terrain, not action.

prefer . . . to "He prefers delegating the duty of firing his subordinates to doing it himself" is correct. Do not mangle the syntax by writing "He prefers delegating the duty of firing his subordinates than doing it himself."

prejudice against, by, for, *or* in favor of

preoccupied with

prepositions This class of short words—*in, on, through, around, by, of, from, under*— can cause writers sleepless nights. Prepositions are highly idiomatic, not logical. Consider the meanings conveyed by *look after, look around, look at, look back, look down, look down on, look for, look forward to, look in, look in on, look into, look on, look out, look out for, look over, look to, look up, look up to,* and *look upon.* For guidance, consult the dictionary.

Careless writers often omit a needed preposition. For example, "she graduated law school" and "he shopped a store" should read "she graduated from" and "he shopped in [*or* at]."

Also, take care to avoid ending a sentence in a preposition that is not part of a fixed phrasal verb. "The plane has taken off" is fine (here, *off* serves as an adverb), but "Bob is the person I studied with" should be recast: "Bob is the person with whom I studied." (An oft-told anecdote provides another solution: The country bumpkin asked the city slicker, "Where's the theater at?" The city slicker replied, "My good man, don't you know that one does not end a sentence with a preposition?" The bumpkin rephrased his question: "Where's the theater at, jackass?")

prerequisite to

presently Historically, *presently* meant "soon" or "immediately." The newer use (many label it a misuse), meaning "now," is pretentious and confusing. When you mean "now," write "now."

principal, principle *Principal* is the main thing, the head of a school, or the money borrowed; *principle* is the rule or course of action we should follow.

prior to Pompous. Use "before."

process Redundant in phrases such as "editing process," "educational process," "litigation process," "negotiation process," "boarding process." Editing, education, litigation, negotiation, and boarding are all processes.

pursuant to An ugly lawyerism that can almost always be avoided. Instead of "pursuant to our phone call," write "As we discussed." Turn "pursuant to Rule 61" into "under Rule 61" or "by Rule 61" or "Rule 61 requires."

pursuit of

quid pro quo One of the rare Latin phrases that has no ready English substitute. It means "giving one valuable thing for another."

quotation marks Place closing quotation marks correctly: after a comma or period, but before a colon or a semicolon. Do not place opening or closing quotation marks around a lengthy passage that is indented and set off from the body of the text.

quote *Quote* is a verb (he quoted the decision); the noun is *quotation* (she deleted the long quotation).

ravage, ravish *Ravage* means "to destroy" (the marauders ravaged the village); *ravish* means "to enrapture or enchant" (the sonata ravished the audience) and also "to rape" (the soldiers ravished her in the barn).

reason about, on, with, *or* for

reason that Avoid the colloquial constructions "the reason is because" and "the reason is why." Instead of "The reason he fled is because he was scared," write "The reason he fled is that he was scared" or "He fled because he was scared."

redundancy Strip your prose of lawyerly redundancies: mutual agreement, written instrument, over and above, connected together, not identically the same, inhabitant actually resident, become progressively more difficult as one goes along. Here's a selection from Eric Partridge's long list (in *Usage and Abusage*): adequate enough, appear on the scene, collaborate together, continue on, equally as, file away, joint cooperation, meet together, mix together, new innovation, pair of twins, past history, penetrate into, really realize, repeat again, revert back, seldom ever, sink down, still continue, unite together, Sahara Desert, skirt around, Sierra mountains, advance planning, as never before in the past, strangled to death, true fate. And who can top Alexander Hamilton, who wrote in *Federalist* 33 that America must develop a "capacity to provide for future contingencies as they may happen." See also p. 124.

reference to A grotesque nominalization. Instead of "the letter makes reference to," write "the letter refers to."

regard for *or* to

regret to, over, *or* about

reluctant. *See* reticent.

remand back Redundant. *Remand* means "to send back."

render Use "give."

requirement for *or* of

res gestae Means "things done," but why say it? Use English.

resemblance among, between, of, *or* to

resentment against, at, *or* for

respect to

responsibility for

reticent, reluctant *Reticent* means "shy, unwilling to talk"; *reluctant* means "unwilling to act."

revert back Redundant. *Revert* means "to go back."

rhetorical questions They are often a weak device, aren't they? Use sparingly.

role of

run-on sentence. See p. 148.

running the gamut, gantlet, gauntlet *Running the gamut* refers to crossing the entire range of something. *Running the gauntlet* (or gantlet) means "taking whatever criticism or punishment is handed out." A *gauntlet* is also a glove, especially one that is thrown down as a challenge to a duel.

said Use only as a verb. Never use this archaic legalism as an adjective (*not* said defendant).

satisfaction of, in, *or* with

save harmless Archaic. Use "hold harmless."

secure in

serious Use sparingly; *see* **emphatics**.

sexism. See p. 121.

singular and plural *Court* is a singular noun; the pronoun referring to a court must be *it* (*not* they). In a series connected with *or*, the verb agrees with the last item in the series. *See also* **plurals**.

so . . . as. *See* **as . . . as**.

split infinitives. See p. 135.

strident, stringent *Strident* means "harsh, grating, shrill, or irritating" (strident language). *Stringent* means "exacting, strict, or severe" (stringent criteria).

subject matter Redundant, though often heard. Outside the discourse of jurisdiction, in which the rule writers have forced us to think about "subject matter jurisdiction," the phrase is never necessary. And there is no call, ever, for "subject matter area."

subsequent to A stuffy substitute for "after."

such as. *See* **like**.

suitable for *or* to

supersede Note the spelling.

supportive of Avoid. Instead of "The court was supportive of plaintiff's position," write "The court supported the plaintiff's position."

surely Avoid; it's surely a weak emphatic.

surprised at *or* by

sympathetic with, to, *or* toward

sympathize in *or* with

taboo words Many vogue words in English serve only to make the writer sound self-important: utilize, infrastructure, parameter. All the following words are too often used as stilted synonyms for simpler words: additionally, at this point in time, bottom line, determinant, disadvantaged, dysfunction, elements, explicate, factor (in a nonmathematical context), finalize, first priority, hopefully, impacts on, in-depth, input, insoluble (meaning "unsolvable"), infrastructure, interface, key (meaning "critical or major"), leanings, lifestyles, meaningful, menu (other than in a restaurant), mode, module, ongoing, outcome, output, paradigm, parameter, quantum, replicate, rubric, segmented (meaning "divided"), stance, subsystem, supportive, symbiosis, time frame, utilize, verbalize, viable.

taste for, in, *or* of

tendency to *or* toward

tortuous, torturous *Tortuous* means "winding, twisting, devious"; *torturous* means "inducing pain."

total and absolute Redundant; avoid.

totaled The use of *totaled* to describe an automobile (he totaled his car) is inappropriate in formal writing. Use "demolished," "destroyed," or "wrecked."

trust in, to, *or* with

try to One tries to do something (*never* try and do it).

undeniably Do not use. Few things are undeniable with two lawyers in town. No matter what point you wish to make, you cannot carry the day simply by asserting that your position is undeniably true or plainly correct.

unfavorable for, to, *or* toward

uninterested. *See* **disinterested.**

unique An either-or word that cannot be modified by "almost" or "very." *See also* **absolute word**s.

unmindful of

unpopular with

up Overused to bolster verbs that can stand on their own; delete the *up* in all of the following: climb up, end up, finish up, head up, loom up, polish up, rest up, rise up, saddle up, settle up, study up.

utilize Pompous and unnecessary. Use "use" instead.

vary from *or* with

venal, venial *Venal* means "corruptible, purchasable" (a politician who takes a bribe is venal). *Venial* means "forgivable," hence minor (jaywalking is a venial offense).

very Use sparingly; *see* **emphatics.**

vexed at *or* with

virtually Avoid this weasel word; if you cannot omit it, rewrite your sentence so that it does not require a hedge. For example: "In virtually every year from 1896 through 1981—with the exception of 1977 and 1978, when we incurred a tremendous oil bill because of the second OPEC crisis—we sold more goods and services abroad than we bought in return," wrote Robert Heilbroner in the *New Yorker;* deleting the "virtually" subtracts nothing from the meaning. In contrast, in "Numerous courts have examined exclusions virtually identical to those contained in the policies," the writer tosses in "virtually" to mask lazy thinking. Either the exclusions are identical or they are not. If they vary by only a word or two, the writer should say so and explain why these differences are insignificant.

vulnerable to

wary of

was, were *See* **were**.

well settled Avoid this overused phrase unless your precise point is that the matter is well settled.

were Use the subjunctive *were* to state a condition that is contrary to fact: "If she were not a corporate director [but she is], she would have no conflict of interest" or "The rule would not apply if this motion were filed in federal court [but it was not]."

where, when *Where* refers to space, location, geography; *when* to time or condition. Thus, "the risk of unintended hardship when (*not* where) a defendant dies during appeal."

whereas Avoid. *See* **lawyerisms**.

wherein Avoid. *See* **lawyerisms**.

whether. *See* **if**.

whether or not Whether to use "whether or not" depends on your meaning. If your point is that something will happen whichever condition comes to pass, include the "or not": "The game will go on whether or not it rains." Otherwise, you do not need the "or not": "Whether the terrorist spoke the truth is unknown."

which. See p. 137.

who, whom *Who* is the subject of a sentence or a clause; *whom* is the object. "Who poisoned whom?" "The defendant became angry and often violent with whoever opposed her" ["whoever" functions as the subject of "opposed"; the object of "angry with" is the clause "whoever opposed her"]. "Sally Smith, who the state says killed six husbands, is on trial here."

with respect to Overused. Reword.

without doubt Few things are without doubt. Avoid this emphatic.

would appear, would seem Avoid using *would* as a hedge. Instead of writing "it would appear that," write "it appears that" or, when possible, drop the "it appears that" and state your point.

AN EDITING CHECKLIST

Like children, flower gardens, and romantic relationships, your writing will benefit immeasurably from close attention. As a professional, you write documents that tell, explain, advocate, and persuade. Your success will depend on the logic, clarity, and strength of your prose. You can produce such prose only if you edit your drafts.

Here is a checklist that offers one reasonable way to ensure that your writing clearly expresses your thought and meaning. It is not the only way to proceed—after a little experimenting, you may find a procedure that suits you better. But this checklist underscores that you will work more efficiently if you edit in several discrete steps. Begin by looking at the structure of your document. Then consider problems related to length, clarity, and continuity. Conclude with a word-by-word proofreading.

EDIT FOR STRUCTURE

Major Sections

Will your reader understand the sequence and logic of the major sections of your document?

Place yourself among your intended audience and determine if the structure of the document makes sense. Consider whether you have incorrectly assumed knowledge of facts and law that your readers might not possess, whether you have answered all questions explicitly or fairly raised by your presentation, and whether each section sensibly flows from the one that preceded it. If the transitions between sections are confusing or do not work, you may need to reorder your discussion. Read through once and home in on the transitions to make sure they are effective.

Have you written a strong lead?

The lead—the first paragraph or two—requires special care. It must orient the reader to the document's content, approach, and purpose, and it should compel the reader to continue reading. Now that you have finished your document, make sure your original lead still works (or rewrite as necessary).

Here is a typical lead sentence in a memorandum written by a young associate in a law firm: "I have been asked to research our options with regard to a potential lawsuit." These are wasted words. First, why identify himself as the one asked to do the research? Of course he was asked or he would not be writing the memo. Second, why recite the assignment instead of giving the results? Third, why be vague about the lawsuit in question? The following lead points the way more quickly and clearly: "Our client, William Jones, has three options to consider before filing his suit against John Smith."

Does your conclusion show the reader you have accomplished what you set out to do?

Just as the lead provides a road map for a document, the concluding paragraph should show that you have reached your destination. Remember that some readers, upon rereading a document, look only at the lead or the conclusion. Take extra time in editing both.

Paragraphs

Does each paragraph have a topic sentence?

Each paragraph should contain one sentence—usually the first sentence—that presents the topic of that paragraph. The reader should be able to glean the substance of the document from the topic sentences alone.

> *A paragraph lacking a topic sentence:* Judge Jones begins by describing the facts. After considering each element of the statute, she summarizes reasons for believing that the plaintiff might prevail. But after 50 pages she shows that each argument was fallacious, and eventually she gives judgment for the defendant.

> *Revision:* Judge Jones's opinion may mislead the reader who does not read far enough. In the first fifty pages, she describes the facts, considers each element of the statute, and summarizes the reasons that the plaintiff might prevail. But she then shows that each argument is fallacious, and she grants judgment to the defendant.

Is the topic flow consistent within each paragraph?

The sentence topics must be closely related in each paragraph. If they are not, you may need to relocate the unrelated points. Look to see whether your sentence tells its story or disguises it by focusing on some other topic.

Are the transitions between sentences and paragraphs coherent?

Make sure that your reader will understand why your sentences follow each other within paragraphs and why one paragraph follows another.

> *Faulty transition:* The lawyers have been working on the brief all week. It is due in court at 3 PM. However, they might cajole the judge into granting an extension.

Revision: The lawyers have been working on the brief all week, and now they are running out of time. The brief is due in court at 3 PM, but it will require at least another day's work. However, they can probably obtain an extension.

EDIT FOR LENGTH

Is every word necessary or useful to the points you are making?
What subsidiary issues and minor points can you prune or eliminate? First (and second and even third) drafts always contain verbiage. You can surely shed more than a quarter of your original words without destroying the document's sense.

Most of us have been taught that length equals quality and effort. The lengthier paper, we falsely assume, takes more time to write than the short one.

Cutting should be done in two steps: take a "macro" chop and then a "micro" slice.
The macro chopping excises unnecessary substantive discussion. The micro slice removes clutter, verbiage, obviousness, windy phrases, and redundancies.

To combat verbosity, play a game: Pretend that you will be paid inversely to the number of words you write—or that *you* must pay for the words you use. Chop, cut, slice.

Are your sentences too long? Can you trim or split them?
Remember that the maxim "one thought per sentence" does not mean "one sentence per thought." A complex thought may require two or three sentences.

A simple test: Read the sentence aloud. If you have to take a breath or if you get lost in your recital, the chances are your sentence is too long.

EDIT FOR CLARITY

Excise Latinisms, legalese, bureaucratese, and pomposity.
Most legal jargon is fuzzy and quite avoidable. In *Plain English for Lawyers,* Professor Richard C. Wydick of the University of California School of Law at Davis writes: "Lawyerisms are words like *aforementioned, whereas, res gestae,* and *hereinafter.* They give writing a legal smell, but they carry little or no legal substance. When they are used in writing addressed to nonlawyers, they baffle and annoy. When used in other legal writing, they give a false sense of precision and sometimes obscure a dangerous gap in analysis."

Eliminate fuzzy phrases.

Why say "concerning the matter of" or "with regard to" when "about" will do just fine?

Fix usage mistakes.

Over the centuries, English usage has become a matter of custom, not logic, and lawyers disregard at their peril the consensus of usage experts. (We discuss the most common errors in the Usage Notes.)

Double-check troublesome words.

Make sure that the words you use mean what you think they mean. You need a comprehensive dictionary as your constant ally.

Delete throat-clearing phrases and clichés.

A throat-clearing phrase is one that you might say aloud to stall for time when thinking about what you want to say. In your writing, you have no reason to stall. Instead of "The next issue I want to deal with is," write "The next issue is . . ."

A cliché is an overworked expression that signals a writer's laziness or fatuousness. Though useful in speech, clichés brand the writer as inexperienced and boring.

Rewrite negatives.

Try to rewrite negative statements in the affirmative. For "he did not remember," substitute "he forgot."

Identify all nominalizations and replace as many as you can.

Nominalization freezes the action of a verb into a noun. Put the action of the sentence in the verb; remove it from the noun and eliminate the flabby verb that carries the nominalization.

> *Unnecessary nominalization:* We carried out an analysis of the blood samples.
> *Revision:* We analyzed the blood samples.

Search for passive verbs and justify them or remove them.

Make the agent of the action the subject of the sentence; don't omit the agent unless you have a good reason.

> *Unnecessary passive:* The lease was signed by the tenants.
> *Revision:* The tenants signed the lease.

Eliminate strings of prepositions.

A string of prepositional phrases obscures the meaning or forces the reader to absorb too many twists and turns of syntax, as in: "If judges will express their ill-informed evaluations *of* cases they know little about, lawyers will make use *of* those expressions, both *as* advocates and occasionally *for* the less worthy purpose *of* passing the buck *of* responsibility *for* the bad news they should have given *to* clients *as* their own judgments *of* the merits *of* the clients' positions."

Rewrite sentences that begin with "there is [are, was, were]."
Impersonal constructions obscure the action, demote your main point to a subordinate *that* clause, and add nothing to the meaning. Instead of "There is no case law that specifically addresses the question," write "No case law specifically addresses the question."

Distinguish between *that* and *which*.
That introduces a clause meant to define the noun it follows. A comma never precedes *that* when used in this way. *Which*, always preceded by a comma, introduces subsidiary information. Compare "He read the brief, which was typed yesterday" with "He read the brief that was typed yesterday." The first sentence suggests that there is only one brief; the information about typing is a subsidiary fact. The second sentence implies the existence of more than one brief; the information about typing serves to identify the particular brief.

Fix the following errors:

FAULTY SUBJECT-VERB AGREEMENT

Faulty agreement: Mere recitations of the legal issue presented to the court does not constitute sufficient pleading.

Revision: Mere recitations of the legal issue presented to the court do not constitute sufficient pleading.

DANGLING PARTICIPLES

Dangling participle: Before addressing the specific paragraphs in the complaint, some general comments are in order.

Revision: Before addressing the specific paragraphs in the complaint, I offer these general comments.

MISPLACED MODIFIERS

Misplaced modifier: Likewise, defendants' assertion that injunctive relief is only to be granted when trade secrets are involved is simply not the law.

Revision: Likewise, defendants err in asserting that injunctive relief is to be granted only when trade secrets are at stake.

SKEWED PARALLELISM

Elements connected by conjunctions (for example, *and, but, or, rather than*) must have the same grammatical form.

Faulty parallelism: Committees usually make recommendations to the full board rather than taking official actions of their own.

Revision: Committees usually make recommendations to the full board rather than take official actions of their own.

SPLIT INFINITIVES

Placing an adverb immediately after the "to" in the infinitive form of a verb ("to rapidly walk") splits the infinitive. Careful writers avoid splitting an infinitive when they can. Some infinitives, however, must be split: "The cost is projected to more than double."

MISSING OR MISPLACED ANTECEDENTS

A missing antecedent—the word to which a later pronoun refers—can make even the simplest sentence confusing. For example, in the sentence "The bank robber brandished his gun about the room, which was seen by all the hostages," the syntax suggests that "which" refers to the room, but the sense suggests that it refers to the action in the preceding clause as a whole. Rewrite it as follows: "The bank robber brandished his gun about the room, a gesture seen by all the hostages."

INCORRECT USE OF POSSESSIVE PRONOUNS

A pronoun that modifies a gerund (a verb ending in "ing" used as a noun) ordinarily must be in the possessive form.

Incorrect: The police objected to them carrying guns.

Revision: The police objected to their carrying guns.

EDIT FOR CONTINUITY

Now start over with a clean version of your document, one that incorporates the changes you made in your earlier edits.

Do first references to persons, cases, or other particular things fully identify them?

Do your transitions still make sense?

Are your cross-references accurate?

If you state that something is mentioned "above" or "below," make sure these locators are correct. Reverify all page-number cross-references. (If you write at the computer, you can eliminate this step by using the automatic update feature for page-number cross-references.)

PROOFREAD

Check your spelling.
Even if your document has been run through a spell-checker, read it again, dictionary at your side. Spell-checkers aren't perfect, and they do not catch homonym errors ("there" for "their").

Correct other typographical errors (missing words, tense endings, plurals).

Enforce a consistent editorial style.
Be consistent in such matters as capitalization, use of honorifics, abbreviations, spelling out of numbers, and citation forms.

Check your punctuation.

Finally, put your document aside; let it rest. Then read it one more time from the perspective of your intended audience.

We have collected the following sentences from lawyers' letters, memoranda, contracts, and articles; judges' opinions; student papers; and newspaper articles. We invite you identify the problems and propose revisions. Our suggestions are in the section that follows, beginning on p. 241.

1. While the Supreme Court frequently makes history through its landmark decisions, it also often uses history to reach them. This practice has not been without its critics.

2. It is the defendants' contention that, conceding everything in the complaint, no viable cause of action is made out.

3. The arbitrator shall deal only with the matter which occasioned his appointment and shall cease to exist on the final decision of that matter.

4. It is the Court's determination that plaintiff's failure to include such information renders the summons jurisdictionally defective. Knowledge of the date of commencement of the action would inform defendant as to whether process was served within the time frame imposed by CPLR 306-b(a) and would necessarily affect defendant's defense strategies relating to the statute of limitations.

5. This will acknowledge receipt of your letter dated November 22, 2001. Unfortunately, in view of the fact that we receive numerous applications for associates, we are unable to interview all qualified applicants.

6. Defendant next moves for a bill of particulars pursuant to C.P.L. §200.95, notwithstanding that the information sought therein is being requested for the first time within the instant motion. A prior filing of a request for particulars is a condition precedent for court intervention to assist a defendant who moves for a bill of particulars. Having failed to previously request this information, this aspect of defendant's motion should be summarily denied.

7. The Governor has not received the letter. We are deeply disappointed with Monsignor Duffy for releasing this to the media simultaneously with it being sent to the Governor.

8. While studios may occasionally edit a movie to conform to looser or stricter foreign standards its almost unheard of for them to show one country a print that ends differently.

9. Since this report contains highly sensitive political information, I'm sending it only to those persons whom I firmly believe will support my candidacy for president.

10. If you are serious about growing your practice, choose Rainmaker as your Marketing Partner. . . . Your success is a direct reflection of our ability, a responsibility we take seriously.

11. Opposing counsel must make an effort to interpose his objection before the witness answers.

12. This statement is written in support of the I-140 petition by The Medical College to classify Dr. X as a permanent immigrant employee of our Center, under the category of outstanding researcher because Dr. X is a versatile scientist and a major contributor to our research he is an invaluable asset to our Medical Center.

13. We are in receipt of your letter requesting our representation with reference to the obtaining of your U.S. permanent residence status. Please note that, with regard to our previous discussion with you during our telephone and office conferences, we do not usually handle your type of case.

14. Although this fire was determined to have originated in arson, there is virtually no evidence implicating the defendant in its responsibility.

15. We would like to thank you for your thoughtfully written letter.

16. There are several possible explanations as to why I and others sometimes tumble over an accounting note or indenture description.

17. The present section 304(a) carries over from section 24 of the 1909 Act the provision for renewal of "posthumous works" by the then copyright owner, but the act continues to have no definition of that phrase.

18. The Illinois supreme court properly recognized that the detective's affidavit might be capable of supplementing the anonymous letter with information sufficient to permit a determination of probable cause.

19. The basis for the defense, according to the lawyers, is a 1990 case in which a federal court in Oregon ruled that a criminal obstruction-of-justice statute couldn't be stretched to apply to a document dispute arising from a civil case.

20. Sworn or certified copies of all papers or parts thereof referred to in an affidavit shall be attached thereto or served therewith.

21. The complaint alleges that the bartender is liable because Hank's injuries were caused by Tex's intoxicated state.

22. We think that the officers' conduct was more intrusive than necessary to effectuate an investigative detention otherwise authorized by the *Terry* line of cases.

23. The Department of State has for some time had under consideration the question whether the practice of the Government in granting immunity from suit to foreign governments made parties defendant in the courts of the United States without their consent should not be changed.

24. We do hereby affix our names to show our waiver of notice of said meeting.

25. The court ordered that his mother permit him to undergo such surgery as in the judgment of the Commissioner of Health upon advice of duly qualified surgeons shall be necessary, and during such surgery the surgeons are authorized to administer such blood transfusions as in their judgment may be necessary.

26. This appeal involves the issue whether a child suffering from Hodgkin's disease whose parents failed to follow the recommendation of an attending physician to have their child treated by radiation and chemotherapy, but, rather, placed their child under the care of physicians advocating nutritional or metabolic therapy, including laetrile, is a "neglected child" within the meaning of section 1012 of the Family Court Act.

27. The trial court refused permission for the plaintiff's counsel to use a blackboard in the examination of a witness to illustrate his testimony with reference to the *locus in quo* of the accident.

28. Senior Management's reaction to the Smith proposal was completely negative.

29. A number of limitations exist with respect to depreciation deductions. Most of these limitations on the depreciation deduction involve the class of property to which the deduction applies. As a general rule only property used in a trade or business or used for the production of income may be the subject of the depreciation deduction.

30. Notwithstanding anything herein contained, if Licensee shall file a voluntary petition in bankruptcy, or be adjudicated a bankrupt or be adjudged insolvent by any State or Federal Court of competent jurisdiction, and such adjudication or appointment shall not be vacated within

sixty (60) days thereafter, or if Licensee shall file under the Bankruptcy
Act a petition or answer for reorganization, or if any involuntary petition shall be filed under the Bankruptcy Act for reorganization and
such petition shall be approved, or if there shall be made a general assignment of Licensee's assets for the benefit of creditors or if a receiver
shall be appointed for the property and business of Licensee and the
same shall not be vacated within sixty (60) days thereafter, or in the
event of any assignment or transfer by Licensee in violation of the provisions of paragraph 11(a) hereof, or the complete liquidation, dissolution or the termination of the existence of Licensee, or any sale, transfer
or assignment by Licensee of the photoplay and the negative and copyright thereof, as distinguished from distribution of the photoplay by Licensor (each of the foregoing being hereinafter referred to as "occurrence"), then, upon the happening of the first said occurrences, all
rights herein granted to Licensee shall terminate and come to an end,
and simultaneously therewith all unpaid, but not due, fixed payments
and all accrued, but unpaid, percentage payments shall then become accelerated and due and payable at that time.

There are many ways to fix each of the problem sentences; in this section we show one or two. In some cases, we have had to guess at the writer's intentions.

1. While the Supreme Court frequently makes history through its landmark decisions, it also often uses history to reach them. This practice has not been without its critics.

   PROBLEM: The negative wording in the second sentence.

   SOLUTION 1: This practice has its critics.

   SOLUTION 2: The Court's use of history has sometimes been criticized.

2. It is the defendants' contention that, conceding everything in the complaint, no viable cause of action is made out.

   PROBLEMS: Nominalizations, vague "everything," puffy emphatic ("viable"), and passive voice.

   SOLUTION: The defendants contend that even if all allegations are true, the complaint does not state a cause of action.

3. The arbitrator shall deal only with the matter which occasioned his appointment and shall cease to exist on the final decision of that matter.

   PROBLEMS: It must be the appointment—not the arbitrator—that will "cease to exist," and "cease to exist" is wordy.

   SOLUTION: The arbitrator shall deal only with the matter for which he was appointed, and the appointment shall terminate when he issues a final decision.

4. It is the Court's determination that plaintiff's failure to include such information renders the summons jurisdictionally defective. Knowledge of the date of commencement of the action would inform defendant as to whether process was served within the time frame imposed by CPLR 306-b(a) and would necessarily affect defendant's defense strategies relating to the statute of limitations.

PROBLEMS: Nominalizations and prepositions galore.

SOLUTION: The Court holds that the summons is jurisdictionally defective because the plaintiff failed to state when the action commenced. The defendant is entitled to know the date, so that he would know whether process was served within the time allowed under CPLR 306-b(a) and could determine whether the statute of limitations applied.

5. This will acknowledge receipt of your letter dated November 22, 2001. Unfortunately, in view of the fact that we receive numerous applications for associates, we are unable to interview all qualified applicants.

PROBLEM: Starchy tone is inappropriate for a note that will disappoint a job seeker.

SOLUTION: Thank you for your letter of November 22, 2001. We receive many applications from able lawyers and, unfortunately, we cannot invite all of them for an interview.

6. Defendant next moves for a bill of particulars pursuant to C.P.L. §200.95, notwithstanding that the information sought therein is being requested for the first time within the instant motion. A prior filing of a request for particulars is a condition precedent for court intervention to assist a defendant who moves for a bill of particulars. Having failed to previously request this information, this aspect of defendant's motion should be summarily denied.

PROBLEM: Wordy and repetitive.

SOLUTION: The defendant for the first time seeks information in its motion under C.P.L. §200.95 for a bill of particulars. This request should be summarily denied because the rule requires the defendant to have sought the information before asking the court for help in obtaining it.

7. The Governor has not received the letter. We are deeply disappointed with Monsignor Duffy for releasing this to the media simultaneously with it being sent to the Governor.

PROBLEMS: The second sentence obscures the sequence of events. The use of "this" (to refer to the letter) is awkward. The "it" is a fused participle.

SOLUTION: We are deeply disappointed that Monsignor Duffy released the letter to the media when he sent it to the Governor.

8. While studios may occasionally edit a movie to conform to looser or stricter foreign standards its almost unheard of for them to show one country a print that ends differently.

PROBLEMS: The misuse of "its" for "it's" is inexcusable—but the contraction "it's" is not acceptable in formal writing. We need a comma after the introductory dependent clause ("While . . . standards"). The sentence could be tightened by eliminating the filler "it is," the bulky "almost unheard of," and the off-key "print that ends differently."

SOLUTION: While studios may occasionally edit a movie to conform to looser or stricter foreign standards, they almost never release a version with a different ending.

9. Since this report contains highly sensitive political information, I'm sending it only to those persons whom I firmly believe will support my candidacy for president.

PROBLEM: The "whom" should be "who," since it is the subject of the clause "will support my candidacy" and not the object of the clause "I firmly believe."

SOLUTION: . . . to those persons who I firmly believe will support my candidacy . . .

10. If you are serious about growing your practice, choose Rainmaker as your Marketing Partner. . . . Your success is a direct reflection of our ability, a responsibility we take seriously.

PROBLEMS: Granted, advertising copy make take some liberties, but the second sentence tells us that the consulting firm takes responsibility for its own ability, rather than for its clients' success. Also, some usage experts counsel against the nonagricultural use of "grow" and would substitute "expand" or "increase."

SOLUTION 1: . . . We take seriously our responsibility to make you successful.

SOLUTION 2: . . . We work hard to ensure your success, a responsibility we take seriously.

11. Opposing counsel must make an effort to interpose his objection before the witness answers.

PROBLEM: Nominalizations.

SOLUTION: Opposing counsel must object before the witness answers.

12. This statement is written in support of the I-140 petition by The Medical College to classify Dr. X as a permanent immigrant employee of our Center, under the category of outstanding researcher because Dr. X is a versatile scientist and a major contributor to our research he is an invaluable asset to our Medical Center.

PROBLEMS: This is a run-on sentence. It is also wordy, and a comma is needed after the clause "under the category of outstanding researcher."

SOLUTION 1: This statement supports The Medical College's I-140 petition to classify Dr. X as a permanent immigrant employee of our Center, under the category of outstanding researcher, because he is a versatile scientist and a major contributor to our research. He is an invaluable asset to our Medical Center.

SOLUTION 2: The Medical College submits this I-140 petition to classify Dr. X as a permanent immigrant employee under the category of outstanding researcher. Dr. X is a versatile scientist, a major contributor to our research, and an invaluable asset to our Medical Center.

13. We are in receipt of your letter requesting our representation with reference to the obtaining of your U.S. permanent residence status. Please note that, with regard to our previous discussion with you during our telephone and office conferences, we do not usually handle your type of case.

PROBLEM: The nominalizations contribute to the stuffiness of a letter to a potential client.

SOLUTION: We have received your letter asking us to assist you in obtaining U.S. permanent residence status. As you may recall from our conversations, we do not usually handle this type of case.

14. Although this fire was determined to have originated in arson, there is virtually no evidence implicating the defendant in its responsibility.

PROBLEMS: Wordy, convoluted, and ambiguous. Does "virtually no evidence" mean that there is *some* evidence or no convincing evidence?

SOLUTION 1: No evidence suggests that the defendant was the arsonist who started this fire.

SOLUTION 2: This fire began as arson, but no evidence points to the defendant as the arsonist.

15. We would like to thank you for your thoughtfully written letter.

PROBLEM: Redundant.

SOLUTION: Thank you for your thoughtful letter.

16. There are several possible explanations as to why I and others sometimes tumble over an accounting note or indenture description.

PROBLEMS: Wordy ("there are," "several possible," "as to"). In this context, "tumble" seems a typographical error.

SOLUTION: Readers, including me, sometimes stumble over an accounting note or indenture description for the following reasons.

17. The present section 304(a) carries over from section 24 of the 1909 Act the provision for renewal of "posthumous works" by the then copyright owner, but the act continues to have no definition of that phrase.

    PROBLEMS: Wordy, owing to nominalizations and the passive voice. The carryover of the provision from the 1909 Act is not the main point, and it can be demoted to a subordinate clause.

    SOLUTION: The present section 304(a), like its predecessor section 24 of the 1909 Act, permits the then copyright owner to renew "posthumous works" but fails to define that phrase.

18. The Illinois supreme court properly recognized that the detective's affidavit might be capable of supplementing the anonymous letter with information sufficient to permit a determination of probable cause.

    PROBLEM: Verbose nominalizations.

    SOLUTION: . . . the detective's affidavit might supplement the anonymous letter with sufficient information to show probable cause.

19. The basis for the defense, according to the lawyers, is a 1990 case in which a federal court in Oregon ruled that a criminal obstruction-of-justice statute couldn't be stretched to apply to a document dispute arising from a civil case.

    PROBLEMS: The actors (the lawyers) and the action (basing their defense on a decision) are both lost in the clutter. Also, the contraction is too informal.

    SOLUTION: The lawyers base their defense on a 1990 federal decision that obstruction-of-justice statutes do not cover a document dispute in a civil case.

20. Sworn or certified copies of all papers or parts thereof referred to in an affidavit shall be attached thereto or served therewith.

    PROBLEMS: Archaic, stuffy, and verbose.

    SOLUTION: Sworn or certified copies of documents (or their parts) must be served with or attached to the affidavit in which they are mentioned.

21. The complaint alleges that the bartender is liable because Hank's injuries were caused by Tex's intoxicated state.

    PROBLEM: Non sequitur: The intoxicated state did not cause the injuries.

SOLUTION: The complaint alleges that the bartender is liable to Hank for injuries caused by Tex while intoxicated.

22. We think that the officers' conduct was more intrusive than necessary to effectuate an investigative detention otherwise authorized by the *Terry* line of cases.

PROBLEMS: The empty "effectuate" lengthens the sentence; the empty "We think" demotes the main point (the characterization of the detention) to the subordinate "that" clause. The "otherwise authorized" turns the matter inside-out, and the "line of" is filler.

SOLUTION: The investigative detention was unlawful because the officers' conduct was more intrusive than permitted under the *Terry* cases.

23. The Department of State has for some time had under consideration the question whether the practice of the Government in granting immunity from suit to foreign governments made parties defendant in the courts of the United States without their consent should not be changed.

PROBLEMS: The subject "practice of the Government" and its predicate "should not be changed" are too far apart, and the question is whether the practice should be changed [*not* "should not be changed"].

SOLUTION: For some time the Department of State has been considering whether to change the practice of the government in granting immunity from suit to foreign governments made parties defendant without their consent in the courts of the United States.

24. We do hereby affix our names to show our waiver of notice of said meeting.

PROBLEMS: Archaisms, two nominalizations, verbose.

SOLUTION: We sign to show that we have waived notice of the meeting.

25. The court ordered that his mother permit him to undergo such surgery as in the judgment of the Commissioner of Health upon advice of duly qualified surgeons shall be necessary, and during such surgery the surgeons are authorized to administer such blood transfusions as in their judgment may be necessary.

PROBLEMS: Overuse of "such" and wordy nominalizations make for a fifty-word sentence.

SOLUTION: The court ordered that his mother permit him to undergo the surgery deemed necessary by the Commissioner of Health and qualified surgeons, and the court authorized the surgeons to administer blood transfusions as needed.

26. This appeal involves the issue whether a child suffering from Hodgkin's disease whose parents failed to follow the recommendation of an attending physician to have their child treated by radiation and chemotherapy, but, rather, placed their child under the care of physicians advocating nutritional or metabolic therapy, including laetrile, is a "neglected child" within the meaning of section 1012 of the Family Court Act.

    PROBLEMS: The subject "a child suffering from Hodgkin's disease" and its predicate "is a 'neglected child'" are too far apart. The constructions "involves the issue whether" and "the recommendation of" clutter this complicated sentence.

    SOLUTION: This appeal asks whether a child suffering from Hodgkin's disease is "neglected" within the meaning of section 1012 of the Family Court Act when the parents do not follow the attending physician's recommendation that their child be treated by radiation and chemotherapy but instead entrust the child to physicians who advocate nutritional or metabolic therapy, including laetrile.

27. The trial court refused permission for the plaintiff's counsel to use a blackboard in the examination of a witness to illustrate his testimony with reference to the locus in quo of the accident.

    PROBLEMS: Nominalizations; unnecessary Latin phrase.

    SOLUTION: The trial court refused to permit the plaintiff's counsel to use a blackboard while examining a witness about the accident site.

28. Senior Management's reaction to the Smith proposal was completely negative.

    PROBLEMS: Nominalization, empty emphatic ("completely"), negative wording. The actors, not their reaction, should be the grammatical subject, and the sentence should tell us what they did.

    SOLUTION 1: Senior Management rejected the Smith proposal.

    SOLUTION 2: Senior Management vehemently denounced the Smith proposal.

29. A number of limitations exist with respect to depreciation deductions. Most of these limitations on the depreciation deduction involve the class of property to which the deduction applies. As a general rule only property used in a trade or business or used for the production of income may be the subject of the depreciation deduction.

    PROBLEMS: Verbose, repetitive, and muddied by irrelevant propositions.

SOLUTION: Depreciation deductions are limited. Generally, the deduction may be taken only for property used in a trade, business, or other income-producing activity.

30. Notwithstanding anything herein contained, if Licensee shall file a voluntary petition in bankruptcy, or be adjudicated a bankrupt or be adjudged insolvent by any State or Federal Court of competent jurisdiction, and such adjudication or appointment shall not be vacated within sixty (60) days thereafter, or if Licensee shall file under the Bankruptcy Act a petition or answer for reorganization, or if any involuntary petition shall be filed under the Bankruptcy Act for reorganization and such petition shall be approved, or if there shall be made a general assignment of Licensee's assets for the benefit of creditors or if a receiver shall be appointed for the property and business of Licensee and the same shall not be vacated within sixty (60) days thereafter, or in the event of any assignment or transfer by Licensee in violation of the provisions of paragraph 11(a) hereof, or the complete liquidation, dissolution or the termination of the existence of Licensee, or any sale, transfer or assignment by Licensee of the photoplay and the negative and copyright thereof, as distinguished from distribution of the photoplay by Licensor (each of the foregoing being hereinafter referred to as "occurrence"), then, upon the happening of the first said occurrences, all rights herein granted to Licensee shall terminate and come to an end, and simultaneously therewith all unpaid, but not due, fixed payments and all accrued, but unpaid, percentage payments shall then become accelerated and due and payable at that time.

PROBLEMS: The point of the provision (the termination of the license) does not appear until the end, the conditions (if . . . or if . . . or if) that trigger the termination are run together, and the redundancies and surplus phrases further obscure the point. (Arthur Ettinger, who submitted this provision from a licensing agreement, asked, "Why do they call it legalese?" It should be called "legalhard.")

SOLUTION: When any of the following conditions occurs, all rights granted to the Licensee shall terminate and both (a) unpaid, but not due, fixed payments, and (b) all accrued, but unpaid, percentage payments shall be accelerated and payable:

(1) The Licensee files a voluntary petition in bankruptcy, etc.

THE ESSENTIAL REFERENCE SHELF

Some books are for fun, some for study, and some for instant reference. Here are books that should be within easy reach at your desk:

1. An unabridged dictionary. Perhaps *Webster's Third New International Dictionary of the English Language,* unabridged ed. (Merriam-Webster, 2000) or the *Random House Unabridged Dictionary,* revised 2d ed. (Random House, 1994).

2. A comprehensive thesaurus, with words arranged in alphabetical order. Perhaps the *Merriam-Webster Collegiate Thesaurus* (Merriam-Webster, 1994).

3. An up-to-date usage book. Probably Bryan A. Garner, *A Dictionary of Modern American Usage* (Oxford University Press, 1998) or *The Merriam-Webster Dictionary of English Usage* (Merriam-Webster, 1989).

4. A basic work on grammar. For example, Karen Elizabeth Gordon, *The Deluxe Transitive Vampire: A Handbook of Grammar for the Innocent, the Eager, and the Doomed* (Pantheon Books, 1993), sugarcoated for delightful reading; George O. Curme, *A Grammar of the English Language,* 2 volumes (Verbatim, 1978), the standard work; or Sidney Greenbaum, *The Oxford English Grammar* (Oxford University Press, 1996), the most comprehensive modern work.

5. R. W. Burchfield, ed., *The New Fowler's Modern English Usage,* 3d ed. (Oxford University Press, 1996).

6. Joseph M. Williams, *Style: Ten Lessons in Clarity and Grace,* 6th ed. (Addison Wesley Longman, 1999). The best short work on how to achieve clarity in prose.

7. William Strunk Jr. and E. B. White, *The Elements of Style,* 4th ed. (Allyn & Bacon, 2000). Thin but essential.

8. David Mellinkoff, *The Language of the Law* (Little, Brown, 1963). Magisterial, a work no lawyer should ignore.

9. A competent book on editing. One of the best is Claire Kehrwald Cook, *Line by Line* (Houghton Mifflin, 1985).

10. A standard composition handbook. One of these will do: Edward D. Johnson, *The Handbook of Good English* (Washington Square Press, 1991), Thomas S. Kane, *The New Oxford Guide to Writing* (Oxford University Press, 1994), or Richard M. Weaver, *A Rhetoric and Composition Handbook* (William Morrow, 1974).

Books on writing and language are plentiful. Listed below are works that we have found interesting, helpful, fun, or quirky.

BOOKS ON USAGE

Bernstein, Theodore M. *The Careful Writer.* Atheneum, 1968.
———. *Miss Thistlebottom's Hobgoblins.* Atheneum, 1971.
———. *Dos, Don'ts & Maybes of English Usage.* Times Books, 1977.
Claiborne, Robert. *Saying What You Mean.* W. W. Norton, 1986.
Copperud, Roy H. *American Usage and Style: The Consensus.* Van Nostrand Reinhold, 1980.
Fiske, Robert Hartwell. *The Writer's Digest Dictionary of Concise Writing.* Writer's Digest, 1996.
Follett, Wilson. *Modern American Usage.* Hill & Wang, 1966.
Fowler, H. W. *A Dictionary of Modern English Usage.* 2d ed. revised by Sir Ernest Gowers. Clarendon Press, 1965.
Hook, J. N. *The Grand Panjandrum.* Macmillan, 1980.
Kilpatrick, James J. *The Writer's Art.* Andrews, McMeel & Parker, 1984.
Morris, William and Mary Morris. *Harper Dictionary of Contemporary Usage.* Harper & Row, 1985.
Partridge, Eric. *Usage & Abusage.* Revised ed. Penguin Books, 1973.
Pei, Mario and Salvatore Ramondino. *A Dictionary of Foreign Terms.* Dell, 1974.
Safire, William. *On Language.* Avon, 1981.
———. *In Love with Norma Loquendi.* Random House, 1994.

SHORTER DICTIONARIES AND THESAURUSES

The American Heritage College Dictionary. 3d ed. Houghton Mifflin, 1997.
The American Heritage Dictionary of the English Language. 4th ed. Houghton Mifflin, 2000.

McCutcheon, Marc. *Roget's Super Thesaurus*. 2d ed. Writer's Digest Books, 1998.

Merriam-Webster's Collegiate Dictionary. 10th ed. Merriam-Webster, 1998.

Merriam-Webster's Collegiate Thesaurus. Merriam-Webster, 1994.

The Oxford Dictionary and Thesaurus, American Edition. Oxford University Press, 1996.

Random House Webster's College Dictionary. 2d revised ed. Random House, 2000.

Webster's New World College Dictionary. 4th ed. Hungry Minds, 1999.

GUIDES TO WRITING

Baker, Sheridan. *The Practical Stylist*. 6th ed. Harper & Row, 1985.

Becker, Howard S. *Writing for Social Scientists: How to Start and Finish Your Thesis, Book, or Article*. University of Chicago Press, 1986.

Bernstein, Theodore. *Watch Your Language*. Atheneum, 1983.

Cappon, Rene J. *The Word: An Associated Press Guide to Good News Writing*. Associated Press, 1982.

Elbow, Peter. *Writing with Power*. Oxford University Press, 1981.

Ewing, David W. *Writing for Results in Business, Government, the Sciences, and the Professions*. 2d ed. John Wiley & Sons, 1979.

Goldberg, Natalie. *Writing Down the Bones*. Shambhala, 1986.

Horton, Susan R. *Thinking through Writing*. Johns Hopkins University Press, 1982.

Lambuth, David and others. *The Golden Book on Writing*. Penguin, 1963.

Lanham, Richard A. *Style: An Anti-Textbook*. Yale University Press, 1974.

Lunsford, Andrea and Robert Connors. *The New St. Martin's Handbook*. Bedford/St. Martin's, 1999.

Murray, Donald. *Writing for Your Readers*. Globe Pequot Press, 1983.

O'Conner, Patricia T. *Woe Is I: The Grammarphobe's Guide to Better English in Plain English*. G. P. Putnam's, 1996.

Payne, Lucile Vaughan. *The Lively Art of Writing*. Mentor Books, 1969.

Read, Herbert. *English Prose Style*. Pantheon, 1952.

Venolia, Jan. *Rewrite Right!* Ten Speed Press, 1987.

Waddell, Marie L. and others. *The Art of Styling Sentences*. Barron's, 1972.

Zinsser, William. *On Writing Well: The Classic Guide to Writing Nonfiction*, 25th Anniversary edition. Harper & Row, 2001.

EDITORIAL STYLE MANUALS

The Associated Press Stylebook and Briefing on Media Law. Norm Goldstein, ed. Revised ed. Perseus, 2000.

The Chicago Manual of Style. 14th ed. University of Chicago Press, 1993.

The MLA Style Manual and Guide to Scholarly Publishing. Joseph Gibaldi and Herbert Lindenberger. 2d ed. Modern Language Association, 1998.

The New York Times Manual of Style and Usage. Allan M. Siegal and William G. Connolly. Revised and expanded ed. Times Books, 1999.

BOOKS ON GRAMMAR AND PUNCTUATION

Curme, George O. *A Grammar of the English Language.* 2 volumes. Verbatim, 1978.

Enquist, Anne and Laurel Currie Oates. *Just Writing: Grammar, Punctuation, and Style for the Legal Writer.* Aspen, 2001.

Gordon, Karen Elizabeth. *The New Well-Tempered Sentence, A Punctuation Handbook for the Innocent, the Eager, and the Doomed.* Ticknor & Fields, 1993.

Greenbaum, Sidney. *The Oxford English Grammar.* Oxford University Press, 1996.

Opdycke, John B. *Harper's English Grammar.* Fawcett Popular Library, 1965.

Shertzer, Margaret. *The Elements of Grammar.* Collier Macmillan, 1986.

BOOKS ON LEGAL WRITING, STYLE, AND USAGE

Charrow, Veda, et al. *Clear and Effective Legal Writing.* 3d ed. Aspen, 2001.

Flesch, Rudolf. *How to Write Plain English: A Book for Lawyers & Consumers.* Harper & Row, 1979.

Garner, Bryan A. *The Elements of Legal Style.* Oxford University Press, 1991.

Goldfarb, Ronald L. and James C. Raymond. *Clear Understandings: A Guide to Legal Writing.* Random House, 1982.

———. *A Dictionary of Modern Legal Usage.* 2d ed. Oxford University Press, 1995.

Gopen, George D. *Writing from a Legal Perspective.* West, 1986.

Katz, Lucy V. *Winning Words: A Guide to Persuasive Writing for Lawyers.* Harcourt Brace Jovanovich, 1986.

Mellinkoff, David. *Legal Writing: Sense and Nonsense.* West, 1983.

————. *Mellinkoff's Dictionary of American Legal Usage.* West, 1992.

Ray, Mary Bernard and Jill J. Ramsfield. *Legal Writing: Getting It Right and Getting It Written.* 3d ed. West, 2000.

Stark, Steven D. *Writing to Win.* Doubleday, 1999.

Weisberg, Richard H. *When Lawyers Write.* Little, Brown, 1987.

Wydick, Richard C. *Plain English for Lawyers.* 4th ed. Carolina Academic Press, 1998.

LAW SCHOOL TEXTBOOKS ON WRITING

Calleros, Charles R. *Legal Method and Writing.* 4th ed. Aspen, 2001.

Edwards, Linda Holdeman. *Legal Writing: Process, Analysis, & Organization.* 3d ed. Aspen, 2002.

Glaser, Cathy; Jethro K. Lieberman; Robert A. Ruescher; and Lynn Boepple Su. *The Lawyer's Craft: An Introduction to Legal Analysis, Writing, Research, and Advocacy.* Anderson Publishing, 2002.

LeClercq, Terri. *Guide to Legal Writing Style.* West, 2000.

Neumann, Richard K., Jr. *Legal Reasoning and Legal Writing: Structure, Strategy, and Style.* 4th ed. Aspen, 2001.

Oates, Laurel Currie; Anne Enquist; and Kelly Kunsch. *The Legal Writing Handbook: Analysis, Research, and Writing.* 2d ed. Aspen, 1998.

Pratt, Diana V. *Legal Writing: A Systematic Approach.* 3d ed. West, 1999.

Ramsfield, Jill J. *The Law as Architecture.* West, 2000.

Schultz, Nancy L. and Louis J. Sirico Jr. *Legal Writing and Other Lawyering Skills.* 3d ed. Matthew Bender, 1998.

Shapo, Helene S.; Marilyn R. Walter; and Elizabeth Fajans. *Writing and Analysis in the Law.* 4th ed. Foundation Press, 1999.

BOOKS ON LEGAL LANGUAGE

Garner, Bryan A., ed. *Black's Law Dictionary.* 7th ed. West, 1999.

Mellinkoff, David. *The Language of the Law.* Little, Brown, 1963.

Rodell, Fred. *Woe unto You, Lawyers.* [1939.] Berkley, 1961.

White, James Boyd. *Heracles' Bow: Essays on the Rhetoric and Poetics of the Law.* University of Wisconsin Press, 1985.

————. *The Legal Imagination.* University of Chicago Press, 1985.

BOOKS ON THE STATE OF THE LANGUAGE

Barzun, Jacques. *A Word or Two Before You Go.* Wesleyan University Press, 1986.

Bryson, Bill. *The Mother Tongue.* William Morrow, 1990.

Chase, Stuart. *The Tyranny of Words.* Harcourt, Brace & Co., 1938.

Claiborne, Robert. *Our Marvelous Native Tongue.* Times Books, 1983.

Cross, Donna Woolfolk. *Word Abuse.* Coward McCann & Geoghegan, 1979.

McArthur, Tom, ed. *The Oxford Companion to the English Language.* Oxford University Press, 1992.

Michaels, Leonard and Christopher Ricks, eds. *The State of the Language.* University of California Press, 1990.

Mitchell, Richard. *Less Than Words Can Say.* Little, Brown, 1979.

———. *The Gift of Fire.* Simon & Schuster, 1987.

Newman, Edwin. *A Civil Tongue.* Warner Books, 1980.

———. *Strictly Speaking: Will America Be the Death of English?* Warner Books, 1980.

Shipley, Joseph T. *In Praise of English.* Times Books, 1977.

Tannen, Deborah. *The Argument Culture.* Random House, 1998.

BOOKS ON CREATIVITY AND WRITING

Adams, James L. *Conceptual Blockbusting.* 2d ed. W. W. Norton, 1979.

———. *The Care and Feeding of Ideas.* Addison Wesley, 1986.

Browne, M. Neil and Stuart M. Keeley. *Asking the Right Questions: A Guide to Critical Thinking.* 2d ed. Prentice-Hall, 1986.

Csikszentmihalyi, Mihaly. *Creativity.* Harper Collins, 1996.

Ghiselin, Brewster, ed. *The Creative Process.* Mentor, 1955.

Goleman, Daniel; Paul Kaufman; and Michael Ray. *The Creative Spirit.* Dutton, 1992.

Howard, V. A. and J. H. Barton. *Thinking on Paper.* William Morrow, 1986.

Koestler, Arthur. *The Act of Creation.* Dell, 1967.

Lewis, David and James Greene. *Thinking Better.* Rawson, Wade, 1982.

Ruggiero, Vincent Ryan. *The Art of Thinking: A Guide to Critical and Creative Thought.* 5th ed., Longman, 1998.

Storr, Anthony. *The Dynamics of Creation.* Ballantine, 1993.

BOOKS ON METAPHOR

Berthoff, Anne E. *The Making of Meaning.* Boynton/Cook Publishers, 1981.

Johnson, Mark, ed. *Philosophical Perspectives on Metaphor.* University of Minnesota Press, 1981.

Lakoff, George and Mark Johnson. *Metaphors We Live By.* University of Chicago Press, 1980.

Ortony, Andrew, ed. *Metaphor and Thought.* Cambridge University Press, 1979.

Sacks, Sheldon, ed. *On Metaphor.* University of Chicago Press, 1979.

ACKNOWLEDGMENTS

ACKNOWLEDGMENTS FOR THE SECOND EDITION

Thanks to Paul Mastrangelo of the New York Law School Library for tracking down elusive information and for other much needed assistance in updating the text; Bert Ross of the New York Law School Class of 2000 for research assistance; Kenneth A. Plevan and Alice Sookhoo for help in arranging interviews with lawyers and paralegal staff at Skadden, Arps, Slate, Meagher & Flom in New York City; Naomi Schneider and Cindy Fulton of the University of California Press; and especially Amy Einsohn, who proved to us that all writers need editing, even the second time around.

ACKNOWLEDGMENTS FOR THE FIRST EDITION

We wish to thank Joe Spieler, Bobbi Mark, and Lisa Frost for their exceptional guidance; Jennifer Crewe for her encouragement; Martha Cooper, Sandor Frankel, Lawrence Grauman Jr., Nancy Ramsey, and Amy Stevens for editing suggestions that greatly improved the manuscript; Elizabeth K. Lieberman for proofreading the galleys; for their research help, Paul Mastrangelo and Mary lin Raisch and the staffs of the libraries at New York Law School, Park City, Utah, and the University of California, Berkeley; Beth Pickett for her administrative help; and Terry Pristin, Mike Keiser, and Phil Friedmann for providing us shelter while we worked on the manuscript. We have also benefited greatly over the years from the published work of and discussions with Joseph M. Williams and George D. Gopen.

We gathered this material from many people, including lawyers in several firms and students at New York and Fordham law schools and the Graduate School of Journalism, University of California, Berkeley.

We are grateful to the following people who took the time to answer our questionnaire. Others answered whom we are unable to acknowledge. Some preferred anonymity. And because of a temporary glitch at the post office, some responses which friends told us had been sent never arrived (and, we suspect, others did not arrive as well). We list respondents with their affiliations as of publication of our hardcover book in 1988.

Beryl A. Abrams, Associate General Counsel, Columbia University, New York City

Prof. Douglas E. Abrams, Fordham University School of Law, New York City

Floyd Abrams, Cahill Gordon & Reindel, New York City

Thomas F. Ahrensfeld, Senior Vice President & General Counsel, Philip Morris, Inc., New York City

Susan Alexander, lawyer and writer, Wilmette, Illinois

C. David Anderson, Tuttle & Taylor, Los Angeles

William L. Anderson, *Minnesota Law Review,* Minneapolis

Lori B. Andrews, American Bar Foundation, Chicago

Hon. Richard T. Andrias, State Supreme Court, New York City

Louis S. Auchincloss, lawyer and author, New York City

Stuart Auerbach, *The Washington Post,* Washington, D.C.

Richard Babcock, *New York Magazine,* New York City

David M. Balabanian, McCutchen, Doyle, Brown & Enersen, San Francisco

Robert S. Banks, Vice President & General Counsel, Xerox Corp., Stamford, Connecticut

Fred Barbash, *The Washington Post,* Washington, D.C.

David A. Barrett, Duker & Barrett, New York City

Prof. Jacques Barzun, Columbia University, New York City

Prof. Paul A. Bateman, Southwestern University School of Law, Los Angeles

James Bays, Vice President & Assistant General Counsel, TRW, Inc., Cleveland

David E. Beckwith, Foley & Lardner, Milwaukee

Hon. Joseph W. Bellacosa, New York Court of Appeals, Albany

Prof. Rebecca White Berch, Arizona State University College of Law, Tempe

Prof. Curtis J. Berger, Columbia University School of Law, New York City

Curtis G. Berkey, Indian Law Resource Center, Washington, D.C.

Albert L. Beswick, Senior Counsel, International Telephone & Telegraph Co., New York City

Lawrence Bodine, Editor, *American Bar Association Journal,* Chicago

Michael Boudin, Covington & Burling, Washington, D.C.

Michael A. Boyd, General Counsel, Donaldson Lufkin & Jenrette, Inc., New York City

Hon. Stephen Breyer, United States Court of Appeals, First Circuit, Boston

David M. Brodsky, Schulte Roth & Zabel, New York City

Prof. Susan L. Brody, Director, Legal Writing, The John Marshall Law School, Chicago

Helman R. Brook, Office of Special State Prosecutor, New York City
Howard D. Burnett, Holly, Troxell, Ennis & Holly, Pocatello, Idaho
W. Peter Burns, Steel Hector & Davis, Miami
Margaret B. Carlson, *Time Magazine,* Washington, D.C.
Bradley Carr, New York State Bar Association, Albany
James H. Carter, Sullivan & Cromwell, New York City
Prof. David Chang, New York Law School, New York City
Richard Cheney, Chairman, Hill & Knowlton, New York City
Dean Jesse Choper, Boalt Hall, University of California, Berkeley
Arthur H. Christy, Christy & Viener, New York City
Roy Peter Clark, The Poynter Institute for Media Studies, St. Petersburg,
    Florida
Hon. Avern Cohn, United States District Court, Detroit
Henry S. Cohn, State Attorney General's Office, Hartford, Connecticut
John T. Connor, Jr., Vice President & General Counsel, PHH Group, Inc.,
    Hunt Valley, Maryland
Randal R. Craft, Jr., Haight, Gardner, Poor & Havens, New York City
L. Gordon Crovitz, *The Wall Street Journal,* New York City
Dean Edward A. Dauer, University of Denver College of Law, Denver
Evan A. Davis, Counsel to the Governor of New York, Albany
James F. Davis, Howrey & Simon, Washington, D.C.
Prof. Joel C. Dobris, University of California School of Law at Davis, Davis
Jean Dubofsky, University of Colorado School of Law, Boulder
Victor Earle III, Cahill Gordon & Reindel, New York City
Charles D. Edelman, Vice President and General Counsel, Fortress Re, Inc.,
    Burlington, North Carolina
Renee Edelman, Edelman Group, New York City
Mary Frances Edwards, Federal Publications, Inc., Washington, D.C.
Richard D. Emery, Lankenau Kovner & Bickford, New York City
Thomas Engel, Engel & Mulholland, New York City
Eli N. Evans, President, The Revson Foundation, New York City
Thomas W. Evans, Mudge Rose Guthrie Alexander & Ferdon, New York
    City
Lisa Evren, *New York University Law Review,* New York City
Herald Price Fahringer, Lipsitz, Green, Fahringer, Roll, Schuller & James,
    New York City
Kenneth R. Feinberg, Kaye, Scholer, Fierman, Hays & Handler, Washing-
    ton, D.C.
Jeffrey Feinstein, Inspector General's Office, Department of Health, New
    York City
Franklin Feldman, Stroock & Stroock & Lavan, New York City
Charles K. Fewell, Jr., Senior Counsel & First Vice President, Deutsche
    Bank AG, New York City

Eugene R. Fidell, Klores, Feldesman & Tucker, Washington, D.C.

Erika S. Fine, WestLaw, New York City

Frank Fioromonti, New York State Attorney General's Office, New York City

Josh Fitzhugh, lawyer, Burlington, Vermont

Stuart Berg Flexner, *Random House Dictionary of the English Language*, New York City

Hon. Marvin E. Frankel, Kramer, Levin, Nessen, Kamin & Frankel, New York City

Sandor Frankel, Bender & Frankel, New York City

Prof. Eric M. Freedman, Hofstra University Law School, Hempstead, N.Y.

Prof. Monroe H. Freedman, Hofstra University Law School, Hempstead, N.Y.

David Freeman, writer, Los Angeles

James C. Freund, Skadden, Arps, Slate, Meagher & Flom, New York City

Prof. Leon Friedman, Hofstra University Law School, Hempstead, New York

Stanley Friedman, Shereff, Friedman, Hoffman & Goodman, New York City

Donald Fry, The Poynter Institute for Media Studies, St. Petersburg, Florida

Martin Garbus, Frankfurt, Garbus, Klein & Selz, New York City

Michael G. Gartner, President, NBC News, New York City

Gibson Gayle, Jr., Fulbright & Jaworski, Houston

Warren B. Gelman, McGee & Gelman, Buffalo

Ted Gest, *U.S. News & World Report,* Washington, D.C.

Robin Gibson, Gibson & Lilly, Lake Wales, Florida

Prof. Stephen Gillers, New York University Law School, New York City

Prof. Donald Gillmor, Silha Center for the Study of Media Ethics and Law, University of Minnesota, Minneapolis

Prof. I. Cathy Glaser, New York Law School, New York City

Marshall Goldberg, writer, Brentwood, California

Robert M. Goldberg, Offices of Robert M. Goldberg & Associates, Anchorage

Sondra Gamow Goldenfarb, Tanney, Forde, Donahey, Eno & Tanney, Clearwater, Florida

Ronald Goldfarb, Goldfarb & Singer, Washington, D.C.

Marshall L. Goldstein, Goldstein and Van Nes, White Plains, New York

James C. Goodale, Debevoise & Plimpton, New York City

Prof. George D. Gopen, Department of English, Duke University, Durham, North Carolina

Robert H. Gorske, Vice President & General Counsel, Wisconsin Electric Power Co., Milwaukee

Milton S. Gould, Shea & Gould, New York City

Joseph Goulden, writer, Washington, D.C.

Chester Graham, Cross Lake, Minn.

Fred Graham, WKRN-TV, Nashville

Lawrence Grauman, Jr., editor, Mill Valley, California

Prof. Eric D. Green, Boston University School of Law, Boston

Matthew Greenberg, Office of Special State Prosecutor, New York City

Jeff Greenfield, ABC-TV, New York City

Linda Greenhouse, *The New York Times,* Washington, D.C.

Robert Gruendel, Burlingham, Underwood & Lord, New York City

Philip Hager, *The Los Angeles Times,* San Francisco

David Halston, Hale & Dorr, Boston

William Hannay, Schiff Hardin & Waite, Chicago

Jane Frank Harman, Surrey & Morse, Washington, D.C.

Hon. Bertram Harnett, Dreyer and Traub, Boca Raton, Florida

Prof. Geoffrey C. Hazard, Jr., Yale University Law School, New Haven

William E. Hegarty, Cahill Gordon & Reindel, New York City

Prof. William E. Hellerstein, Brooklyn Law School, Brooklyn, New York

Lawrence F. Henneberger, Arent, Fox, Kintner, Plotkin & Kahn, Washington, D.C.

Joel F. Henning, writer and lawyer, Chicago

Coleman S. Hicks, Covington & Burling, Washington, D.C.

George V. Higgins, author and lawyer, Milton, Massachusetts

Joseph D. Hinkle, Hill & Barlow, Boston

Alan J. Hruska, Cravath, Swaine & Moore, New York City

Hon. Shirley Hufstedler, Hufstedler, Miller, Carlson & Beardsley, Los Angeles

Prof. Patrick Hugg, Loyola Law School, New Orleans

Prof. Dennis Hynes, Co-Director of Legal Writing, Univ. of Colorado School of Law, Boulder

Linda Ishkanian, Siegal & Gale, New York City

Hon. Jack B. Jacobs, Court of Chancery, Wilmington, Delaware

Herb Jaffe, *Newark Star-Ledger,* Newark, New Jersey

Hon. Matthew Jasen, Moot & Sprague, Buffalo

Alan Jenkins, *Harvard Civil Rights-Civil Liberties Law Review,* Cambridge

Robert D. Joffe, Cravath, Swaine & Moore, New York City

William J. Jones, General Solicitor, AT&T, Berkeley Heights, N.J.

Kenneth Jost, writer, Washington, D.C.

Roberta S. Karmel, Brooklyn Law School and Kelley, Drye & Warren, New York City

Adam Kasanof, Department of Police, New York City

Robert Kasanof, Kasanof & Shannon, New York City

Frank Katz, lawyer, Santa Fe

George Kaufmann, Dickstein, Shapiro & Morin, Washington, D.C.

Hon. John F. Keenan, United States District Court, Southern District of New York, New York City

James M. Kindler, New York County District Attorney's Office, New York City

Dean James M. Klebba, Loyola University School of Law, New Orleans

Hon. J. Anthony Kline, California Court of Appeal, San Francisco

Steven H. Kruis, Higgs, Fletcher & Mack, San Diego

James Simon Kunen, *People Magazine,* New York City

Jack L. Lahr, Foley & Lardner, Washington, D.C.

Newton Lamson, Donley Communications, New York City

A. Van C. Lanckton, Craig & Macauley, Boston

Jay F. Lapin, Wilmer Cutler & Pickering, Washington, D.C.

Mark D. Lebow, Coudert Brothers, New York City

Hon. James J. Leff, State Supreme Court, New York City

Prof. Robert Leflar, University of Arkansas, Fayetteville

Donald G. Leka, General Counsel, Teradyne, Inc., Boston

Thomas B. Lemann, Monroe & Lemann, New Orleans

Prof. Arthur Leonard, New York Law School, New York City

William H. Levit, Jr., Godfrey & Kahn, Milwaukee

Anthony Lewis, *The New York Times,* Boston

Hal R. Lieberman, Disciplinary Committee, Appellate Division, First Department, New York City

Prof. Carol B. Liebman, Boston College Law School, Boston

Carl D. Liggio, General Counsel, Arthur Young Co., New York City

Prof. James Lindgren, University of Connecticut School of Law, Hartford

Martin Lipton, Wachtell, Lipton, Rosen & Katz, New York City

Prof. Daniel H. Lowenstein, University of California at Los Angeles School of Law, Los Angeles

Weyman I. Lundquist, Heller Ehrman White & McAuliffe, San Francisco

Judy Lynch, City Attorney's Office, San Francisco

James E. Lyons, Skadden, Arps, Slate, Meagher & Flom, Los Angeles

Patrick J. Mahoney, Cooley, Godward, Castro, Huddleson & Tatum, San Francisco

Jonathan R. Maslow, editor, San Francisco

Prof. Robert McKay, New York University School of Law, New York City

John F. Meigs, Saul Ewing Remick & Saul, Philadelphia

Prof. David Mellinkoff, University of California at Los Angeles School of Law, Los Angeles

Prof. Michael Meltsner, Northeastern University School of Law, Boston

Elizabeth Mertz, Northwestern Law Review, Chicago

Harry Meyer, Hodgson, Russ, Andrew, Woods & Goodyear, Buffalo

Stephen B. Middlebrook, Vice President & General Counsel, Aetna Insurance Co., Hartford

Prof. Arthur R. Miller, Harvard Law School, Cambridge

Prof. Richard H. Miller, Brooklyn College, Brooklyn, New York

Herbert Mitgang, *The New York Times,* New York City

Prof. Norval Morris, University of Chicago School of Law, Chicago

Alan B. Morrison, Public Citizen, Inc., Washington, D.C.

Justice Stanley Mosk, California Supreme Court, San Francisco

Daniel B. Moskowitz, McGraw-Hill, Inc., Washington, D.C.

Homer E. Moyer, Miller & Chevalier, Washington, D.C.

Hon. William Hughes Mulligan, Skadden, Arps, Slate, Meagher & Flom, New York City

Betty Southard Murphy, Baker & Hostetler, Washington, D.C.

Hon. S. Michael Nadel, Criminal Court, New York City

Stan Naparst, Albany, California

Stephen Natelson, Natelson & Ross, Taos, New Mexico

Robert Stuart Nathan, writer, New York City

Hon. Richard Neely, Supreme Court of West Virginia, Charleston

Maurice N. Nessen, Kramer, Levin, Nessen, Kamin & Frankel, New York City

Prof. Charles R. Nesson, Harvard Law School, Cambridge

Prof. Richard K. Neumann, Jr., Director, Legal Writing, Hofstra University School of Law, Hempstead, New York

Prof. Stephen A. Newman, New York Law School, New York City

Prof. Jacqueline Nolan-Haley, Fordham University School of Law, New York City

J. Michael Parish, LeBoeuf, Lamb, Leiby & Macrae, New York City

Hon. Robert Patterson, Jr., United States District Court, Southern District of New York, New York City

Robert S. Peck, American Bar Association, Washington, D.C.

Prof. Michael Perlin, New York Law School, New York City

Kenneth A. Plevan, Skadden, Arps, Slate, Meagher & Flom, New York City

Milt Policzer, *San Francisco Recorder,* San Francisco

Hon. Richard A. Posner, United States Court of Appeals, Seventh Circuit, Chicago

Prof. Michael Powell, Department of Sociology, University of North Carolina, Chapel Hill

Llewelyn Pritchard, Karr, Tuttle, Koch, Campbell, Jawer, Morrow & Sax, Seattle

Anthony E. Pucillo, West Palm Beach, Florida

Henry Putzel, Jr., Retired Reporter of Decisions, United States Supreme Court, Munsonville, New Hampshire

Henry Putzel III, lawyer, New York City

Prof. Jill J. Ramsfield, Georgetown University Law Center, Washington, D.C.

Charles A. Reich, writer, San Francisco

Prof. Chris Rideout, University of Puget Sound School of Law, Tacoma, Washington

Simon H. Rifkind, Paul, Weiss, Rifkind, Wharton & Garrison, New York City

Marjorie Rawls Roberts, Bureau of Internal Revenue, St. Thomas, V.I.

Charles Robinowitz, lawyer, Portland, Oregon

T. Sumner Robinson, Editor, *The National Law Journal,* New York City

Timothy Roble, Ducker, Gurko & Roble, Denver

Salvatore A. Romano, Arent, Fox, Kintner, Plotkin & Kahn, Washington, D.C.

Prof. Marjorie D. Rombauer, University of Washington School of Law, Seattle

Andy Rooney, CBS-TV, New York City

Prof. Maurice Rosenberg, Columbia University School of Law, New York City

Hon. Albert M. Rosenblatt, Appellate Division of State Supreme Court, New York City

David Rosenbloom, Orrick, Herrington & Sutcliffe, San Francisco

C. Thomas Ross, Craige, Brawley, Lipfert & Ross, Winston-Salem, North Carolina

Prof. Donald Rothschild, George Washington Law School, Washington, D.C.

Arthur W. Rovine, Baker & McKenzie, New York City

Prof. Thomas D. Rowe, Jr., Duke University School of Law, Durham, North Carolina

Prof. Zick Rubin, Brandeis University, Waltham, Massachusetts

Prof. David Rudenstine, Benjamin N. Cardozo School of Law, New York City

Jerry W. Ryan, Crowell & Moring, Washington, D.C.

Elizabeth Sacksteder, Articles Editor, *Yale Law Journal,* New Haven

Joseph R. Sahid, Cravath, Swaine & Moore, New York City

Hon. Leonard B. Sand, United States District Court, Southern District of New York, New York City

Prof. Frank E. A. Sander, Harvard Law School, Cambridge

Justice Leonard H. Sandler (deceased), Appellate Division of State Supreme Court, New York City

David L. Sandor, Simon, McKinsey, Miller, Zommick, Sandor & Dundas, Irvine, California

John P. Scanlon, Edelman Group, New York City

Milton R. Schlesinger, After & Hadden, Cleveland

Prof. David Schoenbrod, New York Law School, New York City

Prof. Peter H. Schuck, Yale Law School, New Haven

Allen G. Schwartz, Proskauer Rose Goetz & Mendelson, New York City
Victor E. Schwartz, Crowell & Moring, Washington, D.C.
Melvin L. Schweitzer, Rogers & Wells, New York City
Eric A. Seiff, Scoppetta & Seiff, New York City
Prof. David. L. Shapiro, Harvard Law School, Cambridge
Prof. E. Donald Shapiro, New York Law School, New York City
Ronald M. Shapiro, Shapiro & Olander, Baltimore
Prof. Marjorie Silver, New York Law School, New York City
Leon Silverman, Fried, Frank, Harris, Shriver & Jacobson, New York City
Robert Siverd, Penn Central lawyer, Stamford, Connecticut
Neil Skene, Executive Editor, *Congressional Quarterly,* Washington, D.C.
Jonathan A. Small, Debevoise & Plimpton, New York City
Chesterfield Smith, Holland & Knight, Miami
Prof. Eva M. Soeka, Marquette University Law School, Milwaukee
Justin A. Stanley, Mayer Brown & Platt, Chicago
John H. Stassen, Kirkland & Ellis, Chicago
Jacob A. Stein, Stein, Mitchell & Mezines, Washington, D.C.
Carl Stern, NBC-TV, Washington, D.C.
Gerald Stern, Administrator, New York State Commission on Judicial Conduct, New York City
Prof. Christopher D. Stone, University of Southern California Law Center, Los Angeles
Fred M. Stone, Executive Vice President & General Counsel, Jamie Securities, New York City
Hon. Eugene B. Strassburger III, Court of Common Pleas, Allegheny County, Pittsburgh
Prof. James F. Stratman, Graduate School of Industrial Administration, Carnegie-Mellon University, Pittsburgh
Prof. Peter L. Strauss, Columbia University Law School, New York City
Fern Sussman, Executive Secretary, Association of the Bar of the City of New York, New York City
Phil Talbert, UCLA Law Review, Los Angeles
Peter Tannewald, Arent, Fox, Kintner, Plotkin & Kahn, Washington, D.C.
Stuart Taylor, Jr., *The American Lawyer,* Washington, D.C.
M. Margaret Terry, Lubell & Lubell, New York City
Texas Law Review staff, 1987–1988, Austin
Evan Thomas, *Newsweek,* Washington, D.C.
Robert Tierney, AT&T, New York City
Sean Tierney, Mudge Rose Guthrie Alexander & Ferdon, New York City
Richard J. Tofel, Gibson, Dunn & Crutcher, New York City
Jay Topkis, Paul, Weiss, Rifkind, Wharton & Garrison, New York City
R. Edward Townsend, Townsend Rabinowitz Pantaleoni & Valente, New York City

Dean David G. Trager, Brooklyn Law School, Brooklyn, New York
Prof. Nicholas Triffin, Pace University School of Law, White Plains, New York
Thomas R. Trowbridge III, Donovan Leisure Newton & Irvine, New York City
Scott F. Turow, Sonnenschein Carlin North & Rosenthal, Chicago
Gerald Uram, Davis & Gilbert, New York City
Andrew Vachss, lawyer and author, New York City
Prof. Jon M. Van Dyke, University of Hawaii, William S. Richardson School of Law, Honolulu
Cyrus Vance, Simpson Thacher & Bartlett, New York City
Prof. Robert Volk, Director, First-Year Writing Program, Boston University School of Law, Boston
George Vradenburg III, General Counsel, CBS, New York City
Hon. Sol Wachtler, New York Court of Appeals, Albany
Hank Wallace, consultant, Washington, D.C.
Irene C. Warshauer, Anderson Russell Kill & Olick, New York City
Kelly R. Welsh, Corporation Counsel, Chicago
Stephen Wermiel, *The Wall Street Journal,* Washington, D.C.
Edwin J. Wesely, Winthrop, Stimson, Putnam & Roberts, New York City
Roger Wilkins, Institute for Policy Studies, Washington, D.C.
Christopher Wren, Wisconsin Department of Justice, Madison
Melvin Wulf, Beldock Levine & Hoffman, New York City
Hon. William G. Young, United States District Court, Boston
Prof. Irving Younger (deceased), University of Minnesota Law School, Minneapolis
Lois Young-Tulin, Wyncote, Pennsylvania
Prof. Donald H. Zeigler, New York Law School, New York City
Sidney Zion, writer, New York City

ABOUT THE AUTHORS

TOM GOLDSTEIN

Tom Goldstein is professor of journalism at the Graduate School of Journalism at Columbia University, where he served as dean from 1997 to 2002. He is also former dean of the Graduate School of Journalism at the University of California, Berkeley. He has been a teacher and journalist on both coasts. From 1973 to 1979 he covered legal affairs for the metropolitan, business, and national desks of the *New York Times*. In 1988 he contributed to the law page of the *Times*. During the 1970s he taught courses on law and journalism as an adjunct professor at the New York University Graduate School of Journalism. During the 1983–1984 academic year, he served as the Gannett Distinguished Visiting Professor at the University of Florida, at Gainesville. The following year he joined the faculty at Berkeley, where he taught courses on newswriting, ethics, and mass media. He was appointed a full professor in 1987 and served as dean from 1988 to 1996.

Professor Goldstein is a graduate of Yale College, Columbia Graduate School of Journalism, and Columbia Law School. In 1970, while still in law school, he served as the first editor of *Juris Doctor*, a magazine for young lawyers that, at its peak, had a monthly circulation of 150,000. After law school, on a Ford Foundation grant, he spent a year studying criminology at Cambridge. In addition to the *New York Times*, he has worked at the *Buffalo Evening News*, the Associated Press, the *Wall Street Journal*, and *Newsday*. He is a member of the New York bar.

From 1980 to 1982 he served as press secretary for Mayor Edward I. Koch. After leaving the mayor's staff, he began to freelance, a career he still pursues. His articles, on media, legal, and political subjects, have appeared in *Rolling Stone, The Nation, Columbia Law Review, Columbia Journalism Review,* and *California Magazine*.

In the last several years, he has lectured widely—in Hawaii, Alaska, Oklahoma, Texas, Illinois, Arizona, Israel, Spain, Japan, at the Kennedy School at Harvard University, and at the New York City Bar Association—on the press and legal subjects. He is the author of *The News at Any Cost* (Simon &

Schuster, 1985), a critique of press ethics; *A Two-Faced Press* (Twentieth Century Fund, 1986), an examination of social responsibility and the press; and editor of *Killing the Messenger* (Columbia University Press, 1988), a volume of press criticism.

JETHRO K. LIEBERMAN

Jethro K. Lieberman is associate dean for academic affairs, professor of law, and director of the Writing Program at New York Law School, and adjunct professor of political science at Columbia University. Since 1982 he has taught Advanced Writing Skills for Lawyers, first at Fordham University Law School, where he began his teaching career, and since 1985 at New York Law School. He also teaches constitutional law and has taught administrative law, dispute resolution, and legal method.

Dean Lieberman took his B.A. at Yale, J.D. at Harvard Law School, and Ph.D. (in political science) at Columbia University, and has had a broad career in writing, with experience in books, newspapers, magazines, and newsletters. The first of his twenty-four books was published in his third year at Harvard, where he was also an editor in the Second-Year Writing Program and contributing editor of the *Harvard Civil Rights–Civil Liberties Law Review.* He has been an associate in a large Washington law firm, a Navy lawyer, and general counsel of a trade publishing house in New York. He was the first legal affairs editor of *Business Week* (1973–1982), was founding editor of *Alternatives to the High Cost of Litigation,* a monthly newsletter on corporate dispute resolution (1982–1985), and has written for many periodicals and journals. He was a charter member of the American Bar Association's Commission on Public Understanding About the Law, special consultant to the Council on the Role of Courts, and principal editor of its report *The Role of Courts in American Society* (West, 1984). He is a member of the New York and District of Columbia bars.

Two of his books—*The Litigious Society* (Basic Books, 1981; Harper Colophon, 1983) and *The Enduring Constitution* (West Publishing Co. and Harper & Row, 1987)—were awarded the Silver Gavel, the American Bar Association's highest prize for writing. The first edition of his *A Practical Companion to the Constitution: How the Supreme Court Has Ruled on Issues from Abortion to Zoning* (University of California Press, 1999) was cited by the American Library Association as an "Outstanding Reference Work of the Year" and was awarded a Gavel Certificate of Merit. He is co-author of a legal writing text, *The Lawyer's Craft* (Anderson Publishing Co., 2002), designed for first-year writing courses in law school.

Designer:	Sandy Drooker
Compositor:	Binghamton Valley Composition, LLC
Text:	11/15 Adobe Garamond
Display:	Copperplate
Printer and binder:	Maple-Vail Manufacturing Group